CRIMINAL MAJOR CASE MANAGEMENT

Persons of Interest
Priority Assessment Tool
(POIPAT)

CRIMINAL MAJOR CASE MANAGEMENT

Persons of Interest Priority Assessment Tool (POIPAT)

Larry Wilson

CRC Press
Taylor & Francis Group
Boca Raton London New York

CRC Press is an imprint of the
Taylor & Francis Group, an **informa** business

Inspector Larry Wilson of the Royal Canadian Mounted Police.

CRC Press
Taylor & Francis Group
6000 Broken Sound Parkway NW, Suite 300
Boca Raton, FL 33487-2742

CRC Press is an imprint of Taylor & Francis Group, an Informa business

No claim to original U.S. Government works

Printed in the United States of America on acid-free paper
Version Date: 20120215

International Standard Book Number: 978-1-4398-9861-1 (Hardback)

Library of Congress Cataloging-in-Publication Data

Wilson, Larry.
    Criminal major case management : Persons of Interest Priority Assessment Tool (POIPAT) / Larry Wilson.
        p. cm.
    Includes bibliographical references and index.
    ISBN 978-1-4398-9861-1 (hardback)
    1. Criminal investigation. 2. Criminal investigation--Psychological aspects. 3. Criminal behavior, Prediction of. I. Title.

HV8073.W5263 2012
363.25--dc23   2012000648

Visit the Taylor & Francis Web site at
http://www.taylorandfrancis.com

and the CRC Press Web site at
http://www.crcpress.com

Contents

Section II

JACK THE RIPPER—CASE STUDY

CD Contents

Jack the Ripper

Jack the Ripper POIPAT Instructional Guide
Jack the Ripper POIPAT

POIPAT Utilities

Element Weighting Chart Card
Elimination Status Coding System Chart
General POIPAT Template
POIPAT Priority Point Ranges Worksheet (20 files)
POIPAT Priority Point Ranges Worksheet (30 files)

Preface

Prioritizing suspects or persons of interest (POIs) is nothing new. As long as investigators have been investigating cases involving multiple suspects, they have been deciding whom on their list they feel is the most likely to have committed their offence(s). Sometimes this is based on the investigation and forensic evidence, and often times on just a gut feeling or intuition.

This approach has served investigators well over the years when the suspect/POI pool was relatively limited. However, when that pool becomes very large as is typically the case in high-profile investigations, establishing a priority ranking is more difficult, but this is when it is most important. It allows management to direct investigative resources to those suspects/POIs who are most likely to have committed the offence(s). This is an effective and efficient use of resources. It not only may save a significant amount of money, but more importantly it could save additional victims.

The problem with using the 'gut feeling' or 'intuitive' approach to prioritizing suspects was illustrated by a research experiment carried out by the author. Twenty-nine files containing background information on 29 individuals who had been identified as POIs in a major serial homicide investigation were given to three very experienced investigators assigned to that investigation. They were asked to evaluate each of the files based on their experience and intuition as to what they thought the priority rating should be on each of the files (POI-1, POI-2 or POI-3). They did this exercise independently of each other without discussion. The results were as follows.

They all agreed on 13 files. Twelve of those files were in the low priority range (POI-3). They disagreed on the remaining 16 files, and in one of those cases all three investigators gave it a different rating.

The purpose of the POIPAT is to provide an objective and consistent means of establishing a priority ranking of suspects/POIs in any given investigation. If created and utilized correctly, the tool can be used to determine if any suspect/POI should be considered a high, medium or low investigative priority.

The goal of this first edition of the *Criminal Major Case Management: Persons of Interest Priority Assessment Tool (POIPAT)* is to provide an instructional manual that will guide the reader step by step through the creation of a POIPAT. It begins by providing an introduction to the POIPAT, followed by some basic development rules. Readers are then provided an 'Element Weighting Guide' which offers some rules and tips on weighting each of the elements. This is followed by a 'Standard POIPAT Elements Library' which lists a number of elements that are typical of most investigations.

This book also includes a chapter on the Elimination Status Coding System (ESCS) which can be used in conjunction with the POIPAT system. The ESCS is utilised when the investigation into any given POI is complete to indicate how that particular POI was eliminated from the investigation.

Perhaps the most interesting section of this book is Section II: Jack the Ripper—Case Study. It uses this famous unsolved case to put into practice the lessons learned in the previous section. Readers are walked through the creation of a POIPAT for that 123-year-old cold case to see how it is used to prioritise some of the best known suspects in that case. Ripperologists[1] will be interested in learning how their favorite suspect scored. The book also includes a CD that contains a POIPAT template that can be modified as a starting point for the creation of a POIPAT for various types of investigations.

The author hopes this book will lead to increased use of the POIPAT in major investigations which in turn should make them more efficient and effective. More importantly it may contribute to the shortening of criminal careers and save potential victims. If just one victim is saved, then the work that went into creating this book was well worth it. The author wishes to thank the many people who assisted with this book.

Endnote

1. A term given to those who study or analyse the Jack the Ripper case.

Acknowledgements

The author wishes to acknowledge the following individuals for their inspiration, assistance and encouragement without whom this book would not have been possible: Beth, Eric, Alex and Danielle Wilson; Retired Deputy Chief Gary Beaulieu (Niagara Regional Police); Retired Supervisory Special Agent Robert R. Hazelwood (FBI); C/Supt. Mike Sekela (RCMP); Retired S/Sgt. Kevin Simmill (RCMP); Retired Sgt. Pat Hayes (RCMP); Supt. Leo O'Brien (RCMP); Insp. Carole Bird (RCMP); Sgt. Larry Burden (RCMP); Spiro Hadjis (RCMP); and Dr. Kim Rossmo (Texas State University).

Special thanks go to Insp. Pierre Nezan (RCMP) who not only reviewed the book for content and accuracy but also wrote Chapter 2, 'Profiling and the POIPAT'.

About the Author

Inspector Larry Wilson has 30 years experience with the Royal Canadian Mounted Police (RCMP). He began his career with the RCMP in 1981 and attended the RCMP training academy in Regina, Saskatchewan. Upon completion of six months of training his first posting was Surrey, British Columbia, where he held a number of positions from general duty policing to serious crimes.

In 1989 he was transferred to the Toronto International Airport where he performed protective policing duties. He was then transferred to the Criminal Intelligence Service Ontario (CISO) where he performed crime analysis duties. While there he was loaned to the 'Green Ribbon Task Force' (Paul Bernardo/Karla Homolka investigation) where he maintained their suspect management system.

Insp. Wilson's next posting was in London, Ontario, as a Division Criminal Intelligence Analyst where he worked until 1997 when he was transferred to Ottawa, Ontario, in the role of Senior ViCLAS Specialist. He worked there for five years and then was transferred to Edmonton, Alberta, as the NCO in charge of the Alberta ViCLAS Centre. He was then transferred to Project KARE in charge of their Behavioural and Tactical Analysis Section. Project KARE was a Joint Forces Operation (JFO) responsible for the investigation of the disappearance and/or homicide of several sex trade workers in the Edmonton area.

In 2007, he was commissioned to the rank of Inspector and assumed his current position of Officer in Charge of the National ViCLAS Policy Centre and then took on the additional responsibility of the RCMP Criminal Investigative Analysis (Profiling) Program.

In 2002 he received the Queen Elizabeth II Golden Jubilee Medal awarded to Canadians who have made outstanding and exemplary contributions to their communities or to Canada as a whole. In 2006, he received the RCMP's 25-Year Long Service Medal with Bronze Clasp, and in 2009 he was awarded a Commander's Commendation for Outstanding Service.

The POIPAT System

I

Introduction to the POIPAT System

Introduction

1

The Persons of Interest Priority Assessment Tool (POIPAT) is a risk management system designed to maximize investigative resources. It is an objective system for assessing the probability of any given persons of interest (POIs) being responsible for any or all of the offences related to any given investigation. This allows the case manager(s) to direct resources necessary to target the high priority POIs first.

The POIPAT is made up of a series of questions that are relevant to the investigation. It is premised on the idea that when a POI is identified, these are questions that an investigator would ask to determine how likely it is that a particular subject is the person responsible for the offence(s). Those questions might include the subject's availability to commit the offence(s), his motivation, his criminal history and his sexually deviant practices (if the case is a sex related offence).

Each of the questions in the POIPAT is weighted based on how important it is to your investigation. For example, it might be more important for you to know whether or not your POI was a long haul truck driver than his level of education. In that case, the weighting system would assign more points to "being a long haul truck driver."

Each POI is assessed based on the questions in the POIPAT, and points are awarded for positive responses. The total number of points that a POI is assessed will determine its priority level. The more points scored, the higher the priority. It is possible to actually rank order all your POIs based on the likelihood that they are responsible for your offence(s).

The POIPAT system creates efficiencies within the investigation. In situations where the investigators receive tasks without prior completion of background checks, they are forced to do the checks themselves. This background work could take anywhere from an hour to a number of days. In some cases, the investigators have neither the knowledge nor the skills to effectively use all of the information systems available to collect this information. The result is an inefficient use of their time, and the eventual information gathered may still be incomplete.

Part of the process with the POIPAT system is to have background checks completed on the POI prior to being assessed. This work would likely be completed by a civilian support employee with the knowledge and skills to operate all of the systems used to conduct the necessary background checks.

By the time a file is received for follow-up by an investigator, all of the background work would already be completed. This ensures that investigators spend much less time in the office and more time on the street following up leads, collecting evidence or interviewing witnesses and POIs.

Although the POIPAT could be used in any high profile investigation, it should definitely be employed in investigations where large numbers of POIs who may be linked to the existing cases have been identified. The POIPAT need not be administered on-site. It may make more sense to do it off-site at another location to take advantage of tools and expertise which are already in place there. It can be used in conjunction with any electronic major case management tool such as 'Evidence and Reports' (E & R).

Given that every investigation is different, it would not be possible to provide one standard POIPAT that could be applied to any and all investigations. In order to be most effective, a new POIPAT that reflects the uniqueness of each case should be created. The same POIPAT could be used in multiple investigations when it is believed the same offender is responsible for all of the cases. It would not be very effective in a case with multiple unrelated investigations that were believed to have been committed by different offenders.

This book will provide all the information required to create a unique POIPAT for any investigation from scratch. It will also provide information on how it should be implemented and identify potential pitfalls. (See Appendix A for a sample POIPAT.)

Applying the POIPAT to Cold Cases

Cold cases are those cases where all investigative leads have been exhausted, and as a result are put aside and looked at only if and when new leads surface. Often these cases are inherited by new investigators, who review the cases if and when they get time. However, in recent history there has been a renewed effort to dust off these cases and examine them in the light of new investigative strategies, techniques and technologies such as DNA. Many large agencies have even created cold case squads dedicated solely to reviewing these cases. This has led to a number of cases being solved many years after the fact.

Typically, these cold cases will have had an extensive amount of work already completed on them. Numerous POIs will have been identified and eliminated for one reason or another. In many of these cold cases, however, the person who turns out to be responsible was identified early in the investigation but eliminated for any number of possible reasons. This does not necessarily mean it was a poor investigation. There are a number of legitimate reasons why this could have happened. For example, the elimination may have been based on a seemingly credible witness who provided the offender a believable alibi that turned out to be false.

One of the strategies employed when reviewing a cold case is to take a critical second look at all POIs who surfaced during the course of the original investigation. Ideally, investigators identify the most likely suspects and take another serious look at them. This usually involves a great deal of work including such investigative steps as taking new statements, collecting DNA, conducting surveillance and perhaps doing under-cover work.

In some instances these cases can involve hundreds of POIs and volumes of information. Cold case investigations normally have the same issue as current investigations in terms of a shortage of investigative resources. In many cases it can be significantly worse because current cases tend to get investigative priority. As such, cold case investigators must also ensure their time is spent focusing on the POIs who are the most likely to have committed the offence(s).

This is an ideal situation for the POIPAT. It could be used during a file review to rank order all of the POIs in order of their likelihood of having committed the offence(s) regardless of how many of them were originally eliminated. Cold case investigators could then focus their investigative energies where they are most likely to be successful. This review would best be conducted by someone who was not connected in any way to the original investigation. If the POIPAT was well constructed, the file review would not necessarily have to be conducted by a police officer provided the reviewer had an understanding of how to apply it.

History of POIPAT

In order to get a thorough understanding of how to create and utilize the POIPAT system, it would be helpful to be aware of the history of its development. In April 1992, the Green Ribbon Task Force was established by the Ontario government to investigate the homicides of two teenagers, Kristen French and Leslie Mahaffy, which occurred in the Niagara Region of Ontario. The task force was led by the Niagara Regional Police but made up of investigators from across Ontario. Larry Wilson, the author, was one of two crime analysts assigned to the case by the Criminal Intelligence Service Ontario (CISO) where he was on loan from the Royal Canadian Mounted Police (RCMP).

The investigation was very high profile with a significant amount of community engagement. The investigators used a number of strategies to solicit tips from the public including a live telethon. This resulted in thousands of POIs being identified.

The problem was that there were only a limited number of investigators to follow up on these tips, so it was important that the most urgent and/or high priority tips were assigned first. There were three operational team leaders who were responsible for assigning tips to investigators, but they did not have any formal priority assessment system in place to assist them in determining what priority to assign to each tip. They had to rely on their intuition and experience to make these assessments, a task which became increasing more difficult as the number of POIs increased. In some instances, except for the most obvious cases, the tips were assigned in the order they were received.

Another problem was that there was no POI tracking system in place. As a result, occasionally the same POI was unknowingly assigned to different investigators because they were identified more than once from different sources.

Wilson recognized a need to establish a priority assessment and tracking system for the POIs that were being identified. He noticed that one investigator in particular was assigning all of his files a priority 1, 2 or 3 based on what he knew about the case and how strongly he felt about the tip. Wilson thought that was a great idea and worked with the operational team leaders to implement and automate that system.

Subsequently, most of the POIs who were identified in the investigation were submitted to Wilson. He would have them added to a database he created to track them and have background checks done on each POI. Once the background check was completed, Wilson evaluated each POI based on how strongly he felt about that POI being a good suspect in the case. He would give the POI a score of one, two or three. Ones were 'good', twos were 'fair' and threes were 'unlikely'.

He then forwarded the POIs to the team leaders, who assigned them to investigators in the priority based on their score. Investigators followed up on the tips and, once completed, they were returned to Wilson, who would update the database to reflect the results of the investigation. The system worked well during the course of the investigation, but the highly subjective assessment process was identified as an issue in a post review of the investigation. Two different people could look at the same information and score the POI differently.

In October 2003, Project KARE, an RCMP led Joint Forces Operation (JFO), was formed to investigate a series of homicides of prostitutes in the Edmonton, Alberta, area. As in the Green Ribbon Task Force case, it was high profile and received a great deal of local and national media attention. Project KARE encountered the same challenges faced by the Green Ribbon Task Force more than 10 years earlier. They were using an electronic major case management system to track tips, but they did not have an objective system in place to prioritize their POIs.

Project KARE's management were aware of Wilson's involvement in the Green Ribbon Task Force and contacted him to see if he could design a tool specifically for their investigation that could be used in conjunction with their major case management system. At that time, Wilson was the manager of the Alberta ViCLAS Centre and as a result was very familiar with all of the Project KARE cases.

He agreed to develop what would eventually be called the Persons of Interest Priority Assessment Tool (POIPAT). Recalling the problem of subjectivity in the scoring system used in the Green Ribbon Task Force system, he set out to make the Project KARE tool as objective as possible. Ideally, anyone using the tool while reviewing the same background information on any given POI would arrive at the same priority assessment.

He started the process by identifying key factors in a POI's background that would make him or her a good suspect in the Project KARE cases. Many of these factors were identified through file reviews, input from the investigative team and a criminal investigative analysis (profile) report that had been done on the cases. Then, in consultation with the investigators and the profiler, he assigned a weighted point value to each factor based on how important it was. The weighting process itself was subjective because it was based on the opinion of those who provided input.

The end product, however, was very objective. All of the factors on the POIPAT were designed to be either true or false with minimal room for interpretation. If the item was true, it received the full weighted value. If not true, it received no points. There were no points awarded for being partially true. As a result, anyone using the POIPAT with the appropriate instructions could review the same file and end up with the same total score. The only differences in score might come as a result of a difference of opinion based on the information available as to whether or not a factor was true or false.

The potential for these types of discrepancies occurring was minimized by creating questions that were as unambiguous as possible. Additionally, there was a guide created that described the purpose of each question as well as the expected response.

Project KARE implemented the POIPAT system shortly after it was developed, and Wilson joined the project in charge of the Tactical and Behavioural Analysis Section. Part of his responsibility was to oversee the POIPAT system.

Over the course of several years, hundreds of POIs were identified and assessed using the tool. It is a very effective tool that has helped Project KARE management maximize the efficiency of the investigative resources available to them. The investigators also understood and appreciated its value. By the time they got a POI assigned to them that had gone through the POIPAT process, all of the background checks had already been done and they knew based on the score whether or not they had a good tip.

The Process

There are a variety of ways POIs come to the attention of police in any investigation. They can come from members of the public, be identified through the investigation, be provided by partner agencies such as corrections, community groups or other police agencies as well as come from proactive strategies.

The POIPAT system begins when a POI first comes to the attention of the investigation. The complexity and resources dedicated to the system will vary from case to case, as will how the system is implemented. These may range anywhere from an investigation with a dedicated POIPAT team, which is integrated into an electronic major case management system, to a small investigation where there are overlapping administrative and operational duties and the case is being run out of a cardboard box.

Regardless of the complexity of the case, the resources available or whether case management is electronic or manual, if the POIPAT system is being used, the principal processes should be the same (see Appendix B: POIPAT Process Map).

New POIs

When POIs are identified to the investigation, they are checked to determine if they have already been identified. If this is the first time the POI has been identified in the case, a POI file should be created and then background checks should be completed. The nature of these checks will be determined by the elements listed on the POIPAT. For example, if there is an element dealing with the POI's access to a vehicle, the POI will be checked against the department of motor vehicle records for a driving history as well as registered vehicles.

The length of time it takes to complete the background checks will depend on the number and complexity of questions on the POIPAT as well as the accessibility of the information. For example, it may take only a few minutes to determine a POI's criminal history, whereas it could take hours of searching various documents to determine if he or she has any connection to the victim(s). This is one reason why it is extremely important when the POIPAT is being developed that the questions be limited and consideration be given to the importance of the information compared to amount of time and effort required to retrieve the information.

Once the background checks have been completed, the POI is assessed using the POIPAT. The POI is awarded points for each element on the tool that is deemed to be true of the POI. The points are then totaled. The total points will determine if the POI is a priority 1, 2 or 3. It will be a management decision as to what score constitutes a priority 1, 2 or 3 (see Chapter 4, 'POIPAT Element Weighting Guide').

After the POIPAT has been scored, it is returned to be assigned to an investigator. Under most circumstances POIs will be assigned in order of priority of their ranking assessment, with ones being assigned first, then twos and eventually threes. Depending on the number of POIs, and the availability of investigators, there may be some delay from the time the POIs receive their POIPAT score until the time they are assigned to an investigator. There may even be incidents where they are scored so low that they are not assigned at all or at least not until all other investigative leads are exhausted.

If a significant amount of time has passed between when the background information was originally collected and the file was assigned to an investigator, it may be necessary to redo some of the background checks in order to ensure the information is still accurate and no new information is available. In some cases the POIPAT score could change based on new information.

Previously Identified POIs

There will be instances when a POI is identified more than once in an investigation through other means and sources. If that POI has not yet been assigned to an investigator, the new information could be added to the POI's background file to be considered when the POI is being assessed by the POIPAT. If the POI has already been scored but not assigned to an investigator, the file can be reassessed which could change the score as well as the priority.

Important Note: If a POI has already been scored and assigned to an investigator, the investigator should be made aware of the new information but the POIPAT should not be re-scored.

Investigators

Once the POIPAT becomes a part of the process, the POIPAT priority ranking will become very important to the investigators. It not only determines the order in which they receive their POIs but also helps them prioritize their own assigned cases. It will also have an impact on how enthusiastic investigators become about their cases. If the POIPAT system is working as it should, when POIs are scored high investigators expect that the leads will be good and, conversely, when they are scored low that the leads won't be so good.

It is good that investigators have confidence in the ranking system, but a word of caution is necessary. In some cases, new or inexperienced investigators may place too much importance on these rankings. Occasionally, they may attempt to increase or decrease the score based on information they have gathered through their investigation. In some incidents, they may not do as exhaustive an investigation or may take short cuts in cases that have been ranked low.

It is important to emphasize to all investigators that the main purpose of the POIPAT is to determine the order in which cases will be assigned. There may be a number of investigative and/or file management processes that precede or follow it, but the POIPAT's job is done once the file has been assigned to an investigator. That is why it is not scored or re-scored after it has been assigned to an investigator.

Investigators must also be aware that it is possible for a number of reasons that the offender responsible for the offence they're investigating is in the list of priority 3s. As such, all investigative steps should be exercised to eliminate POIs once they have been assigned to an investigator, regardless of their POIPAT rating.

Important Note: All investigative steps should be exercised to eliminate POIs once they have been assigned to an investigator, regardless of their POIPAT rating.

POI versus Suspect

Although the terms 'persons of interest' (POI) and 'suspect' are often used interchangeably, there is an important difference for investigators. At one point in time, anyone who came to the attention of police as a person who may have had some culpability in an offence was referred to as a 'suspect'. In those days everyone was a suspect until they were eliminated as such. It was just that some people made better suspects than others.

POIs were usually people whose connection, if any, to the investigation had not yet been established. For example, a witness may have reported seeing someone near the location where a victim's body was recovered. That person may in fact be the offender, a witness who could describe the offender or someone who was simply there by coincidence and had nothing to offer the investigation.

Our legal systems in both Canada and the United States have evolved since then, and the term 'suspect' has come to take on a very important legal distinction. Once a person becomes a 'suspect', he or she is entitled to protection from self incrimination which compels the officer to advise the suspect of that right. This has a significant impact on law enforcement's obligations when dealing with people. Once investigators believe the person they are dealing with is responsible for the offence they are investigating, that person becomes a 'suspect'.

This meant investigators had to be extremely cautious about calling anyone a 'suspect'. As a result, although technically a 'person of interest' (POI) could mean anyone of interest to the investigation regardless of whether he or she is a potential victim, witness or suspect, the term 'POI' has evolved to where it is most identified as describing a 'potential' suspect.

The POIPAT system is aptly named because its purpose is to assess and manage POIs. Those POIs may in fact later turn into 'suspects' after they have been assessed and assigned to an investigator. If a person is a 'suspect' prior to having a POIPAT completed on him or her, chances are he or she has already been assigned to an investigator and as such there is no need to go through the POIPAT process.

Exceptions to Use of POIPAT

Ideally, every person who is identified as a POI would be run through the POIPAT system, but the reality is there will be a number of times in any given investigation when it is not practical, possible or even necessary. There will be instances when a POI is identified and investigators need to act on the tip right away. An example might be a case where the POI is on his way to the airport and not expected to return in the immediate future.

There may also be instances where investigators don't need the POIPAT to tell them a person needs to be made a priority and assigned to an investigator right away. An example would be someone who has made a direct or indirect admission or has been tied to one or more offences through physical evidence.

As a general rule, the POIPAT system should not be used on any POI who has already been assigned to an investigator. Failing to use the POIPAT system on all POIs does not undermine the process. As a matter of fact, using the POIPAT in cases where it is not necessary or after the POI has already been assigned to an investigator would be a waste of investigative resources and counter to the purpose of the system.

Important Note: The POIPAT system should *not* be used on any POI who has already been assigned to an investigator.

Accuracy/Reliability of POIPAT

The only way a POIPAT could be guaranteed to be 100 per cent accurate would be if the offender was known. If that were the case, there would be no need for a POIPAT. Therefore a POIPAT must be created based on what is known or believed to be true of the offender. This is more challenging in cases with no witnesses but not insurmountable.

There are a number of sources of information available to investigators that could help provide some insight into the offender. These could include information about the offence, where it occurred, crime scene examination/analysis, forensic evidence, eye-witnesses and criminal investigative analysis (unknown offender profile). Some elements of the offender's background will be easier to deduce and have a higher potential to be accurate than others. For example, if the offence occurred in a remote area that was accessible only by vehicle, one might infer with some certainty that the offender has access to a vehicle. Conversely, assuming the offender was an outdoorsman because the victim's body was recovered in a wooded area would not be as reliable.

The POIPAT will include a series of these elements which are individually weighted. One of the weighting factors is how likely it is to be accurate. The more accurate we are about each of the elements on the POIPAT, the more accurate the POIPAT will be. That is why it is extremely important that a great deal of thought goes into each of the individual elements.

Important Note: The more accurate each of the elements on the POIPAT is, the more accurate and reliable the POIPAT will be.

If the POIPAT is well constructed, there is a high degree of likelihood that when the offender is identified he or she will score high enough to make him or her a priority 1. However, it is important to note that even in those cases where the POIPAT turns out to be very accurate, there is the possibility that the offender could fall into the priority 2 or 3 categories when he or she first comes to the attention of the investigation.

The primary reason for this would be that when the POI was assessed using the POIPAT, there was limited information available about that person, particularly as it related to the elements on the POIPAT. That is why when elements are identified for the POIPAT, consideration must be given to the availability and accessibility of the information.

Who Should Create the POIPAT?

Ideally, the person creating the POIPAT would be the person who has the most knowledge of the case(s). This person should have unfettered access to every aspect including any hold-back[1] evidence. Although it would be unwise to include anything that could divulge hold-back in the POIPAT, there may be an opportunity to indirectly address it in one of the elements. If, for example, the victim was bound in a very specific and unique way using a certain type of wire that is used in the farming industry, one of your elements might be 'linked to farming or agriculture'. The person creating the POIPAT should also be in a position of knowing how much weight to give to each element of the POIPAT.

In most investigations the lead investigator will have the most knowledge; however, as the case becomes more complex with more people involved, there is less likelihood that even the lead investigator will know every aspect of the case. This is even truer if your investigation involves multiple cases. If the major case management model is being used, the file manager may be the best person. If you have a crime analyst attached to your case, that person may also be a good resource.

If you are going to be using the POIPAT system, chances are your case is suitable for an unknown offender profile. If you have had one completed by a qualified criminal investigative analyst, you have an advantage because it is a great source to assist you in the development of the elements on the POIPAT and it will also help you in determining how much weight to give to each element.

In some cases, this is an extension of the criminal investigative analyst's service and, upon request, the analyst will create a POIPAT for your case based on what he or she knows of your investigation(s) (which should be everything). The Criminal Investigative Analysis Section which is part of the RCMP's Behavioural Analysis Branch in Ottawa offers this service to its clients. They also provide geographic profiles as well which can also be very useful when creating a POIPAT.

Regardless of who creates the POIPAT for your investigation, that individual should have a thorough understanding of the concepts outlined in this book.

Who Should Assess POIs Using the POIPAT?

The person or persons assessing POIs using the POIPAT developed for your case will vary depending on the resources available to the investigation. In some cases it might be one of the investigators; in other cases it might be a civilian employee. It could even be the same person(s) completing the background work. If the POIPAT has been well designed and comes with an instructional assessment guide that explains each element well, anyone with the appropriate training should be able to use the tool effectively.

In the best case scenario, the person who designed the POIPAT for your case would oversee its use for a period of time. This would ensure that it was being used as it was designed, and if necessary the POIPAT itself could be modified to address any issues that may be identified.

POIPAT Instructional Assessment Guide

Even though a well designed POIPAT should be easy to follow and to use on its own, it is a good practice to create a companion instructional assessment guide. The guide should clear up any potential ambiguity and contribute to a consistent approach to the assessment of POIs utilizing the POIPAT you created. The guide should explain not only how each of the elements on the POIPAT should be assessed but also the purpose for each question. Having a good understanding of the rationale behind each element makes it easier to understand what each element is attempting to confirm.

The instructional guide should be written as if the reader has no experience with POIPATs. As such it should start by briefly explaining the POIPAT as a priority assessment tool, how it applies to the case as well as the general methodology behind it. The guide should be set up exactly the same as the POIPAT it was created to accompany. It should be separated into the headings that appear in the POIPAT, and the item numbers from the guide should match the element numbers in the POIPAT. The guide should include the rationale as well as instructions to the assessor for every element in the POIPAT. It should finish by explaining how to score it and then how to assign the appropriate priority ranking.

It would be difficult to provide a step by step instruction on how to create POIPAT instructional assessment guides because they are unique to each case. However, there is a good example of a POIPAT Instructional Guide in Chapter 11 that was created for the Jack the Ripper case study featured later in this book. Readers should be able to use it as a template to create their unique POIPATs. There is also an electronic version of the Jack the Ripper POIPAT Instructional Guide on the companion CD.

POIPAT Development Tools

The POIPAT is simply a collection of elements that are scored, and as such, there are many options available to assist you in its creation. In its basic form it could even be created with just a pen and piece of paper. However, it is most likely you would use one of the many software programs available today, for example a word processing program such as Microsoft Word or WordPerfect. Some word processing programs will even allow you to embed formulas in your document to take care of the math which would reduce the potential for scoring errors.

It is also possible to develop the POIPAT using a database program such as Microsoft Access. This would allow you to maintain a searchable database of all of your POIs with report creating functionality. For example, it would be able to produce a report, rank ordering your POIs based on their score and/or priority assessment. It may also be able to provide an electronic link to your case management program. Regardless of what development tool you decide on, you must first formulate the elements of your POIPAT. The chapters that follow in this book will assist you with that task.

Endnote

1. Highly guarded information or evidence that is known only by the offender and a very limited number of investigators.

Profiling and the POIPAT

2

INSP. PIERRE NEZAN

Introduction

Although in today's modern culture the term 'criminal profiling' has come to mean different things to different people, it is in fact just one of many tools offered in the field of criminal investigative analysis (CIA). Most CIA sections provide services such as interrogation strategies, equivocal death analysis, threat and risk of violence evaluations, geographic profiling and case linkage analysis.

It is, however, the unknown offender profiling service that is the most relevant and useful tool for the purposes of developing a POIPAT. The profile report will detail a description of the unknown offender's traits and characteristics. It is a subjective opinion following the careful analysis of crime scene behaviours and is based on the analyst's experience, specialized training and research. The POIPAT and profiling actually share the same goal of providing investigators with a tool they can use to prioritize persons of interest (POIs). The POIPAT just puts a finer point on it by numerically weighting many of the offender traits and characteristics found in an unknown offender profile. This allows investigators to rank order and prioritize their POIs based on their POIPAT score.

It is possible to create a POIPAT without an unknown offender profile, but it is much better when it is available for this purpose. It is extremely insightful in providing information about the offender which would be unavailable from any other source. The POIPAT is not designed to be a replacement for an unknown offender profile but can be an extension of one. That is why the Royal Canadian Mounted Police (RCMP) Criminal Investigative Analysis Section (CIAS) has introduced it as one of their services. One of the advantages of having the criminal investigative analyst construct the POIPAT (besides the practicality of alleviating a burden for the investigator) is that only those traits and characteristics the analyst feels strongest about will be included. A profile report has many purposes beyond the POIPAT, and as such, some opinions concerning the offender may not be suitable for inclusion. If a member of the investigative team constructs the POIPAT, consultation with the criminal investigative analyst is critical if the unknown offender profile is to be relied upon.

"Of all the animals, man is the only one that is cruel. He is the only one who inflicts pain for the pleasure of doing it."

Mark Twain
(Twainquotes.com)

The rest of the chapter will provide a brief overview of offender profiling which should be helpful when considering elements for any given POIPAT.

History of Profiling

Look for a heavy man, middle-aged, foreign born, Roman Catholic, single, lives with a brother or a sister. When you find him, chances are he'll be wearing a double-breasted suit—buttoned.

Dr. James A. Brussel
(Campbell and DeNevi, 2004, p. 16)

In 1957, when the New York City Police Department turned to a psychiatrist for help in narrowing the search for a serial arsonist dubbed 'the mad bomber', it is unlikely they expected Dr. James A. Brussel to provide such a detailed description of the yet-unknown offender. The sceptics among the investigators probably softened their stance when George Metesky was arrested wearing a buttoned double-breasted suit. In fact, the only point the good Dr. Brussel got wrong was that Metesky was actually living with two sisters. And so the mystical aura surrounding profiling in the modern age began.

Without knowing how Brussel arrived at his opinions, one might think he had a mysterious ability, a paranormal gift or perhaps a good crystal ball. The reality is much less sensational. The mad bomber had been sending a number of angry letters to the media, which Brussel studied for behavioural clues as to the author's ethnicity, age and personal characteristics. His interpretation of the author's personality was based on his experience as a mental health professional and his education and training in human behaviour.

While criminal profiling has existed for many years in Canada and even longer in the United States, its popularity both within and outside the law enforcement community has grown exponentially with the release of successful Hollywood movies such as *Silence of the Lambs*. Today, numerous books, television shows and big screen movies have increased the public's interest and awareness despite the fact that most are inaccurate depictions of the profiling technique and the criminal profilers.

Criminal profiling, which is actually called criminal investigative analysis, was significantly advanced in the law enforcement practice by the Federal Bureau of Investigation's Behavioural Analysis Unit (BAU) in the 1970s and '80s. It is a systematic, logical and analytical method of assessing information gathered from a crime scene. The profiler assesses and interprets the behaviour exhibited by an offender at the scene, and will offer an opinion based on experience, training, education and research on the type of individual who would have committed the crime. The profiler also offers investigative strategies based on the analysis.

The offender profile will assist the investigators in focusing their investigation and establishing a priority suspect list. The purpose of criminal investigative analysis in the truest sense is not to name a specific person as the perpetrator of a crime, but to assist the police officer in focusing the investigation and provide a profile on the type of person who would have committed the crime. Criminal investigative analysts play a supportive role. When crimes are solved, it is the investigators who should be credited, since they are the true architects of the successful conclusion of criminal investigations.

> Criminal Investigative Analysis is an investigative tool, not an investigative solution.
>
> **Roy Hazelwood**
> *(Personal communication)*

Today, criminal investigative analysis has evolved from exclusively providing the unknown offender profile service. In fact, at the RCMP CIAS, it accounts for only approximately 15 per cent of the services provided.

Organized versus Disorganized

A careful crime scene analysis is an integral part of the criminal investigative analysis process. Various studies and classification systems are of assistance to the analyst, such as the organized versus disorganized dichotomy created in the late '80s by Robert Ressler et al.[1] The basic premise is that crime scene behaviours can suggest a preponderance of either organized or disorganized behaviours from which personality traits and characteristics of the offender can be inferred and an unknown offender profile constructed. Rarely, however, will a crime scene exhibit behaviours that will fall exclusively in one category or the other. When you are dealing with human behaviour, it's just not that simple. For this reason, we assess behaviours on an organized/disorganized continuum. This is where the experience/training of the analyst, and to a degree his or her intuition, plays a role.

Typically, the organized crime scene is one that speaks to planning and preparation by the author of the crime. It is one where more of an effort to mitigate the risks of detection and apprehension is undertaken by the offender. Spontaneity may manifest itself through the attack of a victim of opportunity, but even in those cases there have been mental rehearsals by the offender, who is prepared to act when the opportunity presents itself. The organized offender is typically more deliberate and is, in short, your thinking criminal.

Several crime scenes associated to one incident for instance can be suggestive of an organized offender. For example, a murder may involve five crime scenes: the encounter with the victim site, the abduction site, the sexual assault site, the murder site and the body disposal site. The organized offender may have selected these sites ahead of time or may have even improvised, owing to his ability to adapt to changing circumstances. If the encounter site presents too many risks of detection or interruption, he may choose to remove his victim through a ploy or force, relocating to a more private area that will allow him to commit his crime. The sophistication and success of the ruse depends on not only the offender's ability but victimology as well.

Passive victims are usually more desirable in that less effort is required to gain their compliance, allowing the offender to act out his crime, whereas more assertive and aggressive victims will cause him difficulty and, in sexual crimes, negatively impact his ability to see his fantasy play out. Serial offenders will often target prostitutes, who are usually not considered passive individuals but are nevertheless a desirable option because very little effort is required to persuade them to voluntarily accompany the offender. While each offender has his own personal preferences concerning the ideal victim, the most important criteria usually defaults to vulnerability and availability. If the victim has been successfully removed from the high risk area, the body discovery is usually delayed, allowing the offender to place some time and distance between himself and the crime.

The method of body disposal by an organized offender will usually involve concealment or, as is seen less often, the display of the victim. While the former is intended to delay or prevent the discovery of the victim, the latter is done in a manner that will ensure a much more rapid discovery of the body. Ensuring the quick discovery of the body may seem counter-intuitive to the notion of a planned crime by an offender who wishes to mitigate chances of his apprehension. However, the motivation for the offender remains in line with the organized classification since often there is an absence of forensic evidence and the discovery may satisfy an emotional need.

For example, he might derive satisfaction from the shock and panic that he has created in the community. The display may also serve an instrumental purpose by sending a 'message' to competing crime organizations. It may provide a sense of power for the offender, who in some cases will inject himself into the investigation. In the Ressler et al. study, they found that in 20 per cent of the cases, the offender had participated in some way in the investigation. As an example, the RCMP CIAS assisted in a serial offender investigation where the offender orchestrated the discovery of one of his victims by a third party. This type of manipulation concerning body discovery is also seen in cases of staging.

The motivation for concealment of the body is the antithesis of display. Here the offender ideally does not want the body to ever be discovered. When conducting an analysis of the method of body disposal, the degree and sophistication of the concealment effort is considered. Examples of cases that have been referred to the RCMP CIAS have included dismemberment of the body, encasement in cement, burial, destruction through fire and disposal in bodies of water. Clearly, the most efficient disposals are those cases where the victims are never found. This is why it is of vital importance to consider the possibility of a serial offender when a number of persons (especially those who lead high risk lifestyles) are reported 'missing' and to give those investigations the appropriate amount of follow-up.

Tip: While the organized/disorganized system can be helpful in constructing a profile, a normally organized offender's crime scene behaviours may appear disorganized when the offender is under the influence of alcohol or drugs.

The geographic location of the body disposal is often suggestive of the offender's comfort zone. Most offenders operate within a geographic area that is familiar to them and in which they feel comfortable. This applies to both organized and disorganized offenders; however, the former usually have broader comfort zones. In those cases where the area holds no familiarity to the offender, there is usually a preponderance of disorganized behaviours. It is indicative of a spontaneous crime, where the offender did not pre-plan and where body disposal is an afterthought. In some cases, the offender may simply not have an abundance of options, which can be presumed in the Whitechapel murders, which you will read about in the upcoming Jack the Ripper case study.

In that era, it is reasonable to assume that mobility was a luxury (i.e. no cars) and Whitechapel was a populated environment that did not provide much in the way of opportunity for privacy or seclusion. In those cases, opportunities for concealment and significant delay of discovery were limited. As such, you may still have an organized offender despite the rapid discovery of the body, based on the assessment of available options. In other words, he did the best he could with what he had to work with.

Another indicator congruent with an organized offender is the use of bindings and weapons of choice that are brought to the scene by the offender and sometimes removed. Some of these offenders are more aware of the potential for forensic evidence (fingerprints, DNA, hairs, blood, ballistics, etc.) and will undertake efforts to sanitize the crime scene. Removal of the weapons and bindings after the crime, for example, reduces the risk in the offender's mind. Another example that we see more frequently than before involves having the sexual assault victim shower in an effort to eradicate DNA evidence. The disorganized offender may not have used bindings and, consequently, may have had more difficulty controlling his victim. This is not to suggest the disorganized offender does not use weapons; rather, he will usually avail himself of what is at hand during the attack (e.g. a rock, branch, a knife from the kitchen) and usually leave it at or near the scene.

Typically, organized offenders will select victims that are strangers. This is especially true when dealing with serial killers, who overwhelmingly will select victims with whom they have no discernible pre-existing association. The selection of a victim previously unknown to the killer seems incongruent with an organized category that exudes planning and preparation at the hands of a 'thinking criminal'. While selecting an unpredictable stranger as a victim seems at odds with a planned crime, it remains appropriately a feature of the organized killer. According to StatsCan, the average of homicide solve rates in Canada between 1999 and 2008 was 77 per cent. In the vast majority of cases, there was a pre-existing relationship (family or acquaintance) between the offender and the victim.

A key component of any homicide investigation is the intense effort police will dedicate to learning as much as possible about the victim. In reality, that is what a homicide inquiry is—an investigation of the victim that spirals out and usually results in the identification of the killer, linked in some manner to the victim. Clearly, selecting a stranger as a victim offers some advantages for an offender. In crime scenes that depict predominantly disorganized features, we often find that there was a pre-existing victim/offender relationship.

The disorganized murder, a crime scene that is often chaotic and disorderly, frequently occurs as a result of a conflict in the relationship. Because there is strife in the relationship, the scene often reflects intense emotions sometimes manifested by overkill, where the victim's body exhibits much more trauma than was actually necessary to end life. Such features can indicate personalized anger and can suggest that the offender and the victim knew each other.

An example referred to the RCMP CIAS involved an elderly man who was killed by a younger casual acquaintance following an argument. The offender struck the elderly man repeatedly about the head with hammer, even after he was incapacitated and dying. The numerous impacts created a horrific crime scene generated by very significant blood spatter. Yet it is important to note that simply because a scene is gruesome, it does not necessarily equate to overkill.

In the Jack the Ripper murders, especially the Mary Kelly case, the crime scenes were bloody and horrific. Yet they do not necessarily constitute overkill. Rather, the offender killed his victims swiftly, usually by cutting their throats, and the mutilation of the body was done post-mortem. The mutilation is not done to cause death but rather to satisfy an emotional or psychosexual need (fantasy). Death was necessary for Jack the Ripper to get at what was really important to him, the post-mortem activity.

Overkill can be difficult to discern and is not solely based on the severity of the attack, for instance a high number of stab wounds. The RCMP investigated a case where a woman had been stabbed 87 times. In this case the victim resisted her attacker vigorously, and many of the stab wounds were superficial and scattered about the upper body because the offender had difficulty controlling her. Consequently only after he attained vital organs did she cease resisting and died. Yet this was not an overkill situation but, rather, underkill, which is a term used by some analysts. Had the offender (who was intoxicated) been more efficient and attained a vital organ in the first few knife thrusts, there likely would not have been 87 stab wounds. This offender did not do more than was necessary to kill his victim. Rather, his ineptitude caused him to have to stab his victim over 80 times to cause her death.

The RCMP CIAS have found the Ressler et al. organized/disorganized dichotomy to be useful during analysis, recognizing, however, that there are no absolutes when considering human behaviour.

Importance of Fantasy (Ritual) versus MO

Who knows what is in a man's heart? As has been mentioned, the success of criminal investigative analysis hinges on the criminal investigative analyst's ability to recognize and interpret the offender's behaviour. In cases when there is a paucity of discernible behaviour, the analyst's input is hampered. An example would be a bank robbery. Typically, these crimes are perpetrated by a lone male who enters the bank, often with a threatening note he presents to the teller, who will comply with the demands to hand over the cash, after which the offender flees. The time it takes to commit this crime is only a few short minutes and there is very little interaction between the teller and the offender. These are not the types of cases that ideally lend themselves to criminal investigative analysis, certainly not for the unknown offender profile service. These types of crimes are simply not behaviourally rich.

There are a number of crimes where the support offered by criminal investigative analysis is much more valuable. These include but are not limited to crimes of inter-personal violence such as homicides, arsons, bombings and sexual crimes. It is with the latter, however, where the criminal investigative analyst can do his or her best work. This is attributed to the fact that crimes of a sexual nature, especially in serial cases, are often more behaviourally abundant. Sexual crimes are usually based in fantasy, and offenders will often reveal something of themselves and that fantasy during the commission of their crime.

Everyone has fantasies, sexual or otherwise. They are pleasant because you create and imagine them to suit your emotional and psychosexual needs.

Happiness is ideal; it is the work of the imagination.

Marquis de Sade
(Brainyquote.com)

Fantasies respond to a person's wants and desires and are usually intensely private. Consequently, the fantasy is perfect. Reality, however, is usually a proverbial splash of cold water. Take for example the fantasy of winning the lottery, shared probably by most people. In this pleasant daydream the material serendipity solves all of their problems and guarantees their living happily ever after. However, this story-book ending is not so certain. Some of these winners may speak of the strife it caused among the extended family, the ubiquitous charities seeking donations, intrusive and unwanted publicity, complicated decisions concerning investments, etc. This of course does not mean the lottery was unwelcomed by those fortunate few, but rather evidence of how reality and fantasy are rarely, if ever, one and the same.

While many offenders will act out their fantasies with compliant partners, they may fantasize for years before committing their first sexual assault. The fantasy serves as a rehearsal and complements the motivation. Most sex offenders commit their crimes motivated by a need to exercise power/control, anger or a combination of both. The complexity of the fantasy, the theme and the level of aggression and sexual deviance vary from offender to offender. When they ultimately commit their crime, the encounter does not usually develop as was mentally rehearsed, and they are not uncommonly left with a sense of disappointment. However, serial offenders are not deterred by this emotional letdown. Rather, they will continue to offend, making adjustments and refining their crime as they go along in pursuit of that ostensibly elusive fantasy.

One of the original FBI profilers, Roy Hazelwood, has taught us that behaviour can be classified. Regardless of whether or not you are in law enforcement, most people have some familiarity with the term M.O. (modus operandi). In the RCMP Behavioural Sciences Branch, we consider M.O. as those behaviours perpetrated by the offender which are practical in nature. They are intended to ensure the success of the crime, protect the offender's identity and facilitate escape. Common examples include an offender wearing gloves or a condom (protect identity), surveillance of a victim to ensure she is alone (ensure the success of the crime) and binding the victim or cutting phone lines (facilitate escape).

Geography, use of weapons and temporal factors are further examples of M.O. Consequently, they can have important relevance and can be considered for the POIPAT, as will be demonstrated when we create the Jack the Ripper POIPAT in the case study. For example, one of the elements for that POIPAT will be 'lives in Whitechapel'.

When analysing crimes, M.O. behaviours are not necessarily more abundant but frequently much easier to recognize. While M.O. is important when examining a crime and consideration is being given for the POIPAT, it is important to remember that in serial crime, M.O. will usually evolve. Because it is practical behaviour, it is malleable and may change as the offender gains experience, education (sometimes through media) and maturity or in response to changing circumstances.

For example, the RCMP CIAS were called to analyse a series of sexual assaults during which the offender would gain control of victims by threatening them with a knife. During his first few crimes, his victims were appropriately scared and entirely compliant with his demands. During a subsequent attack, however, he encountered a victim who was assertive and defiant and physically resisted him. Consequently, for his next victim he introduced handcuffs and a handgun which he had not used in the earlier crimes. Given the trouble his latest victim had caused, he felt the need to use bindings for control and a weapon that would be perceived as more lethal and threatening. In this case the RCMP CIAS nevertheless linked the crimes, despite this variance in M.O. For the analysts, it was the fantasy based behaviours that persuaded them that this was the same offender.

Tip: 'If it isn't broke, don't fix it'. While you can expect that M.O. will usually be modified, it may remain constant in those cases where the offender is experiencing success.

While we know through our experience that M.O. can evolve and be refined by the offenders, there are occasions when the effort and sophistication of the behaviour may digress. Geography with serial offenders is a good example. During the first few crimes, an offender may travel a significant distance to dispose of a body and take efforts to secrete it at the final resting place. As the months or even years pass, this serial offender's confidence increases because perhaps the bodies have not been discovered and in his mind the police don't even have him on their radar. Why go through that much work next time? The offender may get lazy and not invest as much effort in future disposals. There are a number of examples where serial offenders have gotten 'sloppy', which has contributed to their eventual capture.

One of the primary features that show the differences between M.O. and ritual behaviours is the necessity of the act. Ritual behaviours are those acts that are not necessary to the commission of the crime and are intended to address other offender needs. In sexual crimes, these often complement the motive (power/anger) and fantasy. Another important difference is that in ritual behaviour, while it may evolve and be refined, the theme will remain constant. For example, certain types of sexual offenders are sexually aroused by the suffering and humiliation of their victims. Their crimes commonly reflect elements of torture, humiliation, degradation and bondage. If this offender is serial (which is highly likely with this type of criminal), while the specific acts of violence and torture may vary, the underlying theme will remain constant: the intended suffering of the victim.

With sexual crimes especially, an analyst's focus will be on the offender's verbal, sexual and physical behaviours. These are referred to as offender core behaviours, and close examination and analysis will assist the analyst with understanding the motivation for the crime and the type of person who committed it. As with any group, generalizations should be avoided. Despite some commonalities, not all rapists are created equal. To illustrate, the following two separate cases analysed by the RCMP will be described:

> **Case A:** During the early morning hours, an offender broke into the home of a single mother, who was asleep as was her young boy. He went upstairs and immediately jumped on the woman, who was awakened by his presence. He ripped her clothes off as part of his brutal and sadistic sexual attack, involving violent digital penetration, biting of the breasts, anal penetration and fisting. Her attempts to resist him were immediately put down with repeated punches to her face. His verbal behaviour was degrading, vulgar and commanding. When the victim's young son awoke to investigate the commotion, the offender forced him to participate in sexual acts with his mother, continuing to speak to her in a profane manner.
>
> **Case B:** An offender attacked a young woman walking alone in a park. He produced a knife and threatened her if she resisted. He led her to a secluded area, where he bound her and tried to place a gag in her mouth. She became anxious and said she was concerned she could not breathe and would suffocate. He reassured that she would be okay if she breathed through her nose. Her clothing was removed, as opposed to being torn off her body. He then commenced to penetrate her anally but had difficulty and penetrated her vaginally. The victim was crying and told the offender this is what had happened to her when she was a little girl. This seemed to deflate the offender, and the victim indicated that she believed that the offender felt sorry for her. He stopped his attack and started to cut the bindings to free her. As he was doing so, the victim asked him to be careful not to cut her. He reassured her he would not, after which he fled.

Each of these offenders committed a sexual crime and could be charged under the same Criminal Code section number. When examining the core behaviours (verbal, physical, sexual), however, it is clear that there were some significant differences in the type of and motivation for the attack. Based on this short description of each scenario, you can reasonably hypothesize that these are two separate rapists. This is not to suggest that one is less severe or important than the other. Rather, both of these offenders are serial rapists, and public safety will be assured only if they are both incarcerated for a long period of time.

However, it is clear that offender B demonstrated some concern for his victim and could not carry out his attack. This suggests that injurious violence, such as punching, kicking and biting, does not form part of this offender's fantasy. In his mind, these forced sexual acts are not physically or emotionally hurtful to his victim. Mental health professionals will refer to these as cognitive distortions. A common one for sex offenders is 'it's just sex'. When the young victim in case B made the comment about her abuse history, it shattered his rationalization and conflicted with his fantasy. The reader should not be under the mistaken illusion that this offender's release of the victim was an epiphany for him, recognizing the trauma and pain he was inflicting on others. This type of offender is common among serial rapists. Rather, it is a case of the fantasy not meeting reality and so the mission is aborted—for now.

Conclusion

The POIPAT, used in conjunction with the unknown offender profile, is a strategic tool to help prioritize persons of interest in those cases where the potential leads are overwhelming. Investigative teams will rarely have the sufficient resources to efficiently investigate all of the POIs in short order. The POIPAT will not only improve the efficiency of the investigation, it will provide for a robust, defensible course of action when called upon in future court proceedings. As investigators, we have frequently been asked on the stand why one subject was investigated before others. The POIPAT addresses this question, by providing a standardized and consistent approach.

As one of the most prolific serial killers of the twentieth century once said,

> Since my name came up before the police within a matter of weeks after the Lake Sammamish thing, I suppose they can be faulted for not actually coming out to talk to me. But on the other hand, they can't be faulted because they were working from a huge list. They had hundreds and hundreds of leads. *Which one do they pick?*

Ted Bundy

Endnotes

1. Robert K. Ressler, Ann W. Burgess and John E. Douglas, *Sexual Homicide: Patterns and Motives* (New York: The Free Press), 1988.
2. Robert R. Hazelwood and Ann Wolbert Burgess, *Practical Aspects of Rape Investigation: A Multidisciplinary Approach* (3rd ed.) (Boca Raton, FL: CRC Press), 2001.
3. Stephen G. Michaud and Hugh Aynesworth, *The Only Living Witness: The True Story of Serial Sex Killer Ted Bundy* (Irving, TX: Authorlink Press, 1999), 324, emphasis added.

POIPAT Element Development Basic Rules

3

Introduction

The purpose of this chapter is to provide you with some basic rules and considerations to take into account as you begin developing elements for your POIPAT. Keeping these rules in mind while the POIPAT is being developed will have a significant impact on its reliability and effectiveness.

Conclusions about the Offender Based on Inferences

Every investigation is unique, and so should every POIPAT be unique. In order to be effective, the POIPAT must reflect the unique aspects of each investigation. Therefore you must examine the case(s) to identify those items in an offender's background that would make him or her a good suspect in your case(s). Given that in most cases you will not know who the offender is, there will be little to nothing you really know about him or her for sure. As a result, you will have to do what investigators have been doing for years and that is to draw conclusions about the offender based on inferences.

According to the Merriam-Webster Online Dictionary, an inference is:

> the act or process of inferring, which is the act of passing from one proposition, statement, or judgment considered as true to another whose truth is believed to follow from that of the former.

For example, you might conclude that your offender uses prostitutes which you inferred because your victim was a prostitute and, in your experience, offenders who kill prostitutes are usually consumers of their services. Conclusions based on inferences are in reality educated guesses, and they can range from weak to strong. For example, a weak inference would be that your offender is unemployed because the victim(s) were killed between eight and five on weekdays when most employed people work. This may be correct, but there are many other very plausible explanations such as the offender works night shifts.

An example of a strong inference would be: An autopsy was able to determine the victim died from three gunshot wounds, but the bullets exited the body upon impact and were not recovered; as a result, it was not possible to identify the calibre of gun used. However, you conclude the offender had access to a .357 cal weapon premised on the fact the victim was shot three times and there were three .357 mm bullet casings recovered near the crime scene. Under those circumstances, there would be a strong chance your conclusion was correct even though other, less likely explanations exist.

Once you have determined what elements you will be including in your POIPAT, you will then have to weight each of them. One of the weighting factors will be how strongly you feel about the elements being accurate. The stronger you feel about them, the more points you will assign to them. There will be more on this in the chapter on scoring. However, for the purpose of formulating elements you should try to avoid those that are based on conclusions derived from weak inferences.

Important Point: Avoid using elements on the POIPAT that are based on conclusions derived from weak inferences.

Sources of POIPAT Elements

There are a number of sources that can be drawn upon when considering elements or questions to include in a POIPAT. As indicated early, the person(s) who have the most extensive knowledge of the investigation(s) should be your best source. In very large multiple case investigations, this may be more than one person. If the person who is designing the POIPAT is not the most knowledgeable person, then it is important that he or she has access to the person who is as well as to all aspects of the investigation. Depending on the complexity, size and duration of the investigation(s), it could take weeks or months for one person to review all the material.

One way to shorten this process is to meet with every member of the investigative team including analytical staff to obtain their input. All members of the team should be asked what they believe to be true of the offender, how strongly they feel about it and what, if anything, they have to support their view(s). You could do this individually or in a group brainstorming session. It may be surprising to learn how much is actually known about your offender.

Important Point: When considering elements for the POIPAT, every member of the investigative team including analytical staff should be consulted. They should be asked what they believe to be true of the offender, how strongly they feel about it and what, if anything, they have to support their views.

If an unknown offender profile has been completed for the investigation, it would be an excellent source to consider when formulating questions for the POIPAT. It should be able to provide a very good insight into the offender. Not only will it offer a list of the offender's personality characteristics which could form the basis for many of your elements, it should also include how the profiler came to those conclusions and how strongly he or she feels about them. That would assist in determining how much weight to place on each item.

Number of Elements

When the file review has been completed and everyone has been interviewed, there may be numerous potential elements identified for the POIPAT. That would be a good situation, but it may not be a good idea to include them all. The POIPAT should have a limited number of elements. Every element on the POIPAT contributes to the length of time it takes to complete the background file for each of your POIs. That in turn contributes to the time it takes before it can be assessed, scored, assigned a priority and then assigned to an investigator for follow-up.

The POIPAT system is intended to contribute to the efficiency of the investigation, but if it contains too many elements that take a lot of time to research, it could actually bog down the investigation. The POIPAT is just a tool to identify the likelihood of any particular POI being the person responsible for the offence(s) being investigated. Consider the analogy of investigators explaining to their supervisor why they believe they have a good POI for the investigation. It would likely take no more than five sentences for the investigator to explain why he or she felt the POI would make a good suspect and for the supervisor to form an opinion in that regard.

That is not to suggest the POIPAT should contain only five questions. In reality, the more well founded elements that are on the POIPAT, the more accurate it is likely to be. However, consideration needs to be given to the amount of time and effort required to research each element balanced against the weighted value of that element. For example, it may take only a few minutes on a computer to obtain an offender's criminal history which is likely to be an important element. However, it may take hours, days or weeks to determine a POI's level of education which in most cases is unlikely to be a highly weighted element. In that case you should include the 'criminal history' element and consider dropping the 'education' element.

There are no hard and fast rules about the number of elements on the POIPAT or the amount of time it should take to do the background research for one, but as a general rule you should try to keep them to fewer than 30 elements and no more than a day to research and complete. Ideally, it would take only a few hours to conduct the necessary background research to address all of the elements on a POIPAT.

For the purposes of counting the number of elements in the POIPAT in those cases where there are multiple victims, even though points would be awarded for each victim the POI was linked to, 'links to victim(s)' should be counted as one element regardless of the number of victims. This would also hold true for an 'availability' element. The following are examples of how that might look in a POIPAT:

Linked to Victim			
24	Jane Smith	20	
	Sally Jones	20	
	Bobbi Olson	20	
	Jackie Simpson	20	

The rationale for awarding points to these examples will be explained in a later chapter.

Objective versus Subjective Elements

According to the Oxford Online Dictionary, the definition of 'objective' is 'not influenced by personal feelings or opinions' which is the opposite of 'subjective', the definition of which is 'based on or influenced by personal feelings, tastes, or opinions'. This is a very important distinction because all of the elements on the POIPAT should be designed to be as objective as possible. If the element is objectively worded, different people should be able to look at the same information and arrive at the same answer. This will contribute to the reliability of the tool.

Elements that are subjective are subject to interpretation that is influenced by a person's feelings, opinions and life experiences. This can lead to significant differences in scoring depending on the person assessing the information, and this makes the tool less reliable.

An example of a subjectively worded element would be 'very tall'. 'Very tall' is subject to interpretation. A person who is 5' tall themselves may conclude that anyone over 5' 8" is 'very tall', whereas a person who is 5' 8" may think one would have to be over 6' 2" to be considered 'very tall'. A better way to design that particular element would be to decide what exactly 'very tall' means and reflect it in the wording. For example, '6' 2" or taller'. This wording is objective and leaves no room for interpretation.

Here is an example of subjectively worded elements:

Physical Description			
11	Very tall	10	
12	Very heavy	10	

And here is an example of objectively worded elements:

Physical Description			
11	6' 2" or taller	10	
12	220 lb. or heavier	10	

Although subjectively worded elements should not be included in a POIPAT, there may be situations where they can't be avoided. For example, it may be important to design an element that awards points to POIs who have a sexually deviant history. 'Sexually deviant' is a very broad term and even the experts can't agree on a definition. In that case it would not be possible to define exactly what it means in the wording of the element itself.

Every POIPAT should have an instructional guide that goes along with it. This is where each of the elements can be further explained and/or defined. There may be differences of opinion among analysts on what a particular term used in an element means; however, for the purposes of the POIPAT it is not important. What is important is that the designer of the POIPAT has clearly explained his or her interpretation of the term and what it is he or she is looking for in the POIPAT Instructional Guide. There will be more on creating a POIPAT Instructional Guide for your POIPAT in Chapter 11.

True or False Elements

Each of the elements on the POIPAT should be closed ended and designed so that the only response possible is 'true' or 'false'. Full points are awarded for elements that are 'true' of the POI and no points are awarded for elements which are 'false' or unknown. There should not be an opportunity for them to be partially true or receive partial points (see Chapter 4, 'POIPAT Element Weighting Guide'). The following is an example of an element that could be partially true: 'likes to hunt and fish'.

Offender Lifestyle			
15	Likes to Hunt and Fish	10	

In this case, the POI may enjoy fishing but not like hunting, thereby making the element only half true. If it didn't matter which of those were true, it would be better worded 'likes to hunt *or* fish'.

Offender Lifestyle			
15	Likes to Hunt and Fish	10	

If there was an important distinction between hunting and fishing, then they should be separated into two different elements as follows:

Offender Lifestyle			
15	Likes to Hunt	10	
16	Likes to Fish	10	

Salient Elements

When the task of identifying potential elements for the POIPAT is completed, it is very likely that there will be a small number of salient elements in the list. These are elements that if they were true of any POI, that POI would be of heightened interest to the investigation. They may be considered a high investigative priority regardless of how they scored in any other individual element. An example would be a case where all of the victims were mutilated in the same way and the POI has a history of that type of mutilation. The next chapter, 'POIPAT Element Weighting Guide', will address how these salient elements should be scored to ensure these cases are identified as higher priorities.

Important Note: Given the high importance of salient elements to the investigation and the fact there is likely to be a low number of them, they all should be included in the POIPAT regardless of the availability or accessibility of the information.

POIPAT Element Weighting Guide

4

Introduction

A well designed POIPAT is a very objective tool. As such, if used properly, when the background information of any given POI is assessed, the total POIPAT score should be the same for that POI regardless of who did the assessment. Conversely, when developing the POIPAT, although there are some basic considerations, the weighting of each of the elements is a subjective process.

Ultimately, it will be the person who is creating your POIPAT in consultation with the investigative team who will decide the point value for each element. That person's experience and intuition will play a significant part in that process. This chapter is designed to provide a starting point and factors to consider when deciding the point value for each element.

An Element Weighting Chart (EWC) is included and explained in detail in this chapter. The EWC is really the heart of the POIPAT system and takes most of the mystery out of how many points each element should be weighted based on its level of importance. It explains how to use the 1 to 10 rating system for weighting elements but also offers a textual alternative for those not good with numbers. Those who achieve a firm understanding of how to apply the EWC should have no difficulty weighting the elements of any POIPAT based on the information available to them.

Element Weighting Chart (EWC)

The suggested scoring range for each element on the POIPAT is between 5 and 50 points. The suggested base score which is the starting point for all questions is 20. The POIPAT should be made up of elements which would have an impact on forming an opinion regarding the likelihood of an individual being the person responsible for the case(s) under investigation. If each of these elements were important and had equal influence on your opinion in that regard, you would score them 20 points each. However, in reality that would not likely be the case. For example, if your case was a sexual assault, it would be more important that you know the POI's sexual history than his marital status.

Ultimately, the person accessing the value for each of the elements on the POIPAT will have to decide how important each element is in measuring how likely any given POI is to have committed the offence(s) being investigated. The EWC is designed to assist the evaluator in quantifying a points value for the level of importance placed on each element.

The EWC is designed to allow the evaluator to conceptualize the importance of each element from two perspectives. Firstly, they can look at the element's importance on a scale of 1 to 10 with 1 being the least important and 10 being the most important. POIPAT points are identified for whatever number on that scale the evaluator decides represents how strongly he or she feels about the importance of the element.

Alternatively, the reviewer can consider the element's importance in descriptive terms which reflect various degrees of importance. These terms include: 'unimportant', 'less important', 'important', 'very important' and 'salient'. The numeric scale is fairly straight forward but the descriptive terms will be further explained. A PDF copy of this EWC is available on the companion CD in the POIPAT Utilities sub-directory.

Element Weighting Chart (EWC)		
1 to 10 Scale	POIPAT Points (PPs)	Textual Importance Scale
1	0	Unimportant
2		Unimportant
3	5	Less Important
4	10	Less Important
5	15	Less Important
6	20 (Base Score)	Important
7	25	Very Important
8	30	Very Important
9	50	Salient
10	50	Salient

© Her Majesty the Queen in right of Canada, 2011.

Important Point: All elements should begin with the base score of 20 POIPAT points (PPs) and then be adjusted up or down depending on the other factors considered.

Textual Importance Scale

The following sections describe in detail the different levels of the textual importance scale.

Unimportant

On a scale of 1 to 10 these elements would be scored 1 or 2. They would likely be of little or no value in helping you decide how likely it is that the POI being evaluated is responsible for your offence(s) based on these elements being true. For example, you may have an unknown offender profile that says your offender is likely a loner. As such, you could have an element that reads 'is a loner or asocial'. However, there are two main issues that impact how much weight you should apply to this particular element.

Firstly, it came from an unknown offender profile, and even though these profiles can be very accurate at times, in reality the profiler can never be 100 per cent sure. Most will agree there are some aspects of the profile they feel more confident about than others. If the profiler who created the report is available, you could ask him or her how strongly he or she feels about that element being true. This would help you determine how much weight you should put on it.

Secondly, being 'a loner' or 'asocial' is a personality trait and as such not likely to be readily available, if at all, about most people. If it is available, it would likely take a considerable amount of time and effort to get access to it. When these factors are considered together, 'is a loner or asocial' is not likely to be a very important element of your POIPAT. The impact reliability, availability and accessibility have on scoring will be discussed later in more detail.

General Rule

Elements that are evaluated as 'unimportant' on the textual importance scale or less than 3 on the 1 to 10 scale should not be included in the POIPAT.

Less Important

On a scale of 1 to 10, these elements would be scored 3, 4 or 5 which would equate in POIPAT points to 5, 10 and 15 respectively. These are elements which are not deemed to meet the standard of the base level of importance (described next) but are worthy of consideration anyway. They may also be elements which started off at the base level, but when other factors were considered their value was reduced.

For example, assume the offence you are investigating occurred in a remote off-road area where it was obvious the offender needed to have access to a truck or SUV in order to get to the crime scene. In that case, you may consider 'access to a vehicle' an important consideration when assessing your POIs. However, in reality, depending on the location the majority of the population over 16 is likely to have access to a vehicle. That usually means that the majority of your POIs will have access to a vehicle, so POIs having 'access to a vehicle' is not likely to be of much value to you. It would, however, reduce the overall POIPAT score for the few POIs who do not have access to a vehicle which could provide some value. As such, the element may be included in the POIPAT but have a value of 3 on the 1 to 10 scale or 5 POIPAT points.

A slight rewording of the element in that example to 'has access to truck or SUV' could increase the value of the element. In this case, being more specific about the type of vehicle would reduce the number of persons who would qualify thereby increasing your interest in those particular POIs. It would depend how common owning these types of vehicles is in the population where your offences took place as to how much more weight to place on the element. (See the Vehicle section in Chapter 6, 'Standard POIPAT Elements Library', for more discussion on vehicles.)

Important

Every element included in a POIPAT should be 'important'. However, some are going to be more or less important than the others. When you are considering the importance of each element, there needs to be a benchmark for comparison. In descriptive terms 'important' is the benchmark or base level the EWC uses to compare all elements.

The EWC places 'important' at level 6 on the 1 to 10 scale with a POIPAT points value of 20. This provides the evaluator the flexibility to adjust the value of each element up or down compared to the benchmark on the importance scale.

Ideally, when evaluators begin the element weighting process, they should have all of the elements being considered for the POIPAT available to them. They then need to identify one particular element to use as their benchmark. That item will be scored 6 on the 1 to 10 scale and assigned 20 POIPAT points. All other elements will then be compared against that particular element to determine if it is of more, less or equal value.

For example, assume 'has history of sex offences' was the benchmark element and one of the other elements was 'is an outdoorsman'. Evaluators would have to decide if a person being an outdoorsman was of less, equal or more interest to them than a person who had a history of sex offences.

If evaluators have difficultly identifying an element to use as a benchmark, they should consider 'linked to victim'. In most investigations there will be some link between the victim and offender. The link may be weak or strong, but for the purposes of the POIPAT any type of link between the POI and victim is scored the same and therefore would make a very good benchmark element. (See the Victim section in Chapter 6, 'Standard POIPAT Elements Library'.)

General Rule

'Linked to victim' is an excellent element to use as a benchmark element.

Very Important

In most cases the elements score should not exceed 20 points or 6 on the 1 to 10 scale; however, there are going to be some elements you will feel very strongly about that deserve to be reflected as such in the scoring. These elements could be scored 25 or 30 points depending how strongly you feel about them.

For example, if your case involved the sexual assault of a child, you might score an element 'has history of sex offences' 20 points. However, you might score 'has history of sex offences against children' 30 points. Thirty points should be the maximum points awarded to any element except for salient items which will be discussed next.

General Rule

The number of questions scored higher than the base rate of 20 PPs should be very limited.

Salient Elements

As indicated in Chapter 3, salient elements are elements that if they were true of any POI, that POI would be of heightened interest to the investigation. They may be considered a high investigative priority regardless of how they scored in any other individual element. In order to ensure that cases where these salient elements are true receive a higher relevance, they are scored 50 PPs. That is 20 points higher than the maximum points any element should be otherwise scored. Elements evaluated at 9 or 10 on the 1 to 10 scale should be considered salient elements. An example of a salient element could be 'uses prostitutes' in a case where all of the victims were prostitutes.

It could be argued that if the item is that important, it should be scored high enough to ensure it makes it into the priority 1 category regardless of the scores of the other elements. However, scoring elements so high that the responses to all of the other elements are completely negated will undermine the POIPAT system.

The following is an example that illustrates this point: Assume that in the case where the salient element is 'uses prostitutes' every POI who was identified as using a prostitute was scored so high on this element that it automatically put them in the priority 1 scoring range. At first all goes well, but then an eager investigator (who knows the importance of that particular element) visits his or her vice squad and obtains a database containing the names of hundreds of johns[1] they collected over the last year. Your offender may very well be in the database, but the POIPAT would be useless in helping you prioritize the list because they would all be categorized a priority one.

In reality, although it may be a very important factor to your case, not all johns would be of equal interest. There may be those who have a violent criminal past who were in the area and available during the offence(s) and, conversely, those who have no history of crime or violence and were not in the area or available during the offences. Scoring this element 50 points would ensure that johns scored 50 more points than everyone else in the database. If the POIPAT is well designed, a good POI will score high regardless of any particular salient element. Adding the 50 points in this example would raise the POI's score and should be enough to move him or her up to the next priority level.

It is worth noting that there may be certain elements that, if they were true of any given POI, should become an immediate investigative priority. In those cases it should not be necessary to complete a POIPAT.

Other Factors Affecting Element Weighting

Before making a final decision on the weight value of each POIPAT element, there are a number of other factors evaluators should consider in addition to how they compare to the benchmark element. These factors include, but are not limited to, the availability and accessibility of the information, the frequency or uniqueness of the element in the population, subjectivity and/or the reliability of the source for the element. The following section examines in detail how these factors can increase or decrease an element's weight.

Availability/Accessibility of Information

The availability and accessibility of information relating to POIPAT elements should be a strong consideration in the weighting of an element or even whether the element should be included at all. The element should not be scored higher because the information is readily available or easily accessible, but those factors should reduce the element's weight if the information is difficult to obtain.

For example, you believe your offender is an outdoors person who likes to hunt or fish so you want to use 'likes to hunt or fish' as an element. You believe it would rate a 4 on the 1 to 10 weighting scale which would equal 10 POIPAT points on the EWC. However, the problem is that this type of information may not be readily *available* about most people. As such, you decide you want to keep the element in the POIPAT but reduce its weight from 10 POIPAT points to 5.

Then, you learn there is a government agency who keeps a database of everyone who has obtained a hunting or fishing license in your area. That would make the information available but not necessarily *accessible*. There may be privacy legislation that precludes use of the database by police. However, if you had unfettered access to the database, you could then upgrade the POIPAT points to your original assessment of 10.

In some cases the information may be both available and accessible but would take considerable time and/or effort to obtain. For example, your investigation leads you to conclude that your offender was a very poor academic performer. So you consider adding 'poor academic performer' as an element and assess its weight at 3 on the 1 to 10 weighting scale which would equal 5 POIPAT points.

The most obvious source of a person's academic performance would be school records which would likely be available and accessible. However, the process to obtain those records would probably take considerable effort. This would be compounded by the fact you may not know which school(s) your POI(s) attended so you would have to check them all. At this point, you would have to decide if the value of the element is worth the effort required to confirm it. In this case, given that the initial assessment of the element was 3 out of 10, it is likely that the effort required to confirm it would exceed its value.

General Rule

The POIPAT should not include elements that have been assessed low on the EWC scale and would take considerable effort to verify.

Frequency/Uniqueness of the Element in the Population

The frequency and/or uniqueness of an element could increase or decrease its importance rating. For example, you may have evidence your offender has access to a rifle so you add it as an element. Your initial score on the 1 to 10 EWC scale is 6 which equals 20 POIPAT points because you believe it is of equal importance to the benchmark element 'linked to victim'.

However, it is likely that the location of the offence would also have an impact on how much weight you would place on this element. For example, it is much more likely that POIs living in a rural area are going to have access to a rifle than those living in an urban area. As a result, if your offences occurred in a rural area, owning a gun may be quite common and as such not a significant factor in reducing the pool of POIs. However, owning a rifle in an urban location might be quite rare and make a POI who does stand out from the others.

The more unique or rare the element is in the general population where the offence(s) occurred, the higher the score should be. In the 'access to a rifle' example, the evaluator might score the element 5 on the EWC scale if it occurred in a rural location or 7 if it occurred in an urban location.

Subjectivity of the Information

Objective versus subjective elements were discussed earlier in Chapter 3; however, that section focused on the wording of the element. This section addresses the source or the basis for the element.

When formulating elements for the POIPAT, it is likely that some of them will be subjective in nature. These are elements which were derived from someone's opinion or perception. Two examples of subjective elements include 'offender traits and characteristics' based on an unknown offender profile and offender descriptions based on witness statements.

The subjectivity of the information will not likely increase the weight of the element from your initial evaluation based on its comparison to the benchmark element. However, it could decrease its value. For example, the profile report may suggest the offender is the type of person who would drive a newer four wheel drive pick-up truck so you add it as an element. When doing your comparison of that element to the benchmark element 'linked to victim', you believe it would be less important. The benchmark item is scored 6 on the 1 to 10 EWC scale so you rate the 'owns a newer four wheel drive pick-up truck' element 4.

However, you must then take into account that the element is based on the professional 'opinion' of the profiler and not established 'fact'. Therefore there should be less weight placed on this item. You might then reduce the score from four to three. If this element could be supported by other information, you may let your original evaluation stand. For example, if your offence(s) occurred in an area it would be difficult to get to without a four wheel drive, it would add weight to the profiler's opinion. See the Physical Description section in Chapter 6, 'Standard POIPAT Elements Library', for a discussion on the subjectivity of witness accounts of physical descriptions.

General Rule

The more subjective the source or basis for an element, the less weight it should be given.

Reliability of Source

The old maxim 'consider the source' holds very true when it comes to establishing how much weight to give to any particular element. Like some of the other factors to consider when weighting an element, the reliability of the source of information an element was based on should not increase an element's score beyond its original comparison to the benchmark element but it could decrease it.

For example, you may have an element on the POIPAT that reads 'carries a knife'. If it were substantiated through physical evidence such as knife wounds on the victim, you may have scored it 6 on the 1 to 10 EWC scale, equal to the benchmark 'linked to victim'.

However, if the element was based on the opinion of a highly respected profiler but there was no physical evidence to support it because the victim's body had not been recovered, you might still add it as an element but reduce the weight to perhaps four. If the same element was based on a psychic vision, you might reduce the weight even further or remove the element altogether depending on how you feel about psychic visions.

General Rule

The less reliable the source used to identify an element, the less weight the element should be given.

Endnote

1. A person who uses the services of a prostitute.

Establishing Priority Levels' Points Ranges

5

Introduction

Once you have identified and weighted all of the elements on the POIPAT, the next task will be to decide the priority levels point ranges. Once a POI has been evaluated with your POIPAT, you need to determine what point totals constitute a high, medium or low priority. This is very important because the priority level assigned to a POI will have an impact on the order in which it is assigned to investigators. In some cases where investigative resources are limited and the number of POIs is large, some may not be assigned at all. The priority level may also impact on business rules. For example, team management may decide high priority cases will be assigned to an investigator within 24 hours.

The premise behind the POIPAT is that the higher a POI scores, the more likely he or she is to have been responsible for the offence(s) being investigated. It's like circumstantial evidence—the more you have, the stronger the case. Everyone assessed using the tool is assigned a POIPAT score. That score will determine whether the POI is classified as low, medium or high priority.

There are no hard and fast rules regarding what the range should be for each of these categories. Establishing such strict rules would be difficult because every POIPAT is unique and the total possible POIPAT points will vary from case to case. In many cases it will be a trial and error process and the range may change as the investigation evolves. If for example too many POIs are being assessed as high priority, the threshold can be increased to reduce the number of POIs who fall in that particular range.

As a general rule you should aim to have the following distribution of POIs: 25 per cent high priority, 50 per cent medium priority and 25 per cent low priority. It is not possible to identify a system that will absolutely guarantee the POIs are distributed in this manner. However, the following method should be fairly effective in that regard. We will provide a case example to demonstrate how the method works.

Identify and Score POIs

The first thing you must do is select a number of POI background files to be used for this exercise. The more files you use, the more effective this method will be. However, 20 cases is a reasonable number. The cases should be selected at random without knowing anything about the contents of the file or the background of the POI contained in the file. This should ensure there will be a broad spectrum of scores represented.

For the purposes of our example, the following is a list of 20 names in alphabetical order by last name that we selected at random from our fictitious POI files:

- Allan Bakewell
- Neil Crowl
- Mathew Frady
- Allan Geibel
- Ted Getman
- Ted Hara
- Guy Jinkins
- Fernando Kamin
- Ted Kinch
- Jessie Kornreich
- Neil Krenz
- Jessie La
- Tyrone Lawrie
- Ted Ludden
- Guy Sharper
- Fernando Siegler
- Darryl Sprau
- Clayton Streight
- Allan Whorley
- Daniel Wilkinson

Doing the Calculations

Once you have determined the number of files you will be using for this exercise, you must then determine how many will be in the top 25 per cent, medium 50 per cent and low 25 per cent. This is relatively easy in that the only math you really have to do is determine what 25 per cent of the number of files you will be using is. In this example we are using 20 files, so when we do the math we determine that 25 per cent of 20 is 5. Therefore we know that the five top scoring files will be high priority. We also know that the five bottom scoring files will be low priority. So by default everything between high and low priority files will be medium priority. When you calculate 25 per cent of the number of files you are using, if the result is not a whole number, round the number up.

For example, if you are using 30 files, 25 per cent of 30 is 7.5. In that case you would round 7.5 up to 8.

Once you have determined how many of your cases will be high, medium and low priority, create a table with the following columns left to right: 'number' (can be represented by the # symbol), 'priority level', 'POIPAT score' and 'name of POI'. The table should have the same number of rows as there are POI files, and they should be sequentially numbered in the first column. The following chart is an example for 20 POI files:

#	Priority Level	POIPAT Score	Name of POI
1	High		
2	High		
3	High		
4	High		
5	High		
6	Medium		
7	Medium		
8	Medium		
9	Medium		
10	Medium		
11	Medium		
12	Medium		
13	Medium		
14	Medium		
15	Medium		
16	Low		
17	Low		
18	Low		
19	Low		
20	Low		

Plugging in the Names with POIPAT Scores

Once the priority points range chart has been created, the next step is to score the POI files using the POIPAT. Once they all have been scored, you add the names of the POIs to the chart starting at the top in descending order of their score. The following is an example using the previously listed names:

You may have noticed in this example that POI numbers 5 and 6 both scored 180. The problem here is that position 5 is in the high priority category and position 6 is in the medium priority category. This is a situation that is likely to occur so you must be prepared to address it. It is not possible to have the same score appear in two different category ranges, so you must decide which category that score should be in. In our example we

#	Priority Level	POIPAT Score	Name of POI
1	High	215	Jessie La
2	High	190	Guy Jinkins
3	High	190	Fernando Siegler
4	High	190	Daniel Wilkinson
5	High	180	Allan Geibel
6	Medium	180	Tyrone Lawrie
7	Medium	170	Fernando Kamin
8	Medium	160	Neil Krenz
9	Medium	160	Ted Ludden
10	Medium	150	Allan Bakewell
11	Medium	150	Ted Getman
12	Medium	150	Allan Whorley
13	Medium	145	Mathew Frady
14	Medium	140	Jessie Kornreich
15	Medium	135	Ted Kinch
16	Low	130	Darryl Sprau
17	Low	130	Clayton Streight
18	Low	120	Neil Crowl
19	Low	70	Ted Hara
20	Low	60	Guy Sharper

could place it in high priority which would mean the top 6 scores would make up the high priority range, or it could be placed in medium priority which would mean the middle 11 scores would make up the medium priority range.

There are no strict guidelines to address this situation, but as a general rule it is best in this situation to broaden the high priority range. There is no harm in doing this, but if it is determined that too many POIs end up in the high priority category as a result, it can always be changed at a later date.

Identifying Priority Ranges

Once you have added all of the names with their associated POIPAT score to the priority ranking chart, you can determine the scoring ranges within each of the high, medium and low priority ranges. You can start with the high priority range. In our example the score for the top five POIs ranged from a low of 180 points to a high of 215. However, that was the range for the 20 files we scored in this exercise. It is possible that once the POIPAT goes live in the investigation, some of the new POIs will score higher than our top score of 215. The way to overcome that is to make our high priority range from 180 to whatever the highest possible score that can be achieved on the POIPAT. For the purposes of our example, we will assume the maximum possible score on our POIPAT is 500. Therefore our high priority range would be 180 to 500.

The next step is to determine what the low priority range should be. We do the low priority next rather than medium priority because by default whatever is between high priority and low priority is medium priority. In our example the low priority range was from a low of 60 points to a high of 130 points. However, just as with the high priority range it is possible future POIs could be scored lower than 60 which was the lowest score in the range. To address this issue our low priority range should begin with a low of 0 to a high of 130.

The final step is to determine the medium priority range. The highest score in the low priority category is 130 and the lowest score in the high priority category is 180, so any POIPAT score that falls between 131 and 179 would be in the medium priority category range. However, if you look at the chart in our example, you will see that all of the POIPAT scores are divisible by 5. That would occur if the scoring in each of the elements on the POIPAT were scored this way: 20 points for being from the area, 10 points for having a vehicle and 5 points for being married. Therefore it would not be possible to achieve a total POIPAT score that was not divisible by 5. Thus the lowest possible score that could be achieved in the medium priority range in our example would be 135 and the highest possible score would be 175. So technically, our medium priority range should be 135 to 175.

As a result the following would be the scoring ranges for our example:

Low priority = 0–130
Medium priority = 135–175
High priority = 180–500

Once you have determined the appropriate priority point ranges, they should be added at the bottom of your POIPAT as in the following example:

Priority Point Range: Low = 0–130; Medium = 135–175; High = 180–500	
Completed by: _____	**Date:** ___/___/___
Reviewed by: _____	**Date:** ___/___/___
Note: This assessment was completed with the information available to the assessor at the time of the file review. Additional information could change this assessment.	

Conclusion

Once the priority level scoring ranges have been established using this method, it is likely that future cases will follow the same distribution pattern of 25 per cent high priority, 50 per cent medium priority and 25 per cent low priority. Slight deviations are possible but not likely to be of major concern. If there are significant changes to this distribution pattern, the scoring ranges can be adjusted to address them. Additionally, the 25 per cent, 50 per cent and 25 per cent distribution range for priority categories is not mandatory and can be adjusted either at the outset of the process or even after implementation. You may wish to change these numbers if you feel too many POIs or not enough are falling into a specific category. This system has the flexibility to allow you to do this.

There are two blank POIPAT Priority Point Ranges Worksheets available for your use on the companion CD in the POIPAT Utilities sub-directory. One is for a 20 file sample and the other is for a 30 file sample.

Standard POIPAT Elements Library

6

Introduction

The previous chapters explained the rules for designing, weighting and scoring a POIPAT. This chapter is an excellent source of elements to consider when a POIPAT is being developed. It provides a list of elements that could be important to any investigation. Each element is discussed in detail including its possible relevance to major investigations as well as any pitfalls with including it in the POIPAT. The rationale for assigning points to each element is also explained in detail.

Each of these items is provided as an example for consideration only. Every investigation is unique and as a result many of these items may not apply or be very important. As such only those elements that are relevant or important to the investigation for which the POIPAT is being designed should be used.

The wording of these elements is also only a suggestion and may need to be modified or changed altogether. The weighting of the elements may also need to be adjusted based on their importance to the specific investigation(s).

This chapter will also include examples of how the beginning and end sections of the POIPAT should be constructed. (See Appendix A for an example of a completed POIPAT.)

The Heading

Every POIPAT should begin with the following information: name of POI, date of birth (DOB), fingerprint number (if available) as well as a task/tip reference number. The name of the POI should always be in the same format—for example, surname, first given and second given). This is also true of the DOB. This may seem like a small, unimportant detail, but when you start dealing with hundreds of POIs it will save you a lot of potential confusion and redundancy.

The tip/task number is also very important as it will link this POI to a tip or task which should ensure that it is easily traceable and has been the subject of whatever file management process is being used for your case.

The following is an example of the beginning of a POIPAT:

Persons of Interest Priority Assessment Tool						
Name of POI	**Surname**		**First Given**		**Second Given**	
	Linderman		Mathew		Nelson	
DOB	**YYYY**	**MM**	**DD**	**Fingerprint Number**	**Task/Tip #**	
	1963	07	25	A374658C	1456	
					PP	**Score**
Residence						
1	Alberta (June 1, 2009–Dec. 31, 2009)				20	
2	Calgary (June 1, 2009–Dec. 31, 2009)				20	

Geography

Geography is a very important aspect of any investigation. This can include where the victim and/or offender worked, lived or frequented. In crimes of interpersonal violence such as sexual assault and homicide, there are a number of important scenes. They are where the offender made contact with the victim; where the offence took place; where the victim was released, escaped or was deposited (in the case of homicide); and where evidence is recovered. In some instances two or more of these crime scenes can be at the same location. Examination of these crime scenes can provide either the investigators or criminal investigative analysts (criminal profilers) valuable information about the offender(s). This information can assist with the development of other aspects of the POIPAT.

For the purposes of adding elements to the geographic portion of the POIPAT, we will focus on the POI. This includes where he or she lived during the offence(s) as well as his or her comfort zone. Each of these areas can include a number of questions.

One valuable tool available to investigators in Canada and the United States is geographic profiling. Geographic profilers analyze the locations of crimes and characteristics of local neighbourhoods to predict where the offender likely lives or works. It usually requires a minimum of five crimes or related sites to develop a profile. These profiles can be very useful in developing your POIPAT geography related questions. Even in cases where there are fewer than five sites, a geographic profiler's assessment can offer valuable insight. For more information on geographic profiling visit: http://www.rcmp-grc.gc.ca/tops-opst/geographic-g-profil-eng.htm and http://www.ecri-canada.com/ .

Even if you don't have the benefit of a geographic profile, you can still make some fairly safe assumptions about where the offender lived and his or her comfort zones based on what you know about the investigation(s).

Offender's Residence

It is recognized that offenders do not have to live in the state or province where the crime was committed to have committed the offence, but when they do it makes them better POIs. They make even better POIs when they reside in the city, town or village where the crime(s) were committed. This should be the basis for your first two questions on the POIPAT related to where the POI resided at the time of the offence(s).

The first question should ask if the POI lived in the state(s) or province(s) where the offence occurred, and the second one should ask if the POI lived in the city(s), town(s) or village(s) where the offence(s) occurred. There could be exceptions to this when the geography is unusual or unique. For example, if the crime scene is in the city of Victoria, British Columbia, on Vancouver Island, it might be more appropriate to use 'resided on Vancouver Island' instead of 'resided in British Columbia' as an element.

When assessing if the POI lives in a particular city, you should include adjoining suburbs even if they are not officially part of that city. Your POIPAT Instructional Guide should include this point. The following is an example of these questions assuming all of the offence(s) occurred in Calgary, Alberta, Canada, between June 1, 2007, and December 31, 2007.

		PP	Score
Residence (June 1, 2007–Dec. 31, 2007)			
1	Alberta	20	
2	Calgary	20	

The first column represents the element number. The second is the element description. The third indicates the POIPAT points (PPs) which are the point value assessed if the question is true. The fourth column is to record the number of points if the question is true. It is assumed that if a number is placed in the Score column, then the answer to that question is true. For example, if the POI being assessed with the POIPAT lived in Alberta, the assessor would enter 20 in the Score column on that particular line.

The standard 20 points were assigned to each of these questions as there was nothing that made them any more or less reliable or important than any of the other questions (yet to be created) in this particular POIPAT. These points are cumulative because, in our example, living in Alberta makes one a good POI but living in Calgary makes one an even better POI.

Points are awarded in both these questions if the POI resided in either or both of these areas at any time during the date range for these offences no matter how long he resided there. So, for example, if the POI is known to have resided in Calgary in July and August of 2007, he would get points for both questions. 'Resided' can include limited or full-time incarceration which is something that should be noted in the POIPAT Instructional Guide that you should create for this POIPAT.

This can get more complicated when the offences occur in different cities, but it can also serve to make a POI even stronger. For example, if you have offences that occurred in a number of cities, a POI becomes stronger for every city he lived in during the time of each of those offence(s). In these cases you should add a question for each city, town or village where an offence occurred for which you believe the same offender is responsible. Each of these questions should be qualified by a date range.

The following is an example of a case where it is believed the same offender is responsible for offences in Calgary, Red Deer and Edmonton. Note that the dates are placed on the element line instead of the section title (shaded area) because they are unique to each of the cities mentioned.

		PP	Score
Residence			
1	Alberta (June 1, 2007–Dec. 31, 2007)	20	
2	Greater Calgary area (June–July 2007)	20	
3	Greater Red Deer area (Aug.–Sept. 2007)	20	
4	Greater Edmonton area (Oct.–Dec. 2007)	20	

In this case the offender would get points only for living in those areas during the offence dates. Using the cumulative points awarded in this section, the POI would become a stronger POI for every city he resided in at the time of those offences.

It may appear from this example that you could have a POI who resided in these areas but not during the specific offence dates so as a result would not receive any points. This is true but will be addressed in the next subsection which deals with the offender's comfort zones. These comfort zone related questions are not date specific.

Tip: It is a good practice to include relevant dates in each element description if dates are different for each element or in the section title (shaded area) if one date or date range applies to all elements in that section.

Offender's Comfort Zone(s)

There is a great deal of literature available regarding the comfort zones of offenders. The premise in most cases is that the offender will have some connection to his crime scene(s) which as indicated previously could be where he encountered the victim, where he committed the offence, where he released or deposited the victim or where he disposed of or deposited evidence. It is believed that familiarity breeds comfort which in turn reduces the perceived risk by the offender.

An offender's comfort zone can be a place he lived in, worked at or visited. The connection can be weak or strong. A strong connection could be where the offender grew up as a child, and a weak connection could be a location the offender drove by once. The more times a person visited a particular location, the stronger the connection.

In the case where there are multiple crime scenes, the more scenes the POI can be connected to, the more likely the POI is to have committed the offence(s). For example, in a case where a prostitute is picked up in the city, sexually assaulted and murdered in another location and then deposited in yet another, if you can link a POI to all three locations, that would make him a very strong POI, particularly if those locations were a significant distance apart.

The length of time a person is connected to a location also impacts on the strength or weakness of the connection. Obviously, the more time spent at any given location, the stronger the link. For the purposes of the POIPAT, the strength or weakness of a link does not matter. Full points are awarded if there is a connection to any of the crime scenes regardless of the strength of the connection.

It is not uncommon to have multiple locations within an investigation which is further exacerbated in the case of multiple offences. In these cases you should attempt to reduce the number of comfort zone based questions on the POIPAT by using broader areas. There may be clusters of crime scenes you can refer to, instead of identifying every scene.

The following is an example of a homicide where the victim was picked up in Calgary but the body was deposited in Okotoks and the offence occurred between June 1, 2007 and December 31, 2007. Okotoks is a small community about 65 kilometres south of the city of Calgary.

		PP	Score
Residence (June 1, 2007–Dec. 31, 2007)			
1	Alberta	20	
2	Greater Calgary area	20	
3	Greater Okotoks area	20	
Comfort Zone			
4	Resides in, works in or known to frequent Calgary or surrounding area (25 km radius)	20	
5	Resides in, works in or known to frequent Okotoks or surrounding area (25 km radius)	20	

Notice that in this example the date range for where the POI resided is placed in the section title because it is applicable to all the elements in that section, whereas there is no reference to a date or date range in the Comfort Zone section title or underlying elements.

Physical Description

It is well established that a crime victim's recollection of an offender's actions is far more reliable and accurate than an offender's physical description. Victims have a tendency to retain more about what happened to them than the description of the person who attacked them. This is particularly true if a weapon is involved and there is a surviving victim. This is known as the 'weapon-focus effect'. Additionally, victims' and other witness descriptions can be distorted by their own reality, experiences and perceptions.

As mentioned in a previous chapter, a short person may view a person who is 5' 8" as tall, whereas a tall person may view that person as average or short. A young person may view a 30 year old as old, and a 50 year old may view the same person as young. A thin witness may view a 200 lb person as heavy, and a 250 lb witness may view that person as average.

Another problem with using victim descriptions is that an offender's physical appearance changes over time, some more dramatically than others. These changes can occur intentionally, accidentally or through the aging process. In cases where the offender believes a victim or witness may be able to describe him, he could alter his appearance to reduce his chances of being identified. He could have altered his appearance for cosmetic reasons such as wearing a hair piece or having facial reconstruction. He may have also gained or lost a significant amount of weight.

The dynamic nature of physical characteristics presents another challenge for utilizing it as an element in a POIPAT. In order to be most accurate and effective, the physical description of the POI being considered should be what he looked like on or near the date of the offence. It is usually not difficult to find a source that can provide information about a POI's physical appearance, particularly if he has a criminal background. The difficulty is finding a source that can provide a reliable physical description of the POI for the relevant times.

There will also be cases where there are no witnesses. These could include but are not restricted to homicides, political threats, bombings and arson cases. As such, there is no physical description available. In these cases it may be possible to make some assumptions about the offender's physique based on the investigation or a criminal investigative analysis. For example, you might be able to conclude the offender was a strong person because there was some aspect of the crime that would have required a significant amount of strength.

Based on what we know about the challenges and reliability of using physical description as an investigative aid, you should avoid its use as an element in your POIPAT. It should be considered only in those cases where the offender is believed or known to have a unique or unusual physical attribute that is not likely to change over time. A physical deformity or amputation would be an example of this, but that information is not readily available about most people.

Height would be a good example when all witnesses agree the offender was unusually tall. Yet another could be a tattoo. Information on a person's tattoo(s) should be more available, particularly for anyone who has had involvement with the criminal justice system. It may be found in police Records Management Systems (RMSs), the Canadian Police Information Centre (CPIC), the National Crime Information Center (NCIC), the Violent Criminal Apprehension Program (ViCAP), the Violent Crime Linkage Analysis System (ViCLAS), the National Sex Offender Registry (NSOR) or other law enforcement indices. You must even be cautious with tattoos due to the popularity of temporary tattoos which can be added or removed easily.

The following are examples of questions where it is believed the offender had a tattoo of a lion on his right arm, and he was extremely tall. In reality if you know the offender had a tattoo on his arm, it is likely you also know where on the arm the tattoo appears. However, it is best to leave it open to the entire arm to allow for a small margin of error. You could open this up even more by not qualifying which arm the tattoo appears on.

Physical Description			
7	Tattoo of lion on right arm	30	
8	Very tall (over 6' 2")	20	

You may have noted that the point score for this question was changed to 30 from the standard 20 points. This is an example of weighting a question higher based on its uniqueness. It could be argued that there are likely a large number of people who have a tattoo of a lion on their arm. However, it will be very likely that you would have a lot fewer people in your pool of POIs who have a connection to the city where the offence occurred which is assessed at 20 points than you would have POIs with a tattoo of a lion on their right arm.

The height question was given the standard rating of 20. We could have scored it higher as with tattoos because according to one US government website[1], only 5 per cent of males in the United States 20 years and over are taller than 6' 2". We did not score it higher because it is still subject to a certain amount of perception and the data sources are not always the best. You will note, however, that the element's subjectivity was significantly reduced because it clearly defined what 'very tall' meant by adding '(over 6' 2")'.

Age

Age is another element that is typically of low reliability due to the reasons previously indicated for other aspects of a person's physical description. It is even more problematic when there are no surviving witnesses. However, there are ways of coming up with an estimated age range even when there are no witnesses. There might be certain elements of the offence(s) that could provide clues to the investigator. If, for example, you know the victim was picked up in a licensed establishment by the offender, he would have to be old enough to fit in in that environment. We also know that except for certain offences like paedophilia, offenders tend to slow down their criminal behaviour as they get older. There are of course many exceptions to that rule.

A criminal investigative analysis may be helpful, but as most profilers will concede, age is one of the most difficult categories to evaluate as it is the mental and emotional age of the offender that is being assessed. This does not always correlate with chronological age and therefore no person should be eliminated on the basis of age alone.

For the sake of our continuing example in the physical description category, the following example assumes there were no witnesses, and we had to rely on an unknown offender profile report that said the offender was in his mid- to late 20s.

Physical Description			
7	Tattoo of lion on right arm	30	
8	Very tall (over 6' 2")	20	
9	Age (20–30)	10	
10	Age (31–45)	5	

Given the low reliability of identifying the offender's correct age, two broad age ranges were selected and their scores appropriately weighted. We could have used one age range between 20 and 45 with a weight of 5 or 10 points. However, listing two age ranges with different weights, as in this example, provides the ability to recognize that it is more likely your offender will be between 20 and 30 years than the 31 to 45 range which is outside the profile report's suggested range.

Gender

Even if you had no idea of the gender of the offender in your case, if it was a violent crime, you would be relatively safe in assuming the offender was male. This is particularly true of stranger on stranger crimes of an interpersonal nature. ViCLAS supports this premise in that 97 per cent of the offenders in these cases captured in that system are male. It is also likely that the majority of the POIs who will be identified in your investigation will be male as well.

Given these statistics, it might not seem very useful to add an element dealing with gender. However, adding this element will address those rare situations when a female POI is identified. If a female POI is identified and you believe your offence was committed by a male, you would likely put a low priority on following up on that particular tip. If you did not add this gender element to the POIPAT, you would not be able to rate males higher than females.

If being female significantly reduces the likelihood of a POI being responsible for your offence, you should have that reflected in the scoring. The POIPAT uses a positive cumulative scoring approach so you cannot take points away for being female. You can, however, assign males a stronger weight which reflects how strongly you believe your offender is male.

The following is an example of a gender based element on the POIPAT.

Gender			
9	Male	50	

In this example we scored male 50 points. This high score for being a male will have no effect in raising the priority of POIs who are male because most of the other POIs will also be male, but it will ensure they get a much higher priority than females. This is an exception to the rule that says only salient elements should be scored 50.

Race/Ethnicity/Skin Colour

Relying on witnesses to accurately describe the race or ethnicity of an offender can be problematic. Although a person's appearance may be linked to these, trying to determine what group(s) a person belongs to simply by appearance is in reality only guesswork and as a result not likely to be very reliable. This is further exacerbated by the multitude of different ethnic and racial groups in Canada and the United States. Statistics Canada defines 12 different classifications of race[2] and had over 200 ethnic origins reported in their 2006 census.

Another problem is that due to the sensitivity of this information, it is not always readily available. Most law enforcement agencies collect it for investigative purposes such as describing a missing or wanted person, but not all systems classify it in the same way. For example, one major system, the law enforcement records system, has only 2 classifications for race (white and non-white), whereas another has 13.

Given these challenges, race and ethnicity should be avoided as elements on the POIPAT. However, you could consider using a person's skin colour which can be related to race and/or ethnicity but is easier for a witness(es) to identify. Unfortunately, it also comes with the same difficulties as using other aspects of a person's appearance. As such, it is not recommended; but if you do choose to use it, you should give it a low weighting score and use it only in those cases where you have witnesses who you believe have accurately described that aspect of an offender's appearance.

Accent

A person's accent could be considered as an element on the POIPAT provided it is distinct and easily recognizable. It should also be identified in the broadest context as possible. For example, a francophone might be able to distinguish various French accents such a Québécois, Acadian or Parisian, but others may not be able to make that distinction. Most people, however, would be able to recognize any of those accents as being French.

The score for this question should be weighted on the degree to which the accent stands out from the community in which the offence occurred. For example, if your offence occurred in Newfoundland, Canada, you would likely not be surprised if your offender had a Newfoundland accent or that most of your POIs would also have Newfoundland accents. In that case, having a Newfoundland accent would be corroborative but it would not really make a POI stand out from any others. However, if your offence took place in Victoria, British Columbia, and your offender was known to have a Newfoundland accent, you would likely be quite interested in POIs with that accent, particularly if they were living in Victoria at the time. In that example you would score a Newfoundland accent higher on your POIPAT in British Columbia than in Newfoundland.

For the purposes of the following example, assume the offender was known to have an Irish accent and the offence occurred in Calgary, Alberta. You will note we weighted this question 10. There are probably a large number of people who speak with an Irish accent who live or visit Calgary, but an Irish accent is still likely to stand out there. Based on those demographics, we could have given it the standard score of 20 points. However, the score was reduced because information about a person's accent is not likely to be readily available. Additionally, it involves human interpretation which is always susceptible to error.

Accent			
9	Irish accent	10	

Speech Characteristics

We all have unique speech characteristics that help people identify us just from listening to us speak. This is evident when we recognize a phone caller after only a few spoken words. Some have speech characteristics that are more pronounced than others. These can include fast or slow speech, slurring, stuttering, a nasal tone, a lisp or other speech abnormalities. If you have a victim or witness who can confirm that the offender in your case had an outstanding or unique speech characteristic, it could be used as an element on the POIPAT.

If you do include it, you should try to avoid identifying a specific speech impediment and leave the question open to all types. This increases the reliability of the question because it is not necessary to have to identify the particular impediment.

The example below would give points to any POI with a speech impediment regardless of its nature. It was scored 15 because just as in the case of a person's accent, that information is not readily available but it is not open to as much interpretation as trying to identify a specific accent. You should adjust the score based on your situation. The more a characteristic is subject to a witness's perception or opinion, the lower the score should be. For example, whether a person speaks fast or slow is more a matter of opinion than whether or not a person speaks with a stutter. So speaking with a stutter would be scored higher than how fast or slow a person speaks.

Speech Characteristic			
10	Speech impediment	15	

Lifestyle

You should consider the offender's lifestyle when formulating elements for the POIPAT. This could include such things as whether the offender is an alcohol or drug abuser; whether he likes to socialize or is a loner; whether he is transient, a street person or homeless; whether he uses sex trade workers; whether he engages in frequent criminal activity; whether he is nocturnal; whether he hunts or fishes and so on.

Identifying an offender's lifestyle may be challenging, particularly in those cases where the offender is unknown and there is no one available who can provide this information. However, there are certain elements of the investigation that may be able to help you. For example, if your victim is a prostitute and was believed to be engaged in that activity when he or she met the offender, it would be safe to conclude your offender uses prostitutes. You may have found cigarette butts at the scene that would lead you to believe the offender was a smoker.

An unknown offender profile is also an excellent means of obtaining an insight into the offender's lifestyle. These profiles are specifically designed to help the investigator understand the type of offender who committed the particular offence(s) being investigated. Part of the profile will specifically address certain elements of the offender's lifestyle. See Appendix C for an example of an unknown offender profile report completed by retired FBI SSA John Douglas on the Jack the Ripper investigations.

The following is an example that includes a number of elements of an offender's lifestyle:

Lifestyle			
7	Uses sex trade workers	50	
8	Nocturnal due to choice or circumstance (night person)	5	
9	Engages in activities of an outdoor nature such as hunting or fishing	5	

It is important to note that the first element uses the term 'sex trade workers' rather than 'prostitutes'. The term is broader and includes other areas of the sex trade where clients pay for sexual services such as massage parlors or escort agencies.

You will note that the 'uses sex trade workers' element is weighted at 50 points which is extremely high. We assumed in this example that the victim was in the sex trade which is how she came in contact with the offender. If this was the case, it would be safe to assume the offender has been and may still be a consumer of sex trade services. Therefore any POI with that background would be of heightened interest to the investigation. This information is usually available through police information systems. In some cities 'john' lists are available through local community groups who often record information about people involved in this activity.

The next two elements of the example, 'nocturnal due to choice or circumstance' and 'engages in activities of an outdoor nature ...' may be assumed about your offender through your investigation or included in a profile report. They were scored quite low because they are not likely to narrow the field much. You may be slightly more interested in POIs with this background but not nearly to the extent of those who use sex trade workers. It is also true that this information may not be readily available about most people.

Marital Status

It is very unlikely that you will know the marital status of your offender at the time of the offence(s). This question has more to do with the POI's availability to commit the offence(s) than about a legal status. Your investigation may lead you to believe the offender spends a great deal of time involved in various aspects of the offence. This could include planning or preparing the offence(s), selecting victims, committing the offence(s) and disposing of evidence after the offence(s).

The length and frequency of time the offender spends away from home could indicate he is not likely accountable to a spouse or partner. If he is, he may be in a relationship where he is very dominant and does not need to explain long and/or frequent absences from the home.

Not being accountable to a significant other could also provide the opportunity for the offender to use his home as a crime scene. This could involve anything from storing evidence, souvenirs or trophies to offending against the victim.

The following example addresses both of those possibilities:

Marital Status (June 1, 2007–Dec. 31, 2007) (Select One Only)			
7	Unattached (i.e. single, divorced, separated)	5	
9	Unaccountable (i.e. married but wife is extremely passive or compliant)	5	

This example includes a date range which would cover the dates of the offences in the investigation. There is also a note to 'Select One Only'. That's because a positive response in either element indicates that the POI being assessed is not accountable. These elements are scored 5 based on the importance the POI's lack of accountability would likely have in determining if he is the person responsible for your offence(s). They are also scored lower because this information would not likely be easily accessible for most people.

Employment

As with marital status, it is unlikely you will know the employment status of an unknown offender. However, details of a POI's employment could impact on the probability of his being responsible for the offence(s) you are investigating. If you have an unknown offender profile report for your case, it might give you some suggestions as to whether the profiler believes the offender is employed and the type of work he does. There may also be some aspect of the investigation or trace evidence that leads you to believe the offender works in a certain industry.

The following is an example of how those aspects could be included as elements in a POIPAT:

Employment			
9	Employed—at the time of the incident(s)	5	
10	Employed professional—at the time of the incident(s)	5	
11	Linked to medical industry	20	

For the purposes of our example, assume the first two elements came from an unknown offender profile report. If this was the case, the profiler should be able to tell you how strongly he or she feels about these particular elements. In our example we assumed the profiler did not feel very strongly which is reflected in the low score. You could increase the score if the profile report was supported by some other information you obtained through your investigation.

In the last element, 'linked to medical industry' could have been used if for example you knew your victim(s) was being incapacitated by a drug that was available only to someone working in the medical industry such as a health care worker. We scored this the standard 20 points based on the idea this would be an important aspect of your offence and you would be very interested in any POI who was in this position.

The more specific you can be about the industry or profession, the higher the points you could assign this element. For example, if the drug in question was a narcotic that is normally strictly controlled to the point whereby it can be accessed only by doctors or nurses, you could reword it to 'doctor or nurse (or someone with strong ties to a doctor or nurse)' and score it 50 points as the following example demonstrates:

Employment			
9	Employed—at the time of the incident(s)	5	
10	Employed professional—at the time of the incident(s)	5	
11	Doctor or nurse (or someone with strong ties to a doctor or nurse)	50	

Wording it this way makes it easier for the person assessing the POI. It is much easier to identify whether a POI is a doctor or nurse than whether a POI had access to a specific drug.

Education

There are certain aspects of an offence and/or offender's behaviour that can offer clues about an unknown offender's education level. This is another area where a criminal investigative analysis can be helpful. You may also be able to come to some conclusions based on certain elements of the crime. This is particularly true in cases where the offender has left textual evidence behind as might be the case in extortion or criminal harassment cases. These writings might even be able to point to a particular academic field.

When you are deciding what weight to apply to this element, you should consider how accurate you believe your assessment of the offender's education is. The more confident you are, the more points you should award and vice versa.

You should also consider how important the offender's education was in your offence(s). For example, the offender may have needed a degree in engineering to build a complex explosive device and be able to identify the most vulnerable location for it.

The following is an example where the offender is believed to have a strong academic background due to the content of writings sent to media organizations:

Education		
9	Post-secondary education or higher	10	

In this case we scored it 10 because although it may true of the offender, a large portion of the general population in North America have post-secondary degrees. You could score it higher if this is not true of the population in the community where your offence(s) occurred. Another reason for the low weighting is that determining whether a POI has a post-secondary education may be difficult and time consuming.

Criminal History

There is a generally accepted rule in law enforcement that a minority of criminals are responsible for the majority of crimes. This means there is a good chance the offender in your case has a criminal history even if it does not form part of his official criminal record. It is even more likely if your offence is very serious. Offenders normally don't start off at the most serious extreme end of their crime category.

For example, those who commit non-familial stranger homicides for sexual purpose likely started off committing nuisance offences like exhibitionism and voyeurism. They may have then progressed to sexual assaults and learned through experience that it was not a good idea to leave live witnesses behind.

It is also very common for sex offenders to have a history of property offences such as break and enter, possession of stolen property and theft. Therefore if your case was a sexual homicide, you should be interested in POIs with criminal history involving any type of sex offence as well as property offences.

For the sake of the following example, it is assumed your unknown offender profile report indicated your offender is likely a paedophile and has a history of violence and sex related offences.

Criminal History (Score All That Are Applicable)		
11	Has criminal history	5	
12	Has history of violence	20	
13	Has history of sex related offences	20	
14	Has history of sex offences against children	50	

In this example there are four elements to this section of the POIPAT based on the profile. Each of these elements should be scored cumulatively. This ensures that the more of these elements are true, the higher a priority your POI will be. In this case, number 11 'has criminal history' was scored low. Although that information about your POI would be readily available, its usefulness in determining the likelihood of your POI being the person responsible for your offence would be relatively low. It is likely that a large percentage of your POIs will have a criminal history.

The next two elements, 'has history of violence' and 'has history of sex related offences', were scored the standard 20 points as those elements would likely increase your interest in the POI, and that information should be readily available to law enforcement.

The last element, 'has history of sex offences against children', was scored 50 points because if your offender is a paedophile, it is highly likely he has been previously involved in crimes against children. This could be anything from possession of child pornography to sexual assault. It is important to note here, however, that even if your victim is a child it does not necessarily mean your offender is a paedophile. Some offenders target children because of their availability and/or vulnerability. The type of offender you're dealing with may be one who finds it easier to attack more vulnerable victims such as children, the mentally or physically disabled or the elderly.

This is important for you to know, because in this case it is likely the POI has a history of sex crimes against children but not as likely as would be the case if he was a paedophile. If this were the case, you could still add the 'history of sex offences against children' but lower the score to the standard 20. The priority assessment would still be increased but not to extent of a paedophile.

Unless you have expertise in the field of paedophilia, you should not try to make this determination yourself. Paedophilia is a sexual preference for prepubescent children, and in reality the offender is the only one who can tell you his sexual preference. However, most law enforcement criminal investigative analysts (profilers) do have the expertise to form an opinion in this regard based on an analysis of your case.

For the purposes of the POIPAT, the offender does not need to have an official criminal record or even have been charged with an offence for you to conclude he has a criminal history. This information can come from any credible source such as police reports, databases, intelligence systems or even self-admissions. You just have to believe the information is accurate.

Links to Victim(s)

If the offence you are investigating is a crime against a person, there is a very good chance there is some direct link between the victim and the offender in your case. These links can be very strong and easy to identify such as when the offender kills a spouse, or quite weak and difficult to establish as in a homicide of a sex trade worker. Usually, the weaker the link between the offender and the victim, the more difficult the case is to solve.

It is also true that in most cases where there are multiple victims, the more victims you can link your POI to, the more likely he is the person responsible for the offence. These linkages may be as a result of, but not necessarily restricted to, the following examples: the POI is a relative of the victim(s), a customer or client, an employer/employee, an acquaintance or briefly met the offender on some occasion.

The victim(s) may not even be aware of the linkage. For example, the POI is a janitor at a pub that one or more of the victims frequented. The POI may have known the victim from often seeing him or her there, but the victim(s) never took notice of the janitor.

The following is an example where you believe your offender is responsible for offences against four different victims:

Linked to Victim			
11	Jane Smith	20	
	Sally Jones	20	
	Bobbi Olson	20	
	Jackie Simpson	20	

Establishing a connection between the offender and victim is very important, and as such, even though that information may not be readily available, it was scored the standard 20 points. This is scored cumulatively which ensures the POI's score increases with each victim he is linked to.

In some cases you may not be able to establish a direct connection between the POI and victim(s) but you are able to make an indirect link. For example, you might find that the POI is related to his or her drug dealer. Although this would not be a strong connection, investigators would still be interested.

You can also have an indirect link between a POI and a victim when there are strong connections between victims. The victims could be related, work together, socialize together, belong to the same club, etc. In these cases there may have been some opportunity for the offender to come in contact with those other connected victim(s).

When assessing a POI using the POIPAT, if the connection between victims is as a result of an illegal and/or high risk activity such as prostitution, you should *not* award any points for an indirect connection. In those cases it is likely the victims travelled in the same circles, but their selection as victims would probably have more to do with their illegal or high risk activity than any connection to each other.

Links to Victim(s) in Investigations with Numerous Victims

Investigations with numerous victims are rare but unfortunately they do happen. Ted Bundy, the DC Snipers (John Allen Muhammad and Lee Boyd Malvo), John Wayne Gacy, Jeffrey Dahmer and Clifford Olson are examples. In 2003, Gary Ridgway (the Green River Killer) pleaded guilty to 48 homicides. In 2007, Robert Pickton was convicted of the murders of 6 women. He was charged with murdering 20 others but charges were dropped because he received the maximum possible sentence on the first 6. He is actually reported to have confessed to 49 murders.

As demonstrated in the previous example, it is possible to list multiple victims on the same POIPAT with the view that the more victims the offender is linked to, the higher proportionate investigative priority that POI will be. This linkage principle is no less true of these high profile cases with 10 plus victims. It doesn't take much imagination to appreciate how much investigators would be interested in a POI if that POI could be linked to 10 or more of their victims.

Ideally, all of the victims would be listed on the POIPAT, but there is an alternative approach if that is not practical or the preferred option. Although which victims the POI is linked to would likely interest the investigators, it is not absolutely necessary to list them individually on the POIPAT. The purpose of the POIPAT is to establish a priority ranking, and from that perspective the most important thing is not who but how many. The following example provides an alternative approach to listing each victim individually:

Link(s) to Victim (Maximum Number of Victims = 25)		# of Victims	
11	Multiply number of victims by 20 for total PP score (i.e. 5 victims × 20 PPs = 220)		20	

In this example, rather than listing each victim the number of victims is identified and multiplied by 20 which is the total score for this element. Note that the maximum number of victims was identified for this element. This would indicate that there were 25 victims in this case which would be the maximum number any POI could be linked to. This is important because when identifying the points range for the overall POIPAT, it is necessary to know what the maximum total possible score would be on each element.

Availability of POI

This element of the POIPAT addresses the POI's opportunity and availability to commit any or all of the offences associated with your investigation. In the case where you believe the offender is responsible for multiple offences, the more offences he is available for, the more likely your POI is the offender, and conversely, the fewer he is available for, the less likely he is to be your offender.

Some might argue that if you believe all of your cases were committed by the same offender and the POI was not available or did not have the opportunity to commit *all* of the cases, then the POI should be excluded altogether. This may be true, but you should exercise extreme caution before excluding a POI based on that premise. Unless there is some physical evidence such as DNA that links these cases together, there is always the chance not all of the cases were in fact committed by the same offender.

Another important factor is that it is very difficult to establish absolutely that your POI did not have the opportunity or was unavailable to commit any given offence. Usually the only way to be 100 per cent sure your POI did not commit the offence is to establish that he was dead, in custody or under law enforcement surveillance at the time of the offence.

You also need to be very cautious about using electronic or documentary evidence to conclude an offender was in custody during your offences. There have been occasions when official records have shown that the offender was in custody, but closer examination or investigation revealed that he was on one form of release or another. This is one of the reasons why even if the person doing the POIPAT assessment has indicated that the POI was not available for one or more offences, the file should be assigned to an investigator to confirm.

Important Note: When it comes to scoring this element, if you do not have any information that clears the POI, assume they were available and had the opportunity and as such score the points.

The following is an example where you believe your offender is responsible for offences against four different victims and you have date ranges for when you believe the offences were committed:

Availability (Subject Was Available—i.e. Not Incarcerated at Time of Offence[s])			
12	Jane Smith (2001/6/25–2001/7/30)	10	
	Sally Jones (2001/8/27–2001/9/14)	10	
	Bobbi Olson (2001/10/22–2001/10/29)	10	
	Jackie Simpson (2001/12/14–2001/12/26)	10	

Each of these items has been scored 10 because all of your POIs will be awarded these points unless you can establish they were not available for your offence(s). Additionally, being linked to victims (which is scored 20 points) is more important than being available. Most of your POIs and even the general public will be available for your offences, but not nearly as many are likely to have links to your victims.

You should note that in this example, each of the victims has a date range identified. In these cases you need to determine whether your POI was available during these specific periods. He doesn't need to have been available for the entire date range as long as he was available at any time within that range long enough to have committed the offence(s). If you know the exact date of your offence, you would put that there instead of the date range and worry only about those specific dates.

Availability of POI in Investigations with Numerous Victims

Just as with the 'links to victim' element, ideally all of the applicable dates or date ranges for each victim would be listed on the POIPAT. Although it is not absolutely necessary for the purposes of the POIPAT to list them individually, these dates are extremely important to investigators who will eventually be assigned the task of accounting for the POI during these crucial dates. Having them itemized on the POIPAT provides the investigator with a valuable quick reference tool.

However, if that is not the most practical or preferred approach, it is possible to use a similar method as was described for numerous victims in the 'linked to victim' element. It may be just a bit more complicated. The following is an example:

Availability—Subject Was Available (i.e. Not Incarcerated at Time of Offence[s]) (Maximum Cases = 25)—Assume POI Available Unless There Is Info to Contrary		# of Cases POI Available		
12	Multiply number of cases by 10 (i.e. 5 victims × 10 PPs = 50)		10	

In this example, the person doing the assessing is asked to enter the number of cases where the POI was available to have committed the offence(s). This is then multiplied by 10 to obtain the total score for that element. The maximum number of cases possible is listed in the title bar. There is also a note that indicates the assessor is to assume the POI was available for all of the offences unless there is information to the contrary. For example, if there were 10 cases and there was no information that eliminates the POI from being available for any of them, the assessor would put 10 in the '# of Cases POI Available' box. That would be multiplied by 10 for a total of 100 which would be placed in the last column. However, if a POI was found to have been incarcerated for 4 of the 10 cases, that would make him available for 6 cases. In that instance, 6 would be entered into the '# of Cases POI Available' box, and it would be multiplied by 10 for a total score of 60.

Vehicle

It would obviously be helpful to your investigation to determine firstly if the offender used or had access to a vehicle and secondly the description of that vehicle. There are a number of avenues available to assist you in this regard even if you do not have a witness. Determining if a vehicle was used in the offence should obviously be easier to determine than the description of it. You may be able to conclude this simply based on where the offence took place or the distances between crime scenes.

You might be able to determine the type of vehicle used based on your investigation and/or evidence left at the scene. The type of terrain where the offence(s) took place might also provide you clues to the type of vehicle used. An unknown offender profile might also be helpful. It is often able to even suggest whether or not the offender will be driving a late model car and if it will be well maintained.

The following is an example where it is believed the offence was committed by someone who had access to a truck, SUV or van:

Vehicle			
19	Owns or has access to a vehicle	5	
20	Owns or has access to a truck, SUV or van	15	

Item 19 in this example, 'owns or has access to a vehicle', was scored low because even though it may have been necessary for your offender to have a vehicle to commit your offence(s), it is likely that a very large percentage of the POIs in your case own or have access to a vehicle.

Item 20 in this example was scored 15 because it narrows the field quite a bit more, but it was assumed there would also be a large percentage of the population who own or have access to that type of vehicle. You could weight this higher or lower depending on the nature of the location of your offence and the likelihood of people from that area driving that type of vehicle. For example, you are likely to see more heavy duty pick-up trucks in Fort McMurray, Alberta, than in Toronto, Ontario; therefore you would weight it lower in Fort McMurray because it would be more frequent.

If you have an actual description of the vehicle such as 'it was a late model red Honda', you could add that as an element. However, your weighting should be based on how specific you can be with the description and how confident you are in the accuracy of that description. For example, you would weight 'late model red Honda' higher than 'sporty red compact'. You would also consider the source and reliability of the information. You would weight this higher if it came from evidence found at the crime scene than you would if it came from an eye-witness. You could weight your eye-witness score higher if you had more than one independent witness who described it the same way.

You should be careful though, even when there are multiple witnesses who give a similar description of the same vehicle. For example, in the Paul Bernardo case there were a number of witnesses who described the suspect vehicle involved in the abduction of Kristen French as a beige or yellow Camaro or Firebird. At the time the Camaro and Firebird were nearly identical vehicles in shape and design. The incident occurred in St. Catharines which was strongly connected to the auto manufacturing industry where it was assumed most residents would know their cars. The crime vehicle actually turned out to be a gold Nissan 240SX. A significant amount of investigative resources were dedicated to identifying POIs who drove beige or yellow Camaros or Firebirds.

If you were creating a POIPAT today for that case under those circumstances, your best approach would be to describe this aspect of the Vehicle section as 'owns or has access to a light coloured sports car' and give it 15 points as in the following example:

Vehicle			
19	Owns or has access to a vehicle	5	
20	Owns or has access to a light coloured sports car (i.e. Camaro or Firebird)	15	

Other Elements

All of the preceding elements were factors you are likely to encounter or consider in most investigations. However, every investigation is different and as such there will be one or more elements that are unique. Some may be more important than others. This section is where you can address those elements. Items in this category would typically be scored at the standard score of 20 or higher, based on their uniqueness. We couldn't possibly think of them all but the following are some examples:

If your case is a sexual homicide, there may be certain aspects of the offender's behaviour that are unique. For example, if the offender had sex with the victims post-mortem, you could add an item such as 'history of or documented interest in necrophilia' as in the following example:

Other			
22	History of or documented interest in necrophilia	50	

It is assigned the maximum points because it is assumed that not many of your POIs will have a history of this particular paraphilia, but you would be extremely interested in those who do.

If your case involved an offender who was doing random shootings from a long distance, you could use the following example:

Other		
23	Has access to rifle	20	

This was scored the standard 20 points because for the purposes of this example, it was assumed these offences occurred in a part of the country where it was not uncommon to own a rifle. You could raise or lower this score based how common it is in the area where the offences are occurring for someone to own or have access to a rifle. This would be more likely in a rural area than an urban area.

If you knew the actual make and calibre of the rifle, you could add an additional element as in the following example:

Other		
23	Has access to rifle	20	
24	Has access to Ruger 10-22 CRR rifle	20	

If your case involved an offender who was using explosive devices, you might add an element as follows:

Other		
23	Has access to explosives or materials used in the making of explosives	50	

This example is weighted the maximum 50 points because it was assumed it is a salient feature of your investigation and that not many of your POIs would have access to explosives or related material. However, if the majority of your POIs work in a field such as mining where explosives are common and easily accessible, you could reduce the weighted value.

Comments Section

No matter how exhaustive your POIPAT is, there are likely to be instances where there will be items identified in a POI's background that were not addressed in the POIPAT which would heighten your interest in him. These can be relatively minor to fairly significant. For example, there might be a POI who was scored relatively low on the other elements of the POIPAT but has been collecting newspaper clippings of the offences you are investigating. The Comments section should appear at the end of the POIPAT and is the place where the background reviewer can identify issues in the POI's background he or she believes would be of interest to the investigators. This section is not scored, but the information contained here could be used to elevate the POI's priority regardless of the POIPAT score.

The following is an example of a case where the victims were killed by a specific type of rifle:

Other			
23	Has access to rifle	20	
24	Has access to a Ruger 10-22 CRR rifle	20	
		Total Points	95

Comments
Although this POI scored quite low, an intelligence report revealed that he has a large collection of Soldier of Fortune, Gun and True Crime magazines. It also advises that he has been downloading graphic images from the Internet of homicide victims who have been killed by gunshot.

In this example the POI did not score high on the POIPAT, but his fascination with guns, true crime stories and images of victims who were killed by gunshot was noted in the Comments section as this information would be of interest to investigators.

The End Section

Every POIPAT should have an ending that includes the Priority Point Range (which was explained in detail in Chapter 4, 'POIPAT Element Weighting Guide'), a place for the persons who scored and/or reviewed the POIPAT along with the applicable dates. The dates are very important because the POIPAT is scored based on the information that was available on the date it was scored. New information may become available after that date which may lead to a higher score. However, once the file has been assigned to an investigator the score is not changed. The following is an example of how the end of a POIPAT could look:

Other			
23	Has access to rifle	20	
24	Has access to a Ruger 10-22 CRR rifle	20	
		Total Points	

Comments
Although this POI scored quite low, an intelligence report revealed that he has a large collection of Soldier of Fortune, Gun and True Crime magazines. It also advises that he has been downloading from the Internet graphic images of homicide victims who have been killed by gunshot.
Priority Point Range: Low = 0–175; Medium = 176–225; High = 226–595
Completed by: _____Date: ____ / ____ / ____
Reviewed by: _____Date: ____ / ____ / ____
Note: This assessment was completed with the information available to the assessor at the time of the file review. Additional information could change this assessment.

Endnotes

1. Anthropometric Reference Data for Children and Adults: United States, 2003–2006, http://www.cdc.gov/nchs/data/nhsr/nhsr010.pdf.
2. Statistics Canada, Population Group of Person, 2011, http://www.statcan.gc.ca/concepts/definitions/ethnicity-ethnicite-eng.htm.

POI Elimination Status Coding System

Introduction

The POIPAT and the Elimination Status Coding System (ESCS) are quite different but complement each other. The biggest difference between them is that the POIPAT is applied when a POI is first identified and the ESCS is applied when the POI investigation has concluded. Both of these tools can be plugged into any major investigation utilizing a major case management system whether they are manual or electronic.

Process of Elimination

One misconception held by many who are not familiar with law enforcement investigative techniques is that when investigators have a POI identified or assigned to them, their job is to gather evidence to prove that person is responsible for the offence(s) they are investigating. In fact, in most cases the opposite is true. Unless there is some compelling information or evidence that indicates the POI is the person responsible for the offence(s), the most effective investigative strategy is to use the process of elimination. In most investigations there will be one or two offenders who are actually responsible for the offence(s), so everyone else is innocent and deserve to have their name cleared. This is the approach most investigators take.

In some cases POIs are eliminated right from the start without further investigation because there was no reasonable basis for them to be considered suspects in the first place or they couldn't be responsible because they were incarcerated or deceased at the time of the offence(s). In many cases investigators actually contact the POIs to give them an opportunity to assist in clearing themselves as possible suspects. In instances where there is forensic evidence such as DNA or fingerprints at the crime scene(s), they may be asked to voluntarily provide samples which can be used to exclude them. Often they are asked to provide an alibi which investigators can confirm. In most cases POIs are cooperative and are subsequently eliminated.

Once investigators have completed their POI investigations, the results can range from conclusively eliminated to couldn't be eliminated. The results of their investigation are usually documented in the investigative file. In many cases, there is an elimination coding system in place that quickly identifies how a POI was eliminated. This coding system is often linked to their case management system.

Benefits of Elimination Status Coding Systems

The following elimination status coding system was used by the Green Ribbon Task Force (GRTF) in the Bernardo/Homolka case[1].

GRTF Elimination Status Code System Chart

Code	Title	Description
A	Conclusive Elimination	Supported by conclusive independent evidence (i.e. incarcerated)
B	Eliminated	Supported by independent evidence
C	Probable Elimination	No longer considered suspect despite absence of supporting evidence
D	Status Unknown	Interviewed but cannot substantiate alibi
BLANK	Open	Not yet interviewed

A variation of this coding system was developed and implemented by Sgt. Pat Hayes (Retired) who was the file coordinator for Project KARE. Sgt. Hayes called his elimination tracking system the 'elimination matrix'. It was integrated into the Project KARE major case management system and worked very well.

There are a number of benefits to using an elimination status coding system such as the one used in the GRTF investigation where there were a large number of POIs. In that case they had 3175 POIs. They were rated as follows: 598 good, 1021 fair, 1280 unlikely and 276 not classified due to insufficient information.

One of the benefits of using such a system is that it gives investigators and case managers the ability to quickly identify how subjects were eliminated without having to read through the entire investigative file. This can be particularly useful in cases where new information is received regarding a POI who has already been investigated. For example, if the POI had been coded 'A—Conclusive Elimination' and the new information did not refute previous information used to conclusively eliminate the POI, the new information may simply be placed in the file with a copy to the original investigator. However, if the POI had been coded 'C—Probable Elimination', the POI file may be reopened and reassigned based on the new or additional information.

Another benefit is that if the coding system is integrated into the case management system, whether it is automatic or manual, it provides the ability to easily track all POIs to ensure none fall through the cracks. It also allows the flexibility of implementing investigative or administrative strategies based on these elimination codes. For example, managers may learn through a geographic profile that there is a strong possibility their offender lives in a particular geographic zone. As such, they decide they will now re-examine all of the POIs who live in that zone who had not been scored 'A—Conclusive Elimination'. If they were using the POIPAT as well, they might decide they will first look at all those who were assessed high priority on the POIPAT.

Just as with the POIPAT, a POI elimination status coding system can also be very useful during cold case reviews. It gives cold case investigators the ability to quickly identify those POIs who were not conclusively eliminated or not eliminated at all.

Revised Elimination Status Coding System

The elimination status coding system used by the GRTF worked well in that case, but some of the category titles and descriptions have been updated in the following chart by the author to better define the elimination status they are meant to convey. The term 'suspect' has also been replaced with 'POI' to be consistent with current interpretations of those terms.

Revised Elimination Status Coding System Chart

Elimination Status Coding System (ESCS)		
Code	Title	Description
A	Conclusive Elimination	Supported by conclusive independent evidence (i.e. incarcerated or dead)
B	Supported Elimination	Supported by independent evidence
C	Unsupported Elimination	No longer considered POI despite absence of supporting evidence
D	Couldn't Be Eliminated	All investigative steps have been exhausted but subject could not be eliminated
BLANK	Open	Investigation not yet completed

Each of the categories of elimination including the suggested revision to the titles will be discussed in the following paragraphs.

A—Conclusive Elimination

This category title was not changed as it conveys exactly what the code is meant to describe. This is a situation where investigation has determined there is irrefutable information or evidence that this particular POI could not have committed the offence(s). Examples of this may include an offence where there is offender DNA and this particular POI's DNA does not match. Other examples include the POI being incarcerated, under police surveillance or dead at the time of the offence(s).

Important Point: Investigators should be sure the DNA found on a victim, on a piece of evidence or at a crime scene belongs to the offender before conclusively eliminating a POI based on the fact that his DNA did not match that particular DNA. Locating foreign DNA on the victim or at a crime scene does not necessarily mean it belongs to the offender. Additionally, there may have been two offenders.

Extreme caution should be exercised in all cases before assigning this code to a POI because it could remove that person from further consideration or investigative strategies. For example, new information may be received about the POI but his file is not reopened because the elimination code indicates he has been conclusively eliminated.

An investigator must be convinced that the information or evidence that excludes this person is accurate, reliable and conclusive. Ideally, it would come from a first-hand account or verification and not unsupported sources. For example, if an investigator eliminates a POI because he was incarcerated at the time of the offence, it would be better if the information could be corroborated by someone at the institution. The offender's criminal record may show he was serving time in an institution during the offence(s); however, criminal records do not typically contain information about temporary releases which can occur fairly often. If this information is believed to be accurate but cannot be absolutely confirmed, it should be scored in the next category: 'B—Supported Elimination'.

B—Supported Elimination

The title of this category was changed from 'Eliminated' to 'Supported Elimination' to better reflect how POIs in this category should be classified. The threshold of elimination is just a bit lower than 'Conclusive Elimination' but is still fairly strong. It is important to note, however, that even though in order for a POI to be scored 'B—Supported Elimination' information or evidence must exist to support elimination, that information or evidence is not absolute proof of elimination. It is still possible that the person was responsible for the offence(s) being investigated.

Important Note: Even though elimination of POIs in this category is supported by independent information or evidence, it does not conclusively rule them out.

For example, a POI may suggest he could not have committed the offence because he was on a fishing trip with a friend at the time. Investigators interview the friend, who they find credible, and the friend confirms the POI's story. That POI could then be scored as 'B - Supported Elimination'. However, no matter how credible the friend may seem, there is the possibility that the friend was not being truthful. It is not unheard of for alibi witnesses who were believed to be very credible to knowingly mislead the police. In some cases they may not believe they are doing any harm because they don't believe the person they are protecting committed the offence and are simply doing them a favour by providing them an alibi.

Another example is a POI who indicates he was working at the time of the offence. The investigator goes to the job site and determines from the shift schedule and the POI's time card that he was in fact working that day. This is strong independent evidence to support elimination, but it is not absolutely conclusive. It is still possible for these items to have been manipulated.

There may be occasions when there is independent information or evidence that supports elimination, but the investigator is still not comfortable eliminating the POI. In these cases the investigator's intuition should prevail. If all investigative avenues have been exhausted and there is no evidence to support that the POI committed the offence but neither can he be eliminated, he should be scored 'D—Couldn't Be Eliminated' which will be discussed later.

C—Unsupported Elimination

This category title has been changed from 'Probable Elimination'. The premise of probable elimination remains the same but the new title is more consistent with the other category titles. This category should be used when after all investigative avenues have been exhausted, the investigator believes this person was not responsible for the offence(s) even though there is no independent evidence or information to corroborate it.

In reality it is likely that this is the category in which most POIs will be scored, particularly in those cases where there has been a significant passage of time between when the offence occurred and the POI was interviewed. This is also true when there are multiple offences and/or the offence dates are unknown. These circumstances make it difficult for POIs to provide an alibi or for the police to confirm one. In the end, investigators must make a judgement call as to whether or not, based on the results of their investigation, they believe the POI should be eliminated as a person of interest. In the vast majority of cases they will be correct, but it is important to realize that there will be those rare occasions when they are wrong.

D—Couldn't Be Eliminated

This category title has been changed from 'Status Unknown' and the description changed from 'interviewed but cannot substantiate alibi' to 'all investigative steps have been exhausted but subject could not be eliminated'. The new title is a little more definitive about what it describes which is the elimination status of the POI. The new description recognizes that eliminating POIs is more complex than simply interviewing the POI and confirming an alibi.

Investigators would select this category for those POIs for whom they have exhausted all avenues of investigation but were unable to find information or evidence that supported the POI being eliminated as a person of interest. The difference between this category and 'C—Unsupported Elimination' is that the investigator does not feel comfortable eliminating this subject as a person of interest. This does not necessarily mean the investigator feels the POI would make a good suspect. If he or she did, chances are the file would still be open and there would be no need to decide on the most appropriate elimination code.

Conclusion

The revised ESCS presented in this chapter is a companion major case management tool for the POIPAT. Major case managers can use as is or modify it to their preference. They can use it in cases with a large pool of POIs even if they are not using a POIPAT. It is, however, important to remember that, just as with the POIPAT, it is an administrative tool used to manage POIs and is not designed as an evidentiary tool to prove or disprove criminal culpability.

A PDF copy of the Elimination Status Coding System chart is available in the POIPAT Utilities sub-directory of the companion CD.

Endnote

1. Archie Campbell, *Bernardo Investigation Review*, Report of Mr. Justice Archie Campbell, 1996, http://www.opconline.ca/depts/omcm/Campbell/Bernardo_Investigation_Review%20PDF.pdf, pp. 135–136.

Jack the Ripper— Case Study

II

Jack the Ripper—Investigations 8

Introduction

The previous sections of this guide have provided significant detail on how to create and score a POIPAT. However, the best method of learning and reinforcing a particular skill or knowledge set is to utilize it in a real life situation. This section is designed to do just that. Here, the author utilizes the Jack the Ripper investigation which is one of the oldest and most well known cold cases in history for that purpose.

This investigation makes an ideal case study for creating a POIPAT because it is unsolved, is high profile and has multiple victims and many POIs. There is even an unknown offender profile report available which was completed by well known former FBI profiler John E. Douglas in July 1988 (see Appendix C). In fact, there were two profiles on the case. Police surgeon Dr. Thomas Bond was asked his professional opinion on the extent of the murderer's surgical skill and knowledge. Dr. Bond prepared a report (see Appendix D) based on his post-mortem examination of one of the victims as well as notes from the others' post-mortem examinations. This is believed by many to be the first example of 'criminal profiling'.

This section of the book will walk the reader through the creation of a POIPAT for the Jack the Ripper case, including element selection and weighting. It will then take a number of the better known POIs and rank order them in terms of who would have been the most likely to have committed the offences based on how they score on the POIPAT created for the investigation.

Ideally, when developing a POIPAT you would have access to all of the investigative material including the ability to speak to the investigators. Unfortunately, in this case much of the investigative material is missing and the investigators are deceased. However, some official records still exist, and there have been numerous books, articles, websites, and research papers written on the case.

The following summary of these cases is based on the author's review and interpretation of some of these materials, some of which conflict, and as such it cannot absolutely be guaranteed to be 100 per cent historically accurate. However, the purpose of this chapter is not to provide a historical account of events in the Jack the Ripper case but to provide enough material to demonstrate how to develop a POIPAT. For the purposes of this exercise, we will assume this summary is factual.

Investigational Overview

Approximately 11 homicides occurred between April 1888 and February 1891 in the Whitechapel area of England which became known as the 'Whitechapel Murders'. There has been much discussion and debate by experts over the years on how many of these homicides were actually committed by the offender who would come to be known as Jack the Ripper. No one really knows for sure as there was no forensic evidence such as DNA linking any one individual to one or more of these cases.

However, the general consensus is and a compelling case can be made that he is responsible for five of the cases. The victims in those cases, sometimes referred to as the 'canonical five', are Mary Ann Nichols, Annie Chapman, Elizabeth Stride, Catherine Eddowes and Mary Jane Kelly. For the purposes of this case study, we will accept that they were committed by the same offender.

The lack of absolute proof that cases are linked to the same offender is a situation likely to occur often in present day policing. Sometimes investigators are forced to take this leap of faith as it will have a significant impact on investigative strategies. For the purposes of creating a POIPAT, if the similarities between cases are so strong that it leads the investigators to believe the same person is responsible for them all, chances are that if you create a POIPAT based on what you believe to be true of the offender, that POIPAT with slight modifications will be equally effective, even if it is learned that the cases are not linked and were committed by two different offenders.

For example, let's say we created a POIPAT for the canonical five believing Jack the Ripper was responsible for them all and then we learned he was responsible for only three. The other two cases were actually committed by another offender. We would need to only slightly modify the POIPAT created for the canonical five for it to be as effective in the second series of two cases committed by the second offender.

The canonical five victims were destitute, were heavy drinkers and resided in rooming houses in a very run-down area of Whitechapel in London's East End. Although some were known to have friends and relatives, they were pretty much socially isolated at the time of their deaths. None had a steady income and often relied on prostitution to pay for their room, board and drink.

Most of the victims were believed to have come in contact with the offender by virtue of their profession. They were all killed late at night or early in the morning when it was dark. All but one were killed outdoors, and they all suffered a high degree of violence. They were all cut to some extent by the offender, and most had internal parts of their bodies removed and taken away. This led to speculation that the offender had some anatomical and/or surgical knowledge.

It is likely that the victims did not initially identify the offender as a threat but as a potential client which no doubt contributed to their vulnerability. This lack of vigilance allowed him to overpower and kill them quickly. All of the victims were discovered in a short period of time after the offence which occurred on or very near the weekend.

There are a number of witnesses who were able to provide descriptions of various people they saw with the victims prior to their deaths or close to the crime scenes near the time of the offences. However, these descriptions tend to vary, and none of the witnesses could confirm that the person they described was the person who committed any of the murders.

Mary Ann Nichols

Mary Ann Nichols' lifeless body was discovered at approximately 3:40 a.m. on Friday, August 31, 1888, by a carman on his way to work in a gateway on Buck's Row which was a thoroughfare with two storey houses on one side and warehouses on the other. The carman thought the victim was alive because when he leaned down to see if she was breathing, his hand touched her chest and felt it move. He and a friend decided to go in search of a police officer.

Coincidentally, at 3:45 a police officer on his regular beat patrols along Buck's Row discovered the body and noted blood oozing from a deep cut in her throat. She was lying on her back with her clothes a little above her knees. He sent another constable who arrived on the scene a few minutes later to get a local surgeon. The surgeon arrived on scene shortly after 4:00 a.m. The surgeon did a cursory examination and pronounced life extinct. It was his opinion due to the warmth of the victim's legs that she had not been dead more than 30 minutes. He then ordered the body taken to the mortuary.

Further examination at the mortuary determined Nichols' throat had been cut from left to right, she had been disemboweled and there were small stabs on 'private parts' that appeared to have been done with a strong bladed knife.

She was described as about 45 years old, 5' 2" tall with a dark complexion and dark brown hair. She had a bruise on her right jaw and left cheek, and a slight laceration on her tongue. Several of her front teeth were missing.

Investigation revealed that Nichols had been turned away from her lodging house because she did not have enough money to pay for her bed. One of her friends reported seeing her at 2:30 a.m. at Osborn Street and Whitechapel Road. Nichols was drunk and told her friend she had made twice as much money as she needed for her lodging but had spent it on liquor. Her friend tried to convince her to return to the lodging house, but Nichols refused and headed down Whitechapel Road. The carman discovered her body 1 hour and 10 minutes later.

Nichols was actually 43 at the time of her death. She had been married with five children, but her drinking led to her separation from her husband. Her husband maintained custody of the children and gave her a small weekly allowance until he learned she was working as a prostitute.

Annie Chapman

Annie Chapman's body was discovered at approximately 6:00 a.m. Saturday morning on September 8, 1888, by John Davies in the back yard of 29 Hanbury Street. Davies was on his way to work. This was one day after Mary Ann Nichols' funeral and just over a week since her death.

Police were advised and arrived on the scene shortly after 6:10 a.m. Insp. Joseph Chandler was the first police officer to arrive on scene. According to an official Metropolitan Police, H Division report of September 8, 1888, he reported that he:

> found a woman lying on her back, dead, left arm resting on left breast, legs drawn up, abducted small intestines and flap of the abdomen lying on right side, above right shoulder attached by a cord with the rest of the intestines inside the body; two flaps of skin from the lower part of the abdomen lying in a large quantity of blood above the left shoulder; throat cut deeply from left and back in a jagged manner right around throat.

No physical evidence other than blood was located.

The police surgeon who arrived on scene pronounced Chapman dead and estimated she had been dead at least two hours. Further examination determined that the following body parts were missing: part of the belly wall including navel, the womb, the upper part of the vagina and the greater part of the bladder. The doctor felt that the murderer had anatomical knowledge, and the knife used was a small amputating knife or a well ground slaughterman's knife, narrow and thin, sharp and with a blade of six to eight inches in length. It appeared she may have been wearing rings but they were missing.

A witness reported seeing a woman she later identified as Chapman talking to a man near 29 Hanbury Street at 5:30 a.m. that morning. She said she heard the man say 'Will you' and the woman replied 'Yes'. She described the man as being over 40 years of age, a little taller than the woman and looking like a foreigner. She thought he was wearing a dark coat. She saw him only from behind and would be unable to recognize him again.

Chapman was 45 years old, had a fair complexion, was 5' tall, had wavy dark brown hair, blue eyes and a thick nose and was missing two teeth in her lower jaw. Similarly to Nichols, Chapman was a prostitute who separated from her husband due to her 'drunken and immoral ways'. Her ex-husband gave her a small weekly allowance up to the time of his death 18 months prior to her homicide.

Investigation determined that she returned to the lodging house where she had been residing for the past few months in the evening of September 7, 1888, without the funds to pay for her bed. They allowed her to sit in the kitchen for a while until shortly after midnight when they demanded the money for her bed. She was intoxicated. When she could not pay, they escorted her off the property. That was the last they saw of her.

Elizabeth Stride, aka 'Long Liz'

Elizabeth Stride's body was discovered at approximately 1:00 a.m. on Sunday, September 30, 1888, in a gateway to Dutfield's Yard that led off Berner Street. She was discovered by the secretary of the Jewish Socialist Club which over-looked the yard. He was travelling with a pony and cart which may have alerted the killer to his arrival. The police were advised and arrived within minutes. They were quickly followed by doctors.

According to Chief Inspector Donald Swanson's police report dated October 19, 1888, the body was

lying on left side, left arm extended from elbow, cachous[1] lying in hand, right arm over stomach back of hand & inner surface of wrist dotted with blood, legs drawn up knees fixed feet close to wall, body still warm, silk handkerchief round throat, slightly torn corresponding to the angle of the right jaw, throat deeply gashed and below the right angle apparent abrasion of skin about an inch and a quarter in diameter.

No weapon was found at the scene. They placed the time of death from 20 minutes to a half an hour from the time they arrived on scene.

The difference in this case was, other than the throat being cut, there were no other significant wounds or mutilation on the body. It was specu-lated that the killer was interrupted by the secretary and had to flee the scene before completing his intended acts of mutilation.

Stride, who was also known as 'Long Liz', was 45 years old. She was sepa-rated from her husband who had died a number of years earlier. Like the other victims, she liked to drink and earned money through prostitution. She had been staying at a lodging house where she earned some money cleaning rooms. On September 29, 1888, she spent the afternoon cleaning two rooms and was paid six pence. She went to a local pub after that and then returned to the lodging house to freshen up before going out again.

At approximately 11 p.m. two witnesses reported seeing her in the doorway of a pub with a male who was hugging and kissing her. About an hour and a half later at 12:35 on September 30 (25 minutes before she was found dead), a police constable saw a woman who he later identified as Stride standing with a man in the gateway of Dutfield's Yard. He described the male as about 28 years old, 5' 7" tall and with a moustache and dark complexion. He was wearing a black diagonal coat, a hard felt hat and a white collar and tie.

At 12:45 a.m. Israel Schwartz, who was on his way home, reported seeing a man stop and talk to Stride, who was standing in the gateway of Dutfield's Yard. He said the man tried to pull the woman into the street but ended up turning her around and down on the footway. She screamed three times but not very loudly. As this was happening Schwartz noticed another man standing across the street. The first man shouted 'Lipski', and the second man began following Schwartz. Fearing for his own safety, Schwartz walked away. This caused some to believe the killer was working with an accomplice. However, police believe they identified the second male as an innocent bystander.

The reference to 'Lipski' by the killer led to speculation the killer was Jewish. There was a great deal of anti-Semitism in the area at the time and many residents were already of the opinion that the serial killer was a Jew. They felt that no Englishman would be capable of such crimes. Some thought 'Lipski' may have been the name of an accomplice. Confusing matters more, further investigation determined that 'Lipski' was a term used to insult Jews.

Schwartz described the man who was with Stride as follows: about 30 years old; 5' 5" tall with a fair complexion, dark hair a small brown moustache and a full face; broad shouldered; dressed in a dark jacket and trousers; and wearing a black cap with a peak.

There were only slight differences between the police constable's and Schwartz's descriptions of the man they saw with the woman they believed was Stride shortly before her death. However, it led some to question as to whether they were describing the same person and, if not, which one was the killer.

This situation highlights an important point which is still true of modern day investigations and is relevant to the creation of a POIPAT. It is highly unlikely that two or more subjects witnessing the same event will describe the persons involved exactly the same. Investigators must be careful not to eliminate a potential suspect or POI because he does not perfectly match the description provided by one or more witnesses. This human frailty must also be considered when weighting elements of the POIPAT derived from eye-witness accounts.

Catherine Eddowes

Catherine Eddowes' dead body was discovered at approximately 1:45 a.m. on Sunday, September 30, 1888, in Mitre Square by Police Constable Watkins doing regular beat patrols. Her face was mutilated almost beyond recognition, a portion of her nose was cut off, the lobe of the right ear was nearly severed, her face was cut, her throat was slashed and she was disembowelled with parts of her internal organs placed on top of her. When she was discovered she was missing part of the apron she was wearing. PC Watkins had passed by that location 15 minutes prior, and he did not see Eddowes' body there at that time.

Mitre Square was an enclosed square surrounded by warehouse buildings, shops and a few houses. It was just barely inside the City of London boundaries and therefore the jurisdiction of the City Police rather than the Metropolitan Police, who were investigating the previous three murders.

Shortly after the discovery a number of police officers and two doctors arrived on the scene. It was felt that the murder had taken place within the last 15 to 30 minutes prior to her discovery and that the offender could still be in the area. As a result, police officers were sent off in different directions to attempt to locate the offender or other potential witnesses. This led to the discovery of the missing portion of Eddowes' apron at 2:55 a.m. by PC Long. It was located a short distance away at the bottom of the stairs in front of the Goldston Street Buildings which was in Metropolitan Police jurisdiction. The apron was covered in blood and faecal matter. PC Long said he had been by that same location at 2:20 and the apron was not there then. The area was principally inhabited by Jews of all nationalities as well as English. The Goldston Street tenements where the apron was found were almost exclusively occupied by Jews.

The following was written above the stairs in blurred chalk: 'The Juwes are the men who will not be blamed for nothing'. This led to a serious disagreement between the City Police and the Metropolitan Police over whether it should be removed immediately or remain to be photographed in the daylight. Metropolitan police feared that if local residents became aware of the writing, it would incite a race riot. They had jurisdiction over the location so it was erased.

Later examination of the body determined that death was immediate, caused by haemorrhage from the left common carotid artery, and that the mutilations were inflicted after death. The left kidney was removed along with the womb. Dr. Frederick Brown, who performed the autopsy, felt that the wounds were inflicted by a sharp pointed knife at least six inches long. He also felt that the offender would have had considerable knowledge of the position of the organs in the abdominal cavity and the best way to remove them, such as someone in the habit of cutting up animals. Dr. George Sequeria, who was one of the first doctors to arrive at the crime scene, said at the inquest he agreed with Dr. Brown in every particular but added,

> I formed the opinion that the perpetrator of the deed had no particular design on any particular organ. I do not think he was possessed of any great anatomical skill.

Further investigation revealed that Eddowes had been arrested earlier that night for drunkenness and released at approximately 1:00 a.m., 45 minutes before her lifeless body was discovered. At 1:35 a.m. three men saw a man talking to a woman in Church Passage which leads to Mitre Square. Only one of the three, Joseph Lawende, took notice of the couple. He indicated that he would not be able to identify the man again but described him as follows: about 30 years old, around 5' 9" tall, with a medium build, a fair complexion and a small fair moustache. He could not provide much of a description of the woman as he saw her only from behind. He was sure the woman was Eddowes, but rather than identifying her from physical appearance he made the identification from her clothes which were shown to him at the police station.

Forty-three years old, Eddowes had been living with a man named Kelly at Cooney's Lodging House. She had lived with Kelly for seven or eight years, prior to which she had lived with a man named Conway. He left her because of her 'drunken and immoral habits'. Kelly and Eddowes earned money by hawking. The day before her murder neither had enough money for a bed so Kelly suggested that Eddowes visit her daughter to ask for money. He never saw her again nor did her daughter.

Mary Jane Kelly

Mary Jane Kelly's body was discovered in her rented room at No. 13 Millers Court, Dorset Street, in Spitalfields, on Friday, November 9, 1888. At approximately 10:45 a.m. her landlord sent his assistant to her room to collect her overdue rent. When no one answered his knocks on her door, the assistant looked through the window and noticed blood everywhere. Five minutes later he returned and shared this with the landlord, who immediately went to her room. When he looked in the window he saw what appeared to be a body that had been horribly mutilated and disfigured. They both went to the local police station to report what they had found.

Shortly after being notified, police attended the scene and were quickly followed by Dr. George Phillips, the police surgeon. When he arrived at approximately 11:15 a.m., he found the door to the room locked and two panes in the window near the door broken. He looked through the window and was satisfied from what he saw that the victim was not in need of any immediate medical attention nor did there appear to be anyone else in the room to whom he could render assistance. There was approximately a two hour delay in entry to the room because there was some indication that bloodhounds were going to attend. When it was determined they would not be coming to the scene, entrance was made at 1:30 p.m. by forcing in the door. It was later determined that the key to the door had been lost for some time and that the door was usually unlocked by reaching in through the window where the glass was broken.

Dr. Thomas Bond conducted a post-mortem examination of the body. The following is a brief synopsis of some of his findings: The body was lying naked in the middle of the bed. The shoulders were flat but the axis of the body inclined to the left side of the bed with the head turned on the left cheek. The entire surface of the abdomen and thighs was removed and the abdomen cavity emptied of its viscera. The breasts were cut off, the arms mutilated by several jagged wounds. The face was hacked beyond recognition. The tissues of the neck were severed all around down to the bone. The uterus, kidneys and one breast were under her head. The other breast was by her right foot, the liver between her feet, intestines by her right side and the spleen by the left side of her body. A table contained the flaps removed from her abdomen and thighs. Her face was gashed in all directions with the nose, cheeks, eyebrows and ears being partly removed. The neck was cut through right down to the vertebrae. Further examination showed that the pericardium was open below and the heart was absent.

Kelly was described in a newspaper report as 'twenty-four years of age, tall, slim, fair, of fresh complexion, and of attractive appearance'. She lived with Joseph Barnett for about one year and eight months prior to her death. He was an unemployed fish porter. When they fell behind on their rent, Kelly had to resort to prostitution. On the 30th of October, Barnett left Kelly when she brought another prostitute home to live with them. One witness reported that Kelly was quiet when she was sober but was quite loud when she was drinking. This temperament is believed to account for the broken window-panes in her room.

A few days after the murder, George Hutchinson came to the police station and gave a very detailed statement. It is summarized as follows: At about 2 a.m. on the 9th of November 1888, he was on his way home when he saw Kelly just before Flower and Dean Street. She asked him to lend her six pence. When he told her he did not have any money, she said she needed to go find some and started towards Thrawl Street. He saw her meet a man who was coming from the opposite direction. The man tapped her on the shoulder and said something that made her laugh. Hutchinson heard her say 'All right' and the man responded, 'You will be all right for what I have told you'.

The man then put his right arm around her shoulders. He had what appeared to be a small parcel with a kind of strap round it in his left hand. They both walked past Hutchinson, who was standing against a lamp. When they walked past him the man tipped down his head with his hat over his eyes, so Hutchinson stooped down and looked him in the face. The man gave him a stern look.

Hutchinson said he followed them into Dorest Street where they stood at the corner of the court for about three minutes. The man said something to

Kelly, who responded with 'All right my dear, come along, you will be comfortable'. He then put his arm on her shoulder and gave her a kiss. She told him she had lost her handkerchief and he gave her his. He then saw them go up the court together, and shortly after he went up the court to see if he could see them but did not. He waited there for about 45 minutes to see if they came out but they didn't.

He described the man as follows: 34 or 35 years old, 5' 6" tall, pale complexion with dark eyes and lashes, slight moustache curled up on each end and dark hair. He was wearing a very surly looking long dark dress coat with collar and cuffs trimmed with astracan (Persian lamb pelt), and a dark jacket under a light waistcoat with dark trousers and a dark felt hat turned down in the middle. He had on button boots and gaiters with white buttons. He also wore a very thick gold chain, a white linen collar and black tie with a horseshoe pin. He had a respectable appearance and walked very sharp. He was Jewish in appearance and can be identified.

The degree of detail Hutchinson was able to describe caused some to be sceptical of him. However, Inspector Abberline, who interviewed him, was of the opinion Hutchinson was being truthful. Hutchinson told him he had known Kelly for approximately three years and occasionally given her a few shillings. He also said he was surprised to see her in the company of such a well-dressed man.

One of Kelly's neighbours, Mary Cox, reported seeing her go into her room at about midnight with a man. Kelly was intoxicated and the man had a pot of beer in his hand. She told Cox she was going to have a song. Cox heard her singing for the next 15 minutes until she had to go out. When Cox returned at 1:00 a.m. Kelly was still singing. Cox warmed her hands and went out again. When she returned at 3:00 a.m. the light was out and there was no noise.

Cox described the man she saw as follows: short and stout with a blotchy face and a full, carroty moustache with a clean chin. He was shabbily dressed wearing a longish, shabby dark coat and a hard billy cock black hat.

Two other independent witnesses, one of whom lived in the room above Kelly's, reported hearing someone shout 'Murder' at around 4:00 a.m. Neither knew where it came from and did not pay much attention to it.

Endnote

1. Small aromatic sweetmeats.

Jack the Ripper— Criminal Profiles

9

Introduction

As indicated earlier, there were two profiles prepared on the Jack the Ripper cases. One was completed in 1888 by Dr. Thomas Bond and another 100 years later in 1988 by SSA John Douglas of the FBI National Center for the Analysis of Violent Crime (NCAVC). Dr. Bond conducted the post-mortem examination of Mary Kelly, and at the time he was considered an expert in these types of cases. As such, Assistant Commissioner Robert Anderson of the London Metropolitan Police asked him to review the medical evidence gathered at the inquests of the other cases to offer an opinion 'as to the amount of surgical skill and anatomical knowledge probably possessed by the murder or murderers'. Dr. Bond's response did address that issue but went much further by describing some probable traits and characteristics of the unknown offender.

SSA Douglas conducted a criminal investigative analysis on the cases at the request of Cosgrove-Meurer Productions. His unknown offender profile was based on basic background he was provided on the cases. Although the profiles were over 100 years apart and there were some minor differences, they are not that dissimilar.

Both profile reports were examined, and elements that may be useful in the creation of a POIPAT were itemized. See Appendix C for SSA Douglas' profile report and Appendix D for Dr. Bond's.

Dr. Thomas Bond

The following points were extracted from Dr. Bond's report which could be useful in creating POIPAT elements:

- Mutilation was inflicted by a person who had no scientific nor anatomical knowledge. Does not even possess the technical knowledge of a butcher or horse slaughterer or any person accustomed to cut up dead animals.
- The instrument must have been a strong knife at least six inches long, very sharp, pointed at the top and about an inch in width. It may have been a clasp knife, a butcher's knife or a surgeon's knife. … it was no doubt a straight knife.

- A man of physical strength and of great coolness and daring.
- Subject to periodical attacks of homicidal and erotic mania.
- Mutilations may indicate he had a sexual condition called 'satyriasis'[1].
- In external appearance is quite likely to be a quiet inoffensive looking man probably middle aged and neatly and respectably dressed.
- Must be in the habit of wearing an overcoat.
- Probably solitary and eccentric in his habits.
- Most likely to be a man without regular occupation, but with some income or pension.
- Possibly living among respectable persons who have some knowledge of his character and habits and who may have grounds for suspicion that he is not quite right in his mind at times.

FBI Supervisory Special Agent (SSA)— John E. Douglas (Retired)

The following points were extracted from SSA John E. Douglas' profile report which may be useful in creating POIPAT elements:

- White male between 28 to 36 years old.
- Does not look out of the ordinary. The clothing he wore at the time of the offences was not his ordinary dress because he wanted to project he had money.
- He became detached socially and developed a diminished emotional response towards his fellow man. He became asocial, preferring to be alone. His anger became internalized and in his younger years, he expressed his pent-up destructive emotions by setting fires and torturing small animals.
- As he grew older, his fantasy developed a strong component that included domination, cruelty and mutilation of women. Evidence of this violent destructive fantasy life may be found through personal writings as well as drawings of women being mutilated.
- He would seek a position where he could work alone and vicariously experience his destructive fantasies. Such employment would include a butcher, mortician's helper, medical examiner's assistant, or hospital attendant. He was employed Monday through Friday and on Friday night, Saturday and Sunday is off from work.
- He has carried a knife for defense purposes.
- He has a poor self-image and may have some type of physical abnormality. Although, it would not be severe, he would perceive it psychologically crippling.

- He could be someone who was below or above average in height and/or weight and may have had problems with speech, scarred complexion, physical illness or injury.
- Not expected to be married. If he was married in the past, it would have been to someone older than himself, and it would have been only for a short time.
- He is not adept in meeting people socially and the major extent of his heterosexual relationships would be with prostitutes. He may have been infected with a venereal disease which would have further fueled his hatred and disgust for women.
- He would be perceived as quiet, a loner, shy, slightly withdrawn, obedient and neat and orderly in appearance when working.
- Drinks in local pubs and after a few spirits feels more relaxed and easier to engage in conversation.
- He lives and works in the Whitechapel area. The first homicide would have been in close proximity to his home or workplace.
- Investigators would have interviewed him during the course of the investigation, and he was probably talked to by police on several occasions.
- He would be observed walking all over the Whitechapel area during the early evening hours.
- If the victims were buried locally, he would visit the grave sites of his victims during the early morning hours for the purpose of reliving his lust murders.

Endnote

1. According to the *Collins English Dictionary*, satyriaisis is (psychiatry) a neurotic condition in men in which the symptoms are a compulsion to have sexual intercourse with as many women as possible and an inability to have lasting relationships with them.

Creating the Jack the Ripper POIPAT

10

Introduction

Now that we have a fairly detailed overview of the investigations including two profile reports, we can begin developing the elements for the Jack the Ripper POIPAT. Under normal circumstances we would identify all of the potential elements and then weight them. However, in the interests of ease of explanation and flow, we will weight the elements as they are being identified.

We will utilize the Standard POIPAT Elements Library in Chapter 6 of this book to ensure that we are organized and thorough. We will also make use of the Element Weighting Guide in Chapter 4. You may find it useful to have a copy of the EWC chart from Chapter 4 handy so you can refer to it as we are weighting the elements. It may be easier for you to print off a copy of the chart which is also available in the POIPAT Utilities sub-directory of the companion CD. (See Appendix E or the Jack the Ripper sub-directory of the companion CD for the completed Jack the Ripper POIPAT.)

The Heading

Every POIPAT should have a place to record the following information about the POI being evaluated: name of POI, date of birth (DOB), fingerprint number and a task/tip reference number. The following is the heading for our Jack the Ripper POIPAT investigation:

Persons of Interest Priority Assessment Tool—Jack the Ripper Investigation					
Name of POI	Surname		First Given		Second Given
DOB	YYYY	MM	DD	Fingerprint Number	Task/Tip Number#

Geography Elements

There are two main geographic considerations when developing elements for the Jack the Ripper POIPAT. They are where he most likely resided at the time of the offences and his comfort zone(s). The comfort zone is simply an area where the offender has some type of connection. It could be a place they lived, worked or visited.

All five cases occurred within a quarter mile of each other in Whitechapel which was a suburb of London, England. All of the cases occurred between August 31, 1888, and November 9, 1888.

Residence Section

Although it is possible Jack the Ripper lived in some other location, even a different country, it is most likely he lived not only in London at the time of the offences but also within walking distance of Whitechapel area where the offences occurred.

Therefore our first two POIPAT elements will deal with his residence as follows:

		PP	Score
Residence (Aug. 31, 1888–Nov. 9, 1888)			
1	London (includes suburbs)	20	
2	Whitechapel (10 mile radius)	20	

The last two columns of the first row of this table contain 'PP' and 'Score' respectively. The 'PP' represents the weighted value of POIPAT points. The column titled 'Score' is where the assessor will indicate if the element is true by writing in the PP value. For example, if the POI being assessed lives in London, the assessor will write '20' in the Score column. If he does not live in London the column will remain blank.

The second row of the table which is the section title says 'Residence (Aug. 31, 1888–Nov. 9, 1888)'. It is important here that the dates when the offences occurred are specified. For the purposes of the 'residence' elements, we are interested only in those POIs who resided in these locations at the time of the offences. We could have been even more specific because we know the actual date each of these offences occurred and created a separate POIPAT element for each date. However, this would have unnecessarily given too much weight to residence.

The third row of the table which represents element 1 says 'London (includes suburbs)'. Adding the 'includes suburbs' simply provides some additional guidance to the assessor. This item is weighted the base 20 points. For the purposes of this POIPAT, we will use 'linked to victim' as our benchmark with the base score of 20. We will weight all other elements based on whether we believe they are of less, equal or more importance than 'linked to victim'. If they are of less importance, they will be scored less than 20, of equal importance 20 and more important elements will be scored higher than 20. We assume here that living in London at the time of the offences is equally as important as being linked to a victim.

The fourth row of the table which represents element 2 says, 'Whitechapel (10 mile radius)'. The reason '10 mile radius' was added was because although the offender may not have actually lived in Whitechapel, it is likely he lived within walking distance or a carriage ride. Adding an additional 20 PP for this element will ensure that those POIs living within 10 miles of the crime scenes will be awarded more points than those who simply live in London.

Comfort Zone Section

Even if Jack the Ripper did not live near the crime scenes or even in London, it is very likely he was familiar with the area and had some level of comfort there. All of his crimes took place in the dark of night in some very isolated areas in the back streets of Whitechapel. He was able to move about committing his very high risk offences without being detected. The nature of his offences also indicated he was able to approach his victims without causing them initial alarm. This would support him not only being comfortable with the geographic location but also having social interaction with prostitutes.

His familiarity with the area may come from having lived, worked or visited the area. It is very likely he was a regular consumer of the sex trade in the area and may have even been known to some or all of his victims. It is not uncommon for an offender to be well known and liked by sex trade workers. This makes them even easier prey when the offender suddenly decides to turn against them. The fact all his offences occurred within a quarter mile of each other reinforces the idea that he has a strong connection to the area.

The following comfort zone element addresses this issue:

Comfort Zone			
3	Resides in, works in or known to frequent Whitechapel or surrounding area (10 mile radius)	20	

This comfort zone element is weighted the same as the residence elements but is worded slightly differently. However, the main difference is that there is no time limitation indicated. It doesn't matter when the Ripper resided in, worked in or frequented the area; time does not negate a connection to the area.

Physical Description

Like most cases where the offender is unknown, the victims are deceased and there are no witnesses to the crimes, developing physical description elements for the offender in this case will be a challenge. However, there are a couple of potential sources that may be of assistance in that regard. Firstly, there are the offender profiles by SSA John Douglas and Dr. Thomas Bond. Then there are the witnesses who provide descriptions of males they saw the victims with shortly before they are believed to have been killed.

The following is a list of the descriptions provided by witnesses who are most likely to have seen Jack the Ripper with the victims:

- Forty, a little taller than the victim (who was 5' tall), looked like a foreigner
- About 28, 5' 7", moustache, dark complexion
- About 30, 5' 5", fair complexion, small brown moustache, full face, broad shouldered
- Between 34 or 35 years old, 5' 6", pale complexion, dark eyes and lashes, slight moustache, curled up each end, dark hair, was Jewish in appearance

The information in the profiles and witness statements were considered in the development of the following physical description elements:

Physical Description			
4	Male	50	
5	Age (25–45)	10	
6	Physical abnormality (i.e. speech impediment, scarred complexion, physical illness or injury)	5	

Although there were a significant number of characteristics we could have extracted from the profiles and witness statements, we chose only gender, age and physical abnormality. Utilizing the witness statements in this case to identify offender physical characteristics presented all of the issues inherent in relying on eye-witness accounts. (For more on these issues, see the Physical Description section in Chapter 6, 'Standard POIPAT Elements Library'.) Additionally, in most of the cases there were witnesses who reportedly saw a male who may in fact have been Jack the Ripper with the victim shortly before they were killed; however, there is no way to be absolutely certain it was him.

A review of the profiles was slightly more helpful but also presented issues. Dr. Bond suggested that the offender was a 'quiet inoffensive looking man probably middle aged and neatly and respectably dressed'. Other than being 'middle aged' all of the other characteristics are highly subjective. Even 'middle aged' was open to interpretation, and it is likely to have meant something different in the 1800s than it does today.

SSA Douglas' profile report indicates the offender was a white male, between 28 and 36 years of age. The clothing he wears at the time of the assaults is not his everyday dress because he wants to project that he has money. Douglas also says he would look for someone of below or above average height and/or weight who may have problems with speech, a scarred complexion, a physical illness or an injury.

SSA Douglas formed the opinion he was 'white' because 'white was the predominant race at the crime scene locations and generally crimes such as these are intraracial'. There has been further research since Mr. Douglas wrote this profile in 1988 that indicates that white sex offenders tend to target white victims, but non-white offenders target both white and non-white victims.

Notwithstanding this discussion, as indicated in the Race/Ethnicity/Skin Colour section of the Standard POIPAT Elements Library (Chapter 6), there are a number of issues with using skin colour as an element. This combined with the fact that white was the predominant race in Whitechapel at the time and as such not likely to be a very useful characteristic to cause any given POI to stand out from the others, we have chosen to leave it out.

SSA Douglas said he believed that Jack the Ripper was a male because he had never experienced a female lust murderer[1] either in research or in cases received at the National Center for the Analysis of Violent Crime (NCAVC). This holds true even today. It is virtually unheard of for a female to be responsible for these types of violent sexual homicides. As such, it was added as an element on the POIPAT. We weighted it 50 PPs. The high score for being male will have little effect in raising the priority of POIs who are male because a significant majority of the other POIs will also be male, however it will ensure females get a much lower priority than males.

SSA Douglas used the following logic to support his belief that the offender was between 28 and 36 years old:

> The age of onset for these types of homicides is generally between the mid to late 20's. Based upon the high degree of psychopathology exhibited at the scene, the ability of the subject to converse with the victim until a suitable location is found, and the ability to avoid detection, places him between the age bracket of 28 to 36 years of age.

This also seems to fit with the age range one might expect of someone who would be found lurking in dark back alleys of Whitechapel in the early morning hours engaging with prostitutes. As a result, we added age as an element, but to be a little more cautious the range was expanded to between 25 and 45 years old. It was weighted at 10 PPs instead of the base rate of 20 PPs because even though it is a relatively safe assumption, it is based on a professional opinion and not on known fact.

Mr. Douglas also indicated he would look for someone of below or above average height and/or weight who may have problems with speech, a scarred complexion, a physical illness or an injury. He based this on his opinion that the offender was paranoid, had a poor self-image and:

would be expected to have some type of physical abnormality. However, although not severe, he perceives this as being psychologically crippling.

SSA Douglas has a great deal of experience in these types of cases and his rationale seems to be sound; however, he seems to be going further out on the limb with this than the offender's gender, race or age. The other problem is that in 1888 Whitechapel it is likely a high percentage of the population between the ages of 28 and 36 years suffered from some sort of physical illness or injury—particularly given the poor and overcrowded living and working conditions in the Whitechapel area in 1888. It is for these reasons that 'physical abnormality' was added as an element but given a low weight of five PPs.

Lifestyle

As indicated in the Lifestyle section of the Standard POIPAT Elements Library (Chapter 6), an offender's lifestyle can include such things as whether the offender is an alcohol or drug user; whether they like to socialize or are loners; whether they are transient, a street person or homeless; whether they use sex trade workers; whether they engage in frequent criminal activity; whether they are nocturnal; whether they hunt or fish, etc.

In this case, it is possible to flesh out some elements of Jack the Ripper's lifestyle from what is known of the investigation as well as the criminal profiles. The first and most obvious element is that he frequents and uses prostitutes. Some might argue that because there was no evidence of ante-mortem sexual activity the offender had no interest in sex. He selected prostitutes to fulfil his homicidal fantasies only because they were easy prey and, in his mind, of little societal value. There seems, however, to be a strong consensus that these were in fact sexual crimes because the offender demonstrated a strong interest in the victims' genitalia. SSA Douglas called them 'lust murders', and Dr. Bond felt that the offender had a sexual condition.

For the purposes of creating an element on the POIPAT, Jack the Ripper's motivation for selecting prostitutes as his victims is not important. The fact remains, he killed at least five. Furthermore, it is likely that he did not kill the first prostitute he encountered. He probably knew from experience how to engage them, speak their language and cause them to feel comfortable with him. Therefore creating a 'uses prostitutes' element is a fairly safe decision.

Lifestyle			
7	Uses prostitutes	30	

Assigning a weight to this item was a little more difficult than most of the other elements. If this case were to occur today in any large city in North America, we would likely have made 'uses prostitutes' a salient item[2] which would be scored 50 PPs. However, although in most large cities today there will be a significant portion of the population who use prostitutes, it is likely not to the extent of the 1880s in Whitechapel.

The Metropolitan Police Service estimated there were 1200 prostitutes and about 62 brothels in Whitechapel in 1888. At the time Whitechapel was overcrowded, and there was a significant economic underclass. Robbery, violence and alcohol dependency were common, and the endemic property drove many women to prostitution. Therefore it was very likely that a large number of POIs of 1888 would have been consumers of the sex trade. In view of this, we weighted it 30 PPs which still makes it a very important element on the Jack the Ripper POIPAT.

Another lifestyle characteristic that is fairly apparent for Jack the Ripper is that he was nocturnal. All of his offences occurred after dark, between midnight and 6:00 a.m. It is evident from his offences that he was comfortable moving about the narrow streets and alleys of Whitechapel at that time of the morning. He may have been nocturnal by choice or circumstance. For example, that may have been the best time to encounter prostitutes working alone with minimum risk for interruption or he may have had an occupation such as a night watchman or shift worker at the nearby hospital where he was used to being awake during those hours.

Again, when it comes to the POIPAT, it doesn't matter why he was nocturnal, only that he was.

Although it is quite obvious that the offender was nocturnal in this case, the element was scored only 10 because it is not the type of information that is going to be readily available without a great deal of effort about most of the POIs who would have surfaced at that time. Additionally, when compared to the benchmark element of 'linked to victim' it is likely to be less important.

Lifestyle			
7	Uses prostitutes	30	
8	Nocturnal due to choice or circumstance (night person)	10	

Two other aspects of the offender's personality that both Dr. Bond and SSA Douglas agreed on was that the offender was likely a loner and he would be neatly dressed. Although these characteristics may have been true, they were not used in this POIPAT for the following reasons: they are personality traits based on professional opinion; they are subjective; the information would not readily be available about most POIs; and when compared to the benchmark item they would likely score very low.

Marital Status

It is impossible to know for sure if the Jack the Ripper was married, but the nature of his crimes, particularly when they occurred, as well as their duration, would suggest that he had a low level of accountability to others. Keep in mind that in one morning he had the time to murder two victims in two separate incidents, and in the last case there is evidence that he spent considerable time with the victim. In some of these cases, he is likely to have gotten blood on his clothing, and if he was married or living with someone, he may have had to explain that.

SSA Douglas addressed the issue from an offender personality perspective and said,

> We would not expect this type of offender to be married. If he was married in the past, it would have been to someone older than himself and the marriage would have been for a short duration.

Dr. Bond did not specifically speak to whether or not he was married but indicated that

> he would probably be solitary and eccentric in his habits.

He went on say,

> He is possibly living among respectable persons who have some knowledge of his character and habits and who may have grounds for suspicion that he is not quite right in his mind at times.

For the purposes of the POIPAT, an offender's legal marital status is not important. It is just an indication of his level of accountability which is really what is most important to us. In some cases he may be married but totally dominates the relationship and as a result does not feel accountable to his wife. The following example covers both of those situations.

Marital Status (Aug. 31, 1888–Nov. 9, 1888) (Select One Only)			
9	Unattached (i.e. single, divorced, separated)	5	
10	Unaccountable (i.e. married but wife is extremely passive)	5	

The important thing to notice about this example is the 'Select One Only' instruction in the title box. Even though elements 9 and 10 are worded differently, they both indicate that the offender is not accountable. Allowing the selection of just one of these elements ensures that the POI won't be double scored for being unaccountable.

It is also important to clarify the dates of the offences in the title box because we are concerned only about whether or not the offender was accountable during the time of the offences. These were weighted low because they were based on professional opinion and not fact, and compared to our benchmark 'linked to victim' they would be less important.

Employment

This is one area where Dr. Bond and SSA Douglas disagreed. Bond said,

> He is most likely to be a man without regular occupation, but with some small income or pension.

Mr. Douglas said,

> He would seek a position where he could work alone and vicariously experience his destructive fantasies. Such employment would include work as a butcher, mortician's helper, medical examiner's assistant, or hospital attendant. He is employed Monday through Friday and on Friday night, Saturday, and Sunday is off from work.

For the sake of this POIPAT, we have sided with SSA Douglas' conclusion that the Ripper was employed because it seems to be supported by temporal analysis. All of the offences occurred in the early morning hours of Friday, Saturday or Sunday. This was likely not a coincidence. The times of the offences would have spoken to the victims' and/or the offender's availability. Given that prostitution was a thriving enterprise in Whitechapel during that period, the potential victim pool would have been plentiful and available 24 hours a day, 7 days a week. Therefore the times of the offences were more likely related to the offender's availability.

There could have been any number of reasons the offender was available to commit the offences only on the weekend, but the most likely was that he had a job that precluded him from being out late on weekday nights/mornings. In view of this, 'employed—at time of offences' was added as a POIPAT element in the following example but scored low because of its speculative nature and because it's not likely to be very significant compared to the benchmark element of 'linked to victim'. Although unemployment may have been high during that period, it is likely that the majority of the population were employed.

Employment Status (Aug. 31, 1888–Nov. 9, 1888)			
11	Employed—at time of offences	10	

In this case, being employed would be of less interest to the investigation than the type of employment the offender was engaged in. SSA Douglas suggested he worked in a trade or profession that would have permitted him the opportunity to work alone and vicariously experience his destructive fantasies such as a butcher, mortician's helper, medical examiner's assistant or hospital attendant.

We also agreed with SSA Douglas on these types of professions for the reason he suggested but also because these are all professions which could have involved evisceration and would have required the use of a cutting instrument.

The type of knife he used in his offences could provide a clue as to its source. Although the weapon was never recovered from the crime scenes, Dr. Bond made the following conclusion based on his post-mortem examination and review of the material from the other inquests:

> The instrument must have been a strong knife at least six inches long, very sharp, pointed at the top and about an inch in width. It may have been a clasp knife, a butcher's knife or a surgeon's knife. I think it was no doubt a straight knife.

Dr. Bond's conclusion about the description of the knife supports SSA Douglas' suggestion that the offender may have been a butcher or medical examiner's assistant, but then Bond confused the issue with his statement:

> In each case the mutilation was inflicted by a person who had no scientific nor anatomical knowledge. In my opinion he does not even possess the technical knowledge of a butcher or horse slaughterer or any person accustomed to cut up dead animals.

From a POIPAT perspective the important thing is that we know the offender had access to and utilized a knife. His access to the type of knife used in these offences is likely to have resulted from his employment but could also have been from a hobby such as hunting or some other activity. In order to cover each of these possibilities, the following element was added: 'engaged in an occupation, hobby or other activity where the use of a knife was common'.

Employment Status (Aug. 31, 1888–Nov. 9, 1888)			
11	Employed—at time of offences	10	
12	Engaged in an occupation, hobby or other activity where the use of a knife is common	20	

This element was scored 20 because even though it is also speculative in nature, investigators would be highly interested in POIs who have this type of background, and it would be fairly easy to confirm. Item 12 could have also been placed in the Lifestyle section. The topic of the knife will surface again when the Weapon section is discussed.

Education

Our cursory examination of these cases did not provide any information that would offer information about the offender's level of education. There were a number of letters that were reported to have been written by Jack the Ripper that may have provided clues in this regard, however none were absolutely proven to have been written by him. Sometimes profilers will offer such an opinion but neither SSA Douglas or Dr. Bond did. As such, there will be no education element added to our Jack the Ripper POIPAT.

Criminal History

Both SSA Douglas and Dr. Bond suggested in their profiles that Jack the Ripper had violent mental health issues. Dr. Bond said,

> He must in my opinion be a man subject to periodical attacks of homicidal and erotic mania.

SSA Douglas said,

> His anger became internalized and in his younger years, he expressed his pent-up destructive emotions by setting fires and torturing small animals. By perpetrating these acts, he discovered increased areas of dominance, power and control, and learned how to continue violent destructive acts without detection or punishment. As he grew older, his fantasy developed a strong component that included domination, cruelty, and mutilation of women. We would expect to find evidence of this violent destructive fantasy life through personal writings of his as well as drawings of women being mutilated.

SSA Douglas suggests that in his youth the Ripper may have learned how to continue his violent destructive acts without detection or punishment. It's not clear if he believes this would extend into his adulthood; however, most criminals do not start their criminal careers at the most extreme end of their crime category and, given the horrendously violent and serious nature of these cases, it is unlikely Jack the Ripper started his criminal career with the brutal murder of Mary Ann Nichols.

It is also very common for sex offenders to have a history of property offences such as break and enter, possession of stolen property and theft. Therefore it is likely that Jack the Ripper had a criminal history of not only

violent and/or sexual crimes but also property crimes. For the purposes of
the POIPAT, it does not matter if the offender was charged and/or convicted
of the offence(s) as long as the information comes from a credible source such
as a police report.

Criminal History (Charges and/or Conviction Not Necessary)			
13	History of property crimes, of assault causing bodily harm and of domestic violence	10	
14	History of sex related offences	20	
15	History of throat slashing (includes attempts)	50	

Three elements were added to our POIPAT to address the offender's
criminal past. Each of these element's points are cumulative so for each
item that is true, the offender receives more points which raises his priority level.

Element 13, 'history of property crimes, of assault causing bodily harm
and of domestic violence', was scored only 10 because it is likely that many
of the POIs identified in this case came to the attention of police by virtue of
their criminal past.

Element 14, 'history of sex related offences', was added and weighted 20
PP because police would likely have been very interested in POIs who were
known sex offenders.

Element 15, 'history of throat slashing (includes attempts)', was added
because it was the manner and cause of death in every case. This was an
aspect of his behaviour that could have been both ritual (fantasy based) and
M.O. (modus operandi). It was M.O. because it was an effective means for the
offender to kill the victim with minimal opportunity for her to make noise or
put up resistance. If cutting their throats was part of his enjoyment or thrill,
then that behaviour was both M.O. and ritual. When it comes to history,
the M.O. aspect is the most important of the two because M.O. is learned
behaviour. Offenders' M.O. changes over time as they learn from experience
the most effective means of committing their offence(s). Therefore Jack the
Ripper may have learned from experience that cutting the victim's throat
worked well for him. We deemed this element to be a salient element and as
such weighted it 50 PPs.

Links to Victim

In crimes of a sexually violent interpersonal nature, it is almost a certainty
that there is some connection between the victim and offender. These connections can be strong or weak. As a general rule of thumb, the more difficult
it is to establish the link(s) between victim and offender, the more difficult it

is to solve the crime(s). It is also true that in multiple homicide investigations where it is believed one person is responsible for them all, the more victims you can link a POI to, the more likely the POI is to be the offender.

In this particular investigation, the link(s) between the victim(s) and Jack the Ripper are unknown. There was no indication that his victim selections were anything other than random. They were likely just in the wrong place at the wrong time. His connection to them was likely only as a result of the actual crime itself and only for the duration of the event. However, we don't know that for sure. If investigation revealed that a person who had been identified as a suspect was known to be a former customer of a victim, that would elevate that person as a POI. If it was later determined that the same POI had some sort of connection to one or more of the other victims, he would become a very high investigative priority.

Links between the offender and the victim are scored cumulatively to ensure the POI's score will increase with each victim to which they are linked.

Linked to Victim			
16	Mary Ann Nichols	20	
	Annie Chapman	20	
	Elizabeth Stride	20	
	Catherine Eddowes	20	
	Mary Jane Kelly	20	

Availability

This element addresses the offender's availability and opportunity to have committed any or all of the offences. Just as with links to the victims, the more the POI was available for, the more likely he is to be the offender. In the Jack the Ripper investigation, it is possible to narrow the time of the offences down to a specific date. Each of the victims has been added to the availability element along with the applicable dates.

Availability (Subject Was Available [i.e. Not Incarcerated at the Time of the Offences])			
17	Mary Ann Nichols (Aug. 31, 1888)	10	
	Annie Chapman (Sept. 8, 1888)	10	
	Elizabeth Stride (Sept. 29–30, 1888)	10	
	Catherine Eddowes (Sept. 30, 1888)	10	
	Mary Jane Kelly (Nov. 9, 1888)	10	

Each of the items was weighted at 10 PPs because all POIs should be awarded these points unless it can be established that they were not available for any or all of the offences. Additionally, being linked to victims (which is weighted at 20 PPs) is more important than being available. Most of your POIs and even the general public will have been available for your offences but not nearly as many as are likely to have links to your victims.

Weapon

There is little doubt that Jack the Ripper's weapon of choice was a knife. Although he never actually saw the knife, Dr. Bond believed the knife would be described as follows:

> a strong knife at least six inches long, very sharp, pointed at the top and about an inch in width. It may have been a clasp knife, a butcher's knife or a surgeon's knife. I think it was no doubt a straight knife.

SSA Douglas felt that Jack the Ripper carried the knife for defensive purposes. We also know he brought the knife with him to the crime scenes and utilized it for offensive purposes.

Regardless of whether his use of the knife was defensive, offensive or both, the important thing for the POIPAT is that we know he carried a knife. We just don't know for sure how often. Therefore we added 'known to carry a knife (does not matter how often)' as an element.

Weapon			
18	Known to carry a knife (does not matter how often)	20	

Some might argue that it is not necessary to add this element because the knife issue was addressed in the Employment section. However, that section dealt only with POIs who were engaged in occupations or hobbies where the use of a knife was common. It is likely investigators would be keenly interested in POIs who were known to carry a knife even if the use of a knife was not common in their occupations or hobbies.

This element was weighted 20 PPs because it was assumed to have equal importance to being 'linked to victim' which was the benchmark weighting element.

Other

The previous sections dealt with elements that are likely to be relevant to most investigations. However, nearly all violent sexual homicides have some unique aspect(s) to them. This section provides an opportunity to address those aspects.

One of the most striking aspects of the Jack the Ripper murders was his evisceration and mutilation of the victims, particularly their sexual parts. According to an article titled 'The Lust Murderer' written by Robert Hazelwood and John Douglas, former special agents of the FBI Behavioral Sciences Unit, this would make him a 'lust murderer'. SSA Douglas confirms this in the profile he did of the Jack the Ripper cases.

The article said lust murder is premeditated in the obsessive fantasies of the perpetrator. SSA Douglas was very helpful in his profile by providing insight into how this violent fantasy likely manifested itself for Jack the Ripper and how investigators may find evidence of it. The following is an extract from his profile report:

> He became detached socially and developed a diminished emotional response towards his fellow man. He became asocial, preferring to be alone. His anger became internalized and in his younger years, he expressed his pent-up destructive emotions by setting fires and torturing small animals. By perpetrating these acts, he discovered increased areas of dominance, power and control, and learned how to continue violent destructive acts without detection or punishment.
>
> As he grew older, his *fantasy* developed a strong component that included domination, cruelty, and mutilation of women. We would expect to find evidence of this violent destructive fantasy life through personal writings of his as well as drawings of women being mutilated.

In view of SSA Douglas' comments and the evidence of evisceration and mutilation of the victims, two elements were added to the Other section of the POIPAT. The first element, 'history of setting fires or torturing small animals', was weighted lower than the benchmark element because it was based on professional opinion and not established fact. Additionally, it is not likely to be viewed as important as being 'linked to victim'.

Other			
19	History of setting fires or torturing small animals	10	
20	History of or documented fantasy of evisceration or mutilation of sexual areas of the body	50	

The second element, 'history of or documented fantasy of evisceration or mutilation of sexual areas of the body', was considered a salient element and weighted with the maximum PPs of 50. It is assumed that any POI who fantasizes about the evisceration or mutilation of sexual areas of the body would be of significant interest to investigators. SSA Douglas is quite right when he says evidence of these fantasies is likely to be found in his writings or drawings. Investigators may also find evidence of his fantasies in other collateral materials[3] such as his magazines, books and erotica or pornography. Additionally, although they were obviously not available in the 1800s, ViCLAS and/or ViCAP may be a valuable resource for information regarding a POI's sexual preferences and/or fantasies.

Comments

Thus far, most of the important aspects of these cases have been considered and addressed in the elements used to create this Jack the Ripper POIPAT, however the POIPAT is not yet totally finished. It is quite possible that when an assessor is reviewing a POI's background information to score them on the POIPAT, they will encounter something of interest about that POI that was not addressed by any of the other elements in the POIPAT. The Comments section provides the assessor an area where they can identify such information.

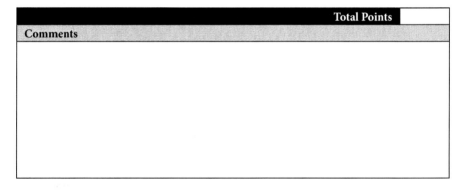

This section is not scored, but the information contained therein could be used to elevate the POI's priority regardless of the total POIPAT score.

The End Section

As the title indicates, this is the final section of the POIPAT. It includes the priority point range, who it was completed and reviewed by as well as relevant dates. There is also a very important note which says:

> Note: This assessment was completed with the information available to the assessor at the time of the file review. Additional information could change this assessment.

For illustrative purposes we have set the following as the priority point range: low = 0–149; medium = 150–199; high = 200–510. In reality, we would not be able to determine this range until we actually tested the POIPAT on a number of POIs. (See Chapter 5, 'Establishing the Priority Levels Points Ranges'.)

	Total Point
Comments	
Priority Point Range: Low = 0–149; Medium = 150–199; High = 200–510	
Completed by: _____ Date: ____ / ____ / ____	
Reviewed by: _____ Date: ____ / ____ / ____	
Note: This assessment was completed with the information available to the assessor at the time of the file review. Additional information could change this assessment.	

(See Appendix E for the complete Jack the Ripper POIPAT. It is also available in PDF form in the Jack the Ripper sub-directory on the companion CD.)

Endnotes

1. Any homicide that involves (post-mortem) mutilation and/or removal of the victim's sexual parts.
2. Elements whereby if they were true of any POI, that POI should be considered a high investigative priority regardless of how they scored in any other individual element.
3. For more information on collateral material, see *Practical Aspects of Rape Investigation* by Robert R. Hazelwood and Ann Wolbert Burgess.

Jack the Ripper POIPAT Instructional Guide

11

Introduction

Even though a well designed POIPAT should be easy to follow and to use without an instructional guide, it is still a good practice to create one. The guide should clear up any potential ambiguity and contribute to a consistent approach to the assessment of POIs utilizing the POIPAT you created. The guide should explain not only how each of the elements on the POIPAT should be assessed but also the rationale of each question. When one understands the reason for an element it makes it easier to understand the expected response.

Every POIPAT instructional guide should be set up exactly the same as the POIPAT it was created to accompany. Every element from that POIPAT should be listed and include its rationale as well as instructions to the reader. This chapter will provide the reader with an example of a POIPAT instructional guide for the POIPAT that was created for the Jack the Ripper case in the previous chapter. The following sections have been laid out exactly as each of the sections would appear in our Jack the Ripper Instructional Guide. The numbers in front of each element in the guide correlate to their matching element number on the POIPAT.

In order to get the most out of this chapter, the reader should follow along with a copy of the Jack the Ripper POIPAT which is available on the companion CD in the Jack the Ripper sub-directory or in Appendix E of this book.

The following sections have been written as they would appear to the reader if following along in the actual Jack the Ripper Instructional Guide which is available in Appendix F.

Methodology

This POIPAT has been created specifically for the Jack the Ripper investigation. It is premised on the belief the same offender is responsible for the homicides of Mary Ann Nichols, Annie Chapman, Elizabeth Stride, Catherine Eddowes and Mary Jane Kelly.

It includes a series of traits and characteristics believed to be true of the offender. It considers where the offender resided at the time of the offences, his comfort zone, lifestyle, marital status, physical characteristics, employment, criminal history, any known association to any or all of the victims and his availability to commit the offence. This composite of the offender was developed after a thorough review of the material available at the time and in consideration of retired SSA John Douglas' profile.

Each of the elements on the POIPAT has been assigned a score. The base score for each element was 20 points. Then each item was weighted based on a number of factors including how important it is compared to the other elements; availability and accessibility of the information; frequency or uniqueness of the element; subjectivity of information; and the reliability of the source. Once this weighting process is completed, it could increase, decrease or have no effect on the initial base score of 20 points.

Once the POIPAT is completed, all the items are added up. The higher the total score, the higher the priority rating that will be assigned to the POI being assessed. The priority ratings are 'low', 'medium' and 'high'. See the 'priority point range' at the end of the POIPAT for the specific point range for each priority level.

General Rules

When scoring each of these elements, either give them full points or no points. No element should receive partial points. Each item is to be considered either true or false. If the element is true, full points are awarded. If the element is false, no points are awarded.

The source of the information to support a true or false response does not have to be an official document such as a criminal record, but it must be believed to be accurate, credible and reliable. This could include, but would not be restricted to, police reports, records management systems, intelligence reports, court records, municipal records, government databases and medical records. It is always a good practice to identify the source of the information that supported the responses to each of the items on POIPAT.

POIPAT Element Assessment

The following sections explain the rationale for each element as well as instruction on how each of the items should be assessed. The number preceding each item is the same as the number of its matching element on the POIPAT.

Residence

1. **Rationale:** All of these incidents occurred in London, England; therefore, it is likely the offender resided in London during the time of the offences.

    Instruction: If the POI resided in London, England, between August 31, 1888 and November 9, 1888, score this element 20. This item is independent of element 2. You score this regardless of whether or not the POI was a resident of Whitechapel at the time.

2. **Rationale:** All of the victims in these cases were believed to have been murdered in or near Whitechapel. It is likely the offender lived in or near Whitechapel.

    Instruction: If the POI resided within 10 miles of Whitechapel, England, between August 31, 1888 and November 9, 1888, score this element 20. This item is independent of item 1. You score this 20 even if you gave the POI points in item 1 for being a resident of London, England.

Comfort Zone

3. **Rationale:** All of the victims in these cases were believed to have been murdered in or near Whitechapel. It is likely that even if the offender did not live there, he was familiar with and comfortable in that area. That comfort may have been a result of living, working or visiting the area. For scoring purposes it does not matter how strong the POI's familiarity is with the area. Full points should be scored regardless of the length or extent of the POI's connection to the area.

    Instruction: If the POI resided in, worked in or was known to frequent within 10 miles of the Whitechapel area, score this item 20 points. It does not matter when.

Physical Description

4. **Rationale:** It is virtually unheard of for a female to be responsible for these types of crimes so it is not very likely Jack the Ripper was a female. However, under POIPAT scoring rules it is not possible to give negative points, so we added 'male' as an element and weighted it very high. This ensures that males receive significantly more points than females.

    Instruction: If the POI is male, score this element 50 points.

5.   **Rationale:** Retired SSA John Douglas' profile report estimated the offender to be between 28 and 36 years old. This age range seems to fit with the age one might expect of someone who would be comfortable engaging prostitutes in the early morning hours in the back alleys of Whitechapel. In the interests of caution, we expanded the age range to between 25 and 45 years old.

     Instruction: If the POI was between 25 and 45 years at the time of *any* of these incidents, score this item 10 points.

6.   **Rationale:** Retired SSA John Douglas indicated in his profile report that he felt that among other physical characteristics the offender would have problems with speech, a scarred complexion, a physical illness or an injury.

     Instruction: If the POI has any known physical abnormality such as a speech impediment, scarred complexion or injury, score this item 5.

Lifestyle

7.   **Rationale:** All of the victims in this investigation were prostitutes, and it is likely that the offender did not kill the first one he met. Furthermore, it is likely that he knew from experience how to interact with them so they would feel comfortable and not in danger around him.

     Instruction: If the POI is known to use prostitutes, score this element 30 points. 'Uses' does not necessarily mean having sex with them. It could also mean he interacts with them in other ways such as buying drugs from or for them, living off them or drinking with them. He does not have to have a criminal record to receive points for this item.

8.   **Rationale:** All of the offences occurred after dark between midnight and 6:00 a.m. This would tend to support the belief that Jack the Ripper was comfortable being out at this time of the night. This may have been a lifestyle choice or a result of his employment.

     Instruction: If the POI is known to be nocturnal (i.e. works shift work or is known to be out at all hours of the night partying or picking up prostitutes), score this element 10 points.

Marital Status

9. **Rationale:** The nature of these crimes is such that the offender likely does not have to account for his whereabouts for extended periods of time, particularly during the late night or early morning hours. This is consistent with someone who is single, divorced or separated or has a passive partner. Retired FBI profiler John Douglas' profile report agreed that he would not likely be married: 'We would not expect this type of offender to be married'.

   Instruction: If the POI was unattached such as being single, divorced or separated (includes common-law relationships), score this item 5.

10. **Rationale:** See item 9.

    Instruction: If the POI was married (includes common-law relationship) but had a very passive wife during the time of the incidents, score this item 5. If you awarded points in item 9, do *not* score this item.

Employment Status

11. **Rationale:** All of these offences happened during the early morning hours of Friday, Saturday or Sunday. This was likely because the offender had a conventional Monday to Friday day job which precluded him from being able to stay out late during the regular week days. Mr. Douglas said the following in his profile report: 'He would seek a position where he could work alone and vicariously experience his destructive fantasies. Such employment would include work as a butcher, mortician's helper, medical examiner's assistant, or hospital attendant. He is employed Monday through Friday and on Friday night, Saturday, and Sunday is off from work'.

    Instruction: If the POI was employed at the time of the offences, score this item 10 points. Item 12 is related to this element but each is to be scored separately.

12. **Rationale:** See item 11.

    Instruction: If the POI was employed in an occupation, hobby or other activity where the use of a knife was common, score this item 20 points.

Criminal History

13. **Rationale:** It is common for sex offenders to have a history of property offences such as break and enter, possession of stolen property and/or theft. It is also likely that the offender had a history of violent crimes such as assault causing bodily harm and domestic violence.

    Instruction: If the POI has a criminal history involving theft, break and enter, minor frauds, domestic violence, assault causing bodily harm and other such similar crimes, this item should be scored 10 points.

14. **Rationale:** Chances are, given the number of cases the offender is believed to be responsible for and the fact criminals don't usually start committing offences at the most extreme end of their crime category, it is likely that Jack the Ripper was involved in other sex crimes. It is also known that it is common for sex offenders to have a number of psychosexual disorders such as exhibitionism and voyeurism.

    Instruction: If the POI has been known to be involved in any sex related criminal offences of any type, this item is to be scored 20 points.

15. **Rationale:** All of the victims had their throats slashed. In most if not all of the cases, this led to the incapacitation and death of the victims. This was a consistent behaviour for Jack the Ripper and is very likely to be present in any other offences he committed or attempted. It does not necessarily have to have led to the victim's death.

    Instruction: If the POI has been known to have slashed or attempted to slash a victim's throat whether or not it led to their death, score this item 50 points.

Linked to Victims

16. **Rationale:** The purpose of this item is to acknowledge any linkages that can be identified between the POI and any or all of the victims. The more victims the POI can be linked to, the higher the probability that this POI is the offender. The linkage may be a result of but not

restricted to the following examples: the POI is a relative, a customer or client, an employer/employee or an acquaintance of the victim(s) or briefly met the offender on some occasion.

The victim(s) may not even be aware of the linkage. For example, the POI was an attendant at the hospital where the victims were patients. The POI may know the victim(s) from seeing them there often, but the victim never took notice of the attendant.

Instruction: Score 20 points for each of the cases where there is a linkage between the POI and the victim.

Availability

17. **Rationale:** The rationale of this element is to assess the POI's opportunity and availability to commit any or all of the offences. If for example it can be proven he was in prison at the time of Mary Ann Nichols' murder, then he would not be available or have the opportunity to commit that particular murder.

    Instruction: Score 10 points for each case where the POI would have been available and had the opportunity at the time of the offence. In this case, *if you do not have any information that clears the POI, assume he or she was available and had the opportunity.*

Weapon

18. **Rationale:** Given that all the victims had their throats slashed and most were cut open and had parts of their bodies removed, there is no doubt that Jack the Ripper used a knife as a weapon. Dr. Bond, who conducted one of the autopsies, said he thought the knife was 'a strong knife at least six inches long, very sharp, pointed at the top and about an inch in width. It may have been a clasp knife, a butcher's knife or a surgeon's knife. I think it was no doubt a straight knife'.

    It is also likely that Jack the Ripper brought the knife to each of the crime scenes, so we can be quite confident that he carried a knife even if it was only on those occasions he planned to murder.

    Instruction: If the POI is known to carry a knife no matter how often, score this element 20 points.

Other

19. **Rationale:** This element comes from retired SSA John Douglas' profile report: 'His anger became internalized and in his younger years, he expressed his pent-up destructive emotions by setting fires and torturing small animals'.

    Instruction: If the POI has a history of setting fires or torturing animal, score this item 10 points.

20. **Rationale:** Almost all of the victims were eviscerated and had parts of their body removed post-mortem. It is highly likely that Jack the Ripper derived psychosexual gratification from this activity which would likely be present in other similar cases he was involved in.

    Instruction: Score 50 points if the POI has a history of or documented fantasy of evisceration, mutilation and/or removal of body parts. This information can come from any believed reliable source such as police information systems or sources close to the offender such as a girlfriend or ex-wife.

Comments

Rationale: The Comments box was designed for important information that may not have been addressed in other areas of the POIPAT. Although this item is not scored, it may be very important to the investigation and regardless of the total POIPAT score may cause this POI's priority level to be elevated.

Instruction: If during the course of the review of this POI's background material you discover information you believe has not been covered in other areas of the POIPAT but may be of interest to investigators or management, record the information here.

The End Section

Once all of the elements have been considered and scored, they should be added and the total placed in the Total Points box. This score will determine the priority ranking for this POI. These rankings are located under the Comments box. If the total points are between 0 and 149, the priority ranking will be 'low'. If they are between 150 and 199, the priority ranking will be 'medium'. If the total score is higher than 199, it will be a 'high' priority. You can circle the applicable priority level.

There is a location for two signature blocks including a place for a date. The person conducting the POI assessment should sign the 'Completed by' signature block. It is very important that it be dated when the assessment was completed, because the score is based on the information that was available to the assessor on that date. New information could be received later that could change the score.

The second signature block is there for the person who reviews the POIPAT once it has been completed. This could be a supervisor, file manager, lead investigator or whoever's job it is to oversee the POIPAT system for this case.

Jack the Ripper Suspects 12

Introduction

Just as with most high profile investigations, there were a large number of POIs in the Jack the Ripper investigation who were identified as suspects for a number of reasons and from a variety of sources. Unfortunately, many of the investigative case records including the suspect file went missing during the 1970s and early 1980s before they could be deposited in the Public Record Office. Many of the documents have resurfaced over the years, but the location of the suspect file still remains a mystery.

The identities of many of the most famous suspects and what is known or believed to be true of them have surfaced as a result of the determination of researchers, writers and Ripperologists dedicated to solving this case. Everyone seems to have their favourite suspect. Some would have made strong suspects, whereas others were very unlikely and occasionally bordered on the ridiculous.

Three of the better known suspects actually surfaced in 1894 in response to a newspaper article suggesting that Thomas Hayne Cutbush was Jack the Ripper. Sir Melville Macnaghten, who was then chief constable of Scotland Yard, wrote a confidential report that indicated that although there were many homicidal maniacs identified as suspects,

> no shadow of proof could be thrown on any one. I may mention the cases of 3 men, any one of whom would have been more likely than Cutbush to have committed this series of murders.

Regardless of how the suspects were identified or how strongly anyone felt about them, if the POIPAT was available at the time, it could have been used as an objective and unbiased means of prioritizing them.

In this chapter we will provide some basic information on 10 better known Jack the Ripper suspects including Thomas Hayne Cutbush and the three identified by Sir Melville Macnaghten. In some cases there were reams of secondary material available about these suspects, including books, magazine articles, television programs, movies, documentaries and Internet sites. In some cases there was very little information. Some of these secondary sources were contradictory or took opposing views on the viability of these individuals as suspects.

The purpose of this chapter is not meant to be a definitive historic account of these suspects but to provide the reader with enough information about each of them to evaluate them using the POIPAT we created in the previous chapter. The information provided here is believed to be accurate, but it was derived from secondary sources that in some cases developed conclusions based on their own inferences, assumptions and deductions so we cannot absolutely guarantee its accuracy.

These POIs are listed here in alphabetical order of their last name. As you read the details of each of these subjects, try to rank order them in your own mind based on who you believe was most likely Jack the Ripper. Then in the next chapter we will score each of them using our Jack the Ripper POIPAT, followed in the next chapter by a rank-ordered list of the POIs based on his POIPAT score.

Thomas Hayne Cutbush

Thomas Hayne Cutbush was 23 years old at the time of the murders. He lived with his mother and aunt in Kennington, England. He was born in and lived in Kennington all his life. His father died when he was young. He worked as a clerk and traveller in the tea trade at the Minories and then canvassed for a directory in the East End. He was noted to have been of good character during that time. He is believed to have contracted syphilis around 1888 after which he was not known to ever have had a job.

His illness apparently affected his brain because he began to think people were trying to poison him. He wrote to a number of people complaining that a Dr. Brooks supplied him with bad medicines. On March 5, 1891, he was detained as a wandering lunatic at Lambeth Infirmary. Within a few hours he escaped, and while on the loose, he stabbed Florence Grace Johnson in the buttocks and tried to do the same to another lady, named Isabelle Frazer Anderson.

He was arrested again four days later on March 9, 1891, and shortly afterwards was declared insane and sent to Broadmoor Criminal Lunatic Asylum.

He came to light as a suspect on February 13, 1894, by a newspaper when it published an article claiming to know the identity of Jack the Ripper. They did not mention him by name but it was apparently obvious they were writing about Cutbush. He became of even more interest when it was learned he was the nephew of Executive Superintendent Charles Cutbush of the Metropolitan Police.

Subsequent investigation determined that a knife found on Cutbush was purchased in Houndsditch about a week before he was detained in the infirmary which was more than two years after the Whitechapel murders. Although no one could account for his whereabouts during the Whitechapel murders, they were unable to link him to the Whitechapel area which is a fair distance from his home in Kennington, England.

Montague John Druitt

Montague John Druitt was the first of three subjects mentioned in Sir Melville Macnaghten's report as 'more likely to have committed this series of murders' than Thomas Cutbush. His report said the following:

(1) A Mr. M.J. Druitt, said to be a doctor & of good family, who disappeared at the time of the Miller's Court murder, & whose body (which was said to have been upwards of a month in the water) was found in the Thames on 31st. Decr., or about 7 weeks after that murder. He was sexually insane and from private inf. I have little doubt but that his own family believed him to have been the murderer.

His support for Druitt as a good suspect was likely bolstered by his theory that the murders stopped because the murderer either committed suicide or was confined to an asylum. The following is an excerpt from his report:

A much more rational theory is that the murderer's brain gave way altogether after his awful glut in Miller's Court, and that he immediately committed suicide, or, as a possible alternative, was found to be so hopelessly mad by his relations, that he was by them confined in some asylum.

Druitt was born on August 15, 1857, at Westfield, Wimborne, Dorset, and was 31 years old at the time of the murders. He was a barrister-at-law and an assistant schoolmaster at a boarding school in Blackheath, London, England. He was believed to have been in good physical shape and was noted to have excelled in a number of sports, particularly cricket. Although Macnaghten apparently claimed that Druitt lived with his family, records indicate that he actually lived alone at 9 Eliot Place, Blackheath. Blackheath is approximately 7.5 miles from Whitechapel.

His father died in 1885 of a heart attack. There was a history of mental illness and suicide in his family. His mother became mentally ill and had attempted to take her own life with an overdose of medicine. She was eventually admitted to an asylum. She died there in December 1890.

On Monday December 31, 1888, Henry Winslade, a waterman, found Druitt's body floating in the Thames River. He was fully clothed except for a hat and collar. There were no marks of injury on the body but it was quite decomposed. The following items were found on the body:

- Four large stones in each pocket in the top coat
- £2 10s. in gold
- 7s. in silver
- 2d. in bronze

- Two cheques on the London and Provincial Bank (£50 and £16)
- First-class season pass from Blackheath to London for the South-Western Railway)
- Second half return Hammersmith to Charing Cross dated 1 December
- Silver watch
- Gold chain with spade guinea attached
- Pair of kid gloves
- White handkerchief

According to a report from the *Acton, Chiswick & Turnham Green Gazette* (January 5, 1889), Druitt's brother, William H. Druitt, a solicitor, gave evidence at the subsequent inquest that his brother Montague had stayed with him at Bournemouth for a night near the end of October. Then on December 11 he learned from a friend that his brother had not been heard of at his chambers for more than a week. As a result, he travelled to Blackheath where he learned Montague had been dismissed due to getting into serious trouble at the school. He subsequently had Montague's residence searched, and a paper addressed to William was located. The paper was produced at the inquest and read to the effect: 'Since Friday I felt I was going to be like mother, and the best thing was for me to die'. According to William, his brother had never attempted suicide before. The verdict of the inquest was suicide while in an unsound state of mind.

As indicated previously, Sir Melville Macnaghten claimed to have private information that Druitt was sexually insane and his family believed he was the murderer. However, even though there is no reason to disbelieve Macnaghten, there was no apparent independent evidence to support those claims. There was also no evidence to connect Druitt to the Whitechapel area.

Sir William Withey Gull

Sir William Gull was born on December 31, 1816. In 1837, before he was 21, he left home to begin his medical training at Guy's Hospital, London, England. He later obtained his MB degree with honours in surgery, physiology, medicine and comparative anatomy. He went on to have an impressive medical career. He attained a number of important medical positions and honours. He made numerous contributions to medical science particularly in the fields of anorexia nervosa, Gull-Sutton syndrome, myxoedema and paraplegia. He married Susan Anne Lacey on April 18, 1848.

In 1872 Dr. Gull was made the First Baronet of the Baronetcy of Brook Street after being credited for leading the recovery of HRH the Prince of Wales from typhoid fever. In addition to being the Prince of Wales' physician-in-ordinary, he was also appointed to be physician-in-ordinary to HM Queen Victoria which was in large part an honourary appointment.

Dr. Gull died from a stroke on January 29, 1890, at his home in 74 Brook Street, London. He had suffered a number of strokes prior to his death. The first stroke occurred in the fall of 1887 while he was at his home in Scotland which caused slight paralysis on his right side. He recovered enough after a few weeks to allow him to return to London. During the next two years he lived in London, Reigate and Brighton where he suffered a number of strokes.

Speculation that Dr. Gull was Jack the Ripper came from a couple of different sources and became the subject of a published article, books, television programs and movies. The first suggestion he was the Ripper came from a series of newspaper articles published in various newspapers in the United States between 1895 and 1897. The first article reported that a Dr. Howard from London told a prominent citizen from San Francisco that the murderer was a 'medical man of high standing'. His wife became alarmed by his erratic behaviour during the Jack the Ripper murders and disclosed her concern to some of her husband's medical colleagues. They subsequently interviewed him and searched his house where they 'found ample proofs of murder' which gave them grounds to commit him to an asylum. Dr. Howard's identity was never established.

Later variants of the story suggested the murderer was 'a demented physician afflicted with wildly uncontrollable erotic mania'. It reported that Robert James Lees, who was a preacher and spiritualist, helped police identify the killer with his clairvoyant powers, leading them to Gull's house in Mayfair. The police allegedly entered the house of the distinguished physician and took him to a private asylum under another name. The physician's funeral was faked to explain his sudden disappearance.

The second suggestion that Gull was Jack the Ripper came in 1973 during a six-part mini-series docudrama titled 'Jack the Ripper'. The royal conspiracy theory was suggested by Joseph Sickert, who claimed to be Walter Sickert's (see Walter Richard Sickert below) illegitimate son. Joseph Sickert said his father told him that Prince Albert Victor had a child named Alice Margaret Crook with Joseph Sickert's grandmother, Annie Elizabeth Crook, who was a Catholic. His father, Walter, raised the child with the help of friends, including Mary Jane Kelly, who had been one of his models.

The fact there may have been a Catholic heir to the throne would have been major scandal at the time. In an attempt to cover this up, Prime Minister Lord Salisbury (Robert Gascoyne-Cecil) supposedly conspired with Queen Victoria and senior Freemasons including high ranking police officials.

Kelly apparently became aware of the plot and hid the child with nuns. Then she took off into the East End where she told the story to Mary Nichols, Elizabeth Stride and Annie Chapman, who in turn decided to make some money with the information by blackmailing the royal family. It was suggested that Gull murdered the women including Kelly with the assistance of a coachman, John Netley, to ensure their silence. Catherine Eddowes was allegedly killed by mistake because she often went by the name of Mary Kelly.

Joseph Sickert apparently retracted his story several years later in an interview with the London *Sunday Times* indicating that it was a hoax he had made up.

Although it would be easy to conclude that Jack the Ripper had a serious dislike of or disrespect for women, this was not the case for Dr. Gull. At a time in history when women were discouraged from entering the male dominated medical profession, Dr. Gull was a strong advocate for them. In 1886 he chaired a meeting of a medical society to establish a medical scholarship for women. He made a small personal financial contribution to the scholarship himself.

Severin Antoinovich Klosowski, aka George Chapman

Severin Klosowski was born on December 14, 1865, in Poland. At the age of 15 he became a surgeon's apprentice and later enrolled in a course in practical surgery at the Warsaw Praga Hospital. Although the exact date is unknown, it is believed he moved to London sometime between 1887 and 1888.

His first job was a hairdresser's assistant at a shop located at 70 West India Dock Road, London. Several months later he ran his own barber shop at 126 Cable Street, St. George's-in-the-East, which is believed to have been his residence at the time of the Whitechapel murders. St. George's-in-the-East was situated next to Whitechapel in London's East End.

When he moved to London he left his wife behind in Poland, but this did not prevent him from marrying Lucy Baderski in 1889 just a few weeks after meeting her. In 1890 he began working at a barber shop located in the basement of the White Hart Pub at George Yard just off Whitechapel High Street.

In 1891 the couple moved to the United States together where Klosowski got a job as a barber. On one occasion his wife reported that she got into an argument with him which led to him pinning her on a bed in the back of the shop. As this was happening a customer walked into the shop and Klosowski went to tend to him. That is when she noticed 'a sharp and formidable knife' under the pillow which she promptly hid from him. He later told her he had planned to kill her and showed her the place in the room where he intended on burying her body.

Baderski returned to London in 1892 shortly after the incident where she gave birth to their daughter. Klosowski later returned to London, and they reunited for a short period of time. In 1893, Klosowski went to work at another barber shop in South Tottenham where he met Annie Chapman. She coincidentally had the same name as one of Jack the Ripper's victims. They lived together for about a year before they split up, but he took her surname as his own and became known as 'George Chapman'.

Between 1895 and 1901 Klosowski entered into illegitimate marriages using his new identity with three other women whom he abused physically and mentally. All three women died from systematic poisoning by Klosowski. In October 1902, Klosowski was arrested shortly after the doctor who conducted the autopsy on the third victim found poison in her stomach, bowels, liver, kidneys and brain. The other two victims were later exhumed and both were found to have had large amounts of poison in them. He was charged, convicted and then hanged on April 7, 1903, at Wandsworth Prison.

Klosowski took prominence as a Jack the Ripper suspect on March 24, 1903, when comments made by retired Chief Inspector F. G. Abberline of Scotland Yard were published in an article in the *Pall Mall Gazette*. Mr. Abberline was the lead investigator in the Whitechapel murders and likely knew as much or more than anyone associated with the cases until he retired in 1892. When one of the *Gazette*'s representatives called him to ask his opinion regarding the theory printed in a morning newspaper that Chapman (Klosowski) was Jack the Ripper, the *Gazette* quoted Mr. Abberline as saying,

> What an extra-ordinary thing it is that you should just have called upon me now. I had just commenced, not knowing anything about the report in the newspaper, to write to the Assistant Commissioner of Police, Mr. Macnaghten, to say how strongly I was impressed with the opinion that 'Chapman' was also the author of the Whitechapel murders.

The following paragraph printed in the same article encapsulates most of Mr. Abberline's rationale for believing Chapman was responsible for the Whitechapel murders:

> 'As I say', went on the criminal expert, 'there are a score of things which make one believe that Chapman is the man; and you must understand that we have never believed all those stories about Jack the Ripper being dead, or that he was a lunatic, or anything of that kind. For instance, the date of the arrival in England coincides with the beginning of the series of murders in Whitechapel; there is a coincidence also in the fact that the murders ceased in London when Chapman went to America, while similar murders began to be perpetrated in America after he landed there. The fact that he studied medicine and surgery in Russia before he came here is well established, and it is curious to note that the first series of murders was the work of an expert surgeon, while the recent poisoning cases were proved to be done by a man with more than an elementary knowledge of medicine. The story told by Chapman's wife of the attempt to murder her with a long knife while in America is not to be ignored, but something else with regard to America is still more remarkable'.

The remarkable issue had to do with a discussion between Dr. Phillips, who had conducted the post-mortem on one of the victims, and the coroner. Dr. Phillips described the skill of the offender with the knife and overwhelming evidence that the body was mutilated so the offender could obtain one of the organs. The coroner in turn commented that he was told by the sub-curator of a pathological museum that he had been approached by an American a few months before to procure a number of specimens for which he was willing to pay £20 each. A similar request had been made at another institution in London.

This, in addition to the fact the Whitechapel murders stopped after Klosowski moved to the United States and then a similar case occurred there, seems to have led Mr. Abberline to the theory that Klosowski was supplying the unknown American with body parts as this excerpt from the article seems to suggest:

> 'It is a remarkable thing', Mr. Abberline pointed out, 'that after the Whitechapel horrors America should have been the place where a similar kind of murder began, as though the miscreant had not fully supplied the demand of the American agent'.

There were a few other issues in the article that Mr. Abberline felt supported his suspicions as follows:

> There are many other things extremely remarkable. The fact that Klosowski when he came to reside in this country occupied a lodging in George Yard, Whitechapel Road, where the first murder was committed, is very curious, and the height of the man and the peaked cap he is said to have worn quite tallies with the descriptions I got of him. All agree, too, that he was a foreign-looking man,—but that, of course, helped us little in a district so full of foreigners as Whitechapel. One discrepancy only have I noted, and this is that the people who alleged that they saw Jack the Ripper at one time or another, state that he was a man about thirty-five or forty years of age. They, however, state that they only saw his back, and it is easy to misjudge age from a back view.

Contrary to Mr. Abberline's comments, Klosowski didn't actually move to George Yard in Whitechapel until 1890 (about two years after the first murder). He did, however, live in the East End of London very close to Whitechapel during the murders.

Mr. Abberline's contention that there was a series of similar murders in the United States after Klosowski moved there was not supported by research with the exception of the murder of prostitute Carrie Brown. Her mutilated body was discovered in a hotel room at the East River Hotel in New York on April 24, 1891. She appeared as though she had been strangled and had cuts and stab wounds all over her body. Although Klosowski lived in New Jersey, which is just across the river, around the time of this murder, there was no evidence to link him to it.

Aaron Kosminski

Aaron Kosminski was the second person mentioned in Sir Melville Macnaghten's report. The following is what he had to say about Kosminski:

> (2) Kosminski, a Polish Jew, & resident in Whitechapel. This man became insane owing to many years indulgence in solitary vices. He had a great hatred of women, specially of the prostitute class, & had strong homicidal tendencies; he was removed to a lunatic asylum about March 1889. There were many circs connected with this man which made him a strong 'suspect'.

Macnaghten did not mention Kosminski's first or middle name, and there is no mention of a 'Kosminski' as a suspect in official police records, so it is not possible to determine conclusively who he was writing about. However, in 1987 Martin Fido, author of *The Crimes, Detection and Death of Jack the Ripper*, went searching asylum records in the UK and Wales for the name 'Kosminski' and was able to find only Aaron Kosminski, who was admitted to the Colney Hatch Asylum in 1891. It has become generally accepted that Macnaghten's 'Kosminski' and Martin Fido's 'Aaron Kosminski' are the same person.

Aaron Kosminski was believed to have been born in Poland on September 11, in either 1864 or 1865, which would have made him either 24 or 25 at the time of the homicides. He emigrated to England around 1880 or 1881 with his sisters and their husbands where he was believed to have resided with his family in Whitechapel. Although his asylum record lists his previous occupation as a hair-dresser, there doesn't appear to be any evidence he actually ever had any job after moving to England.

There is not a lot of material available regarding his physical description, but case notes indicate he had been showing signs of insanity since 1885. Some of his symptoms included auditory hallucinations and a paranoid fear of being fed by other people. This caused him to refuse food provided to him by others and resort to eating food that had been discarded as garbage. This poor diet led to his emaciation. He also refused to wash or bathe.

In 1890, he was admitted to Mile End Old Town Workhouse for a few days as a result of exhibiting mental problems and was later released into the care of one of his brothers. On February 7, 1891, he was admitted to the Colney Hatch Asylum. His abode was listed as 16 Greenfield St., Mile End (Whitechapel) which was believed to be the residence of his sister and brother-in-law.

According to *The Complete Jack the Ripper A to Z* (p. 271) by Begg, Fido, and Skinner, the following notes were made in the admissions book of the Colney Hatch Lunatic Asylum:

> Facts indicating insanity observed by Medical Man
> He declares that he is guided and his movements altogether controlled by an instinct that informs his mind; he says that he knows the movements of all

mankind; he refuses food from others because he is told to do so, and he eats out of gutters for the same reason.

2.   Other Facts Indicating Insanity Communicated by Others

Jacob Cohen, 51 Carter Lane, St Paul's EC says that he goes about the streets and picks up bits of bread out of the gutter and eats them, he drinks water from the tap & he refuses food at the hands of others. He took up a knife and threatened the life of his sister. He is very dirty and will not be washed. He has not attempted any kind of work for years.

It was noted in his initial physical and emotional examination at Colney Hatch Lunatic Asylum in 1891 that he suffered physically from self-abuse (some believe this was a euphemism for masturbation), was manic and incoherent, was in fair physical state and was not dangerous to others, suicidal or epileptic.

We did not uncover any information that supported Kosminski having been suspected, accused, charged or convicted of any criminal offences. There was one violent incident mentioned in a medical log in 1892 as follows:

1892 Jan 9: Incoherent: at time excited & violent—a few days ago he took up a chair, and attempted to strike the charge attendant: apathetic as a rule, and refuses to occupy himself in any way: habits cleanly. Health fair.

Other than the chair incident and the mention of threatening his sister with a knife, these are the only indications of violent behaviour for Kosminski.

There is some information that Kosminski was identified by a witness as having been with one of the victims just before her murder. Assistant Commissioner Sir Robert Anderson claimed in his memoirs titled *The Lighter Side of My Official Life* that Jack the Ripper had been identified by the 'only person who had ever had a good view of the murderer', but they could not prosecute because the witness and culprit were both Jews and the witnesses would not testify against a fellow Jew. Notes made in the margins of his copy of *The Lighter Side of My Official Life* by Chief Inspector Donald Swanson, who led the Jack the Ripper investigation, indicated that 'Kosminski' was identified at the Seaside Home in Brighton.

Swanson's notes also indicate that Kosminski knew he had been identified, and after the identification he was returned to his brother's house in Whitechapel where he was watched by police day and night. Soon thereafter he was sent to Stepney Workhouse and then to Colney Hatch and died shortly afterwards. Kosminski actually died several years later at Leavesden Asylum in 1919.

There has been a great deal of discussion and debate about this identification. Some are sceptical because it is believed to have been made a significant time after the murder. It was not clear which witness or even which victim they were referring to. It is likely that they were referring to Israel Schwartz, who said he saw a male with Elizabeth Stride 15 minutes before she was murdered. However, it could also have been Joseph Lawende, who had seen a man talking with Catherine Eddowes about 10 minutes prior to her body being discovered, although he said he would not be able to identify the man if he saw him again.

There was nothing in Kosminski's background material to indicate he was either married or in a relationship with anyone at the time of the murders.

Michael Ostrog

Michael Ostrog was the third person mentioned in Macnaghten's memo as one of the men who would have been more likely than Cutbush to have committed this series of murders. The following is a quote from the memo:

> (3) Michael Ostrog, a Russian doctor, and a convict, who was subsequently detained in a lunatic asylum as a homicidal maniac. The man's antecedents were of the worst possible type, and his whereabouts at the time of the murders could never be ascertained.

It is unclear who or what Macnaghten's sources were for the information he had on Ostrog, but some of it with the benefit of hindsight and further research appears to be inaccurate or somewhat exaggerated. Ostrog had a very extensive criminal history of petty crimes such as fraud and theft but there is no record of more serious or violent offences. He was prone to violent resistance when confronted with arrest which may be where his reputation for being a dangerous person originates. There was one such incident in 1873 in which he apparently produced a revolver at a police station after having been arrested for several thefts.

According to a record in the Habitual Criminals Register for 1904, he went by a number of aliases including: Matters Ostroy, Bertrand Ashley, Claude Clayton, Dr. Grant, Stanistan Sublinsky, John Sobieski and Michael Ostrog. It also says he was born in 1830 at sea. It also mentions his date of liberation, intended address and occupations as: '17-09-1904, 29 Brooke St., Holbron Doctor'.

In July 1887, he was arrested for stealing a metal tankard from the Royal Military Academy at Woolwich, in southeast London. He was sentenced to six months hard labour and subsequently certified insane. As a result, he was sent to the Surrey Pauper Lunatic Asylum in Tooting on September 30, 1887, where he was registered as a 50 year old, married Jewish surgeon who was suffering mania. Research has been unable to provide evidence that Ostrog was a medical doctor or had any medical training.

Ostrog was released from the Asylum on March 10, 1888, with the condition to report regularly to police which did not happen. This, combined with the theory that Jack the Ripper was a lunatic with some medical training, likely elevated Ostrog to suspect status with the investigators, who would have been interested in anyone at large during the Whitechapel murders who fit that profile.

On October 26, 1888, a warrant for his apprehension for failing to report was posted in the police *Gazette*. It described him as follows:

> age 55, height 5ft. 11in., complexion dark, hair dark brown, eyes grey, scars right thumb and right shin, two large moles right shoulder and one back of neck, corporal punishment marks; generally dressed in semi-clerical suit. A Polish Jew.

The article concluded with

> Special attention is called to this dangerous man.

He was described as 'a surgeon by profession, and stated to be a desperate man' on an index card.

The fact that Ostrog's whereabouts were unknown to police in London during the Whitechapel murders could be because he was actually in custody in France under another alias. There was some evidence that he was arrested in July 1888 in France under one of his aliases. If this was true, he would not have been available for the Whitechapel murders because he remained in custody in France until November 1888, when he began a two year prison term.

John Pizer, aka Leather Apron

John Pizer, a Polish Jew, was believed to have been born in 1850. He became one of the earliest of the better known suspects to be identified in the Jack the Ripper cases. He was initially brought to the attention of police during the Mary Ann Nichols investigation by a number of prostitutes who knew him at the time only as 'Leather Apron'. They accused him of being violent towards them when they did not comply with his blackmail demands.

According to a police report on the Mary Ann Nichols homicide, dated September 7, 1888, submitted by Inspector J. H. Helson and Superintendent J. Keating:

> A man named Jack Pizer, alias Leather Apron, has, for some considerable period been in the habit of ill-using prostitutes in this, and other parts of the metropolis, and careful search has been, and is continued to be made to find this man in order that his movements may be accounted for on the night in question, although at present there is no evidence whatsoever against him.

His notoriety as a suspect really took off when a number of newspapers began to report on 'Leather Apron'. The following is an excerpt from the *Star* newspaper on September 5, 1888, prior to Pizer being identified as 'Leather Apron':

He is a more ghoulish and devilish brute than can be found in all the pages of shocking fiction. He has ranged Whitechapel for a long time. He exercises over the unfortunates who ply their trade after twelve o'clock at night, a sway that is *BASED ON UNIVERSAL TERROR.*

He has kicked, injured, bruised, and terrified a hundred of them who are ready to testify to the outrages. He has made a certain threat, his favorite threat, to any number of them, and each of the three dead bodies represents that threat carried out. He carries a razor-like knife, and two weeks ago drew it on a woman called 'Widow Annie' as she was crossing the square near London Hospital, threatening at the same time, with his ugly grin and his malignant eyes, to 'rip her up'.

The *Star* also printed that one of their reporters got a description of 'Leather Apron' from about '50 of the unfortunates', who described him as follows:

He is five feet four or five inches in height and wears a dark, close-fitting cap. He is thickset, and has an unusually thick neck. His hair is black, and closely clipped, his age being about 38 or 40. He has a small, black moustache. The distinguishing feature of his costume is a leather apron, which he always wears, and from which *HE GETS HIS NICKNAME.*

His expression is sinister, and seems to be full of terror for the women who describe it. His eyes are small and glittering. His lips are usually parted in a grin which is not only not reassuring, but excessively repellant. He is a slipper maker by trade, but does not work. His business is blackmailing women late at night. A number of men in Whitechapel follow this interesting profession. He has never cut anybody so far as known, but always carries a leather knife, presumably as sharp as leather knives are wont to be.

Pizer became aware of his newly found notoriety and as a result feared going out into public. Consequently, he went into hiding with the help of his relatives.

When Detective-Sergeant William Thicke learned that a person named 'Leather Apron' was a suspect in the case, he knew they were referring to John Pizer. He had known Pizer for a number of years. On September 10, 1888, two days after Annie Chapman's murder, Detective-Sergeant Thicke arrested Pizer at 22 Mulberry Street in Whitechapel which had been his family home for a number of years. He was unmarried at the time of the homicides.

The September 11, 1888, edition of the *Pall Mall Gazette* reported that in the course of apprehending Pizer, Detective-Sergeant Thicke, he seized five long-bladed knives. These knifes however are commonly used by those working as boot finishers which was Pizer's profession.

Pizer cooperated with the police and provided them with an account of his whereabouts for both the Mary Ann Nichols and Annie Chapman homicides. He said that on the night of the Nichols murder, August 31, 1888, he slept at a common lodging house on Holloway Road. This was confirmed by the proprietor, who knew Pizer. Holloway Road, London, was about five miles from Whitechapel. His alibi was further bolstered by the fact that around 1:30 p.m. he had gone out for a walk near the lodging house and encountered the lodging house manager and one or two police officers. He could see the glow of a fire which was coming from the London docks and asked one of the police officers where the fire was.

On September 8, the night of the Chapman murder, he said he stayed at 22 Mulberry St. because he was afraid to leave due to the reports that had been published about him in the press. This was corroborated by several persons.

After his alibis were confirmed by witnesses, he was subsequently cleared as a suspect and released from custody. In a further attempt to clear his name, he later appeared as a witness at the Chapman inquest. There is no indication the police had any interest in him as a suspect beyond that time even when the later murders occurred. It is also believed that he received a payment from at least one newspaper for slandering him.

Walter Richard Sickert

Walter Sickert was born in Munich, Germany, on May 31, 1860, to painter Oswald Sickert and Eleanor Louisa Moravia Henry. Walter was the oldest of their six children. In 1868 the family moved to England where Sickert attended a number of colleges. After graduating he began a short lived acting career and then studied art. He also became an assistant to well known artist James McNeill Whistler for a short time. He went on to become a well known artist in his own right.

Many of his paintings were fairly controversial for the time period. One series of paintings in particular, known as 'The Camden Town Murder', was inspired by the true case of a part-time prostitute who had been found murdered in her bed with her throat cut in September 1907. Another was a painting in 1908 titled "Jack the Ripper's Bedroom' which was motivated by a story that the landlady of one of the rooms he had stayed in told him about her belief that Jack the Ripper had stayed in the same room.

Sickert was married three times and is believed to have had a few mistresses. He did not have children from those marriages, but Joseph Gorman, who changed his name to Joseph Gorman-Sickert, claimed to be Walter Sickert's illegitimate son (see Sir William Withey Gull above). He married Ellen Cobden in 1885 and lived at 54 Broadhurst Gardens, South Hampstead, London, which is approximately nine miles from Whitechapel. They divorced in 1899 apparently due to his infidelities, and he moved to Dieppe until 1905. He occasionally travelled to Venice where in 1903 he painted a series of prostitutes in shabby rooms.

He moved back to London in 1905 where he resided at a number of locations including 6 Mornington Crescent, Camden Town, the inspiration for his 'Jack the Ripper's Bedroom' painting. Camden Town is about five miles from Whitechapel. In 1911 he married his student Christine Drummond Angus, and they moved to Dieppe together after World War I. She died in 1920, and he returned to London in 1922 where he married the painter Thérèse Lessore in 1926. He died in 1942 at Bathampton, Wiltshire, where he was living at the time.

Walter Sickert's fame as a suspect came about on two fronts from two different modern day writers: Jean Overton Fuller, *Sickert and the Ripper Crimes* (revised 2003), and Patricia Cornwell, *Portrait of a Killer: Jack the Ripper Case Closed* (revised 2003). Fuller claims in her book that on April 12, 1948, her mother said to her, 'She says he knew who Jack the Ripper was!'. Her mother, Violet Overton Fuller, was speaking about something Humphrey Holland, née Florence Pash, told her Walter Sickert confided to her.

Artist Florence Pash had been a very close friend of Walter Sickert for many years and had exchanged a number of letters with him. Pash was also good friends with Jean Fuller's mother, Violet, and they agreed to write a book titled *Letters to Florence, from Sickert, Conder and Moore* that included some of Sickert's letters to her. Neither the letters nor the proposed book had anything to do with the Whitechapel murders. However, Pash did disclose information to Violet Overton Fuller about Sickert's possible connection to the murders.

Ms. Fuller indicates in her book that not only had Sickert admitted to seeing the bodies of the victims, he also painted them from memory. There was apparently a series of paintings Pash felt could never be exhibited because they were too horrible: 'She could not bear to look at them. Paintings of bleeding, mutilated corpses, which he had done from his memory'. Fuller and her mother concluded that if Sickert saw all of the bodies, he must be Jack the Ripper.

Pash told Fuller that the memories weighed on him. He was afraid to talk about them outright but wanted it known after his death so he painted clues into his pictures. One of the clues was supposed to be a gull which he had placed on Queen Victoria's shoulder. This was interpreted later in the book as a possible link to Sir William Gull (see Sir William Gull above), who figured prominently in the Joseph Gorman-Sickert royal conspiracy theory. There were a number of other not so subtle inferences of Sickert's connection to the royal conspiracy theory in the book including a reference to a 'Mary Kelly' who was reportedly employed by Sickert as a nanny, but who left and later began to blackmail him.

In her book *Portrait of a Killer: Jack the Ripper Case Closed*, Patricia Cornwell describes a number of reasons why she was convinced Sickert was

Jack the Ripper. This includes forensic evidence that may link him to a number of Jack the Ripper letters. One reason she suspected him had to do with an apparent medical condition (penal fistula) that may have caused him to be impotent.

Cornwell found evidence that he underwent a number of surgeries for the condition, twice in Germany and once in London. However, there are detractors who point out that the doctor who performed the surgery was a proctologist and that both he and the hospital where he worked specialized in rectum, anus and vagina surgeries. Based on this, they conclude that he was more likely to have suffered from the more common anal fistula. They also point out that his three marriages, allegations of adultery, several mistresses and accusations of having at least one illegitimate child don't support the theory he was impotent.

Ms. Cornwell was able to locate some of Sickert papers, and when they were compared by Peter Bower, a highly regarded paper examiner, to Ripper letters bearing the same watermark, he concluded that some of them came from the same batches of paper. She concluded from this that Sickert might have written some of the Ripper letters.

Her claim was somewhat bolstered by another examination of papers made by Mr. Bower. According to *The Complete Jack the Ripper A to Z* (p. 467), he examined another collection of Sickert letters supplied by another source and Ripper letters watermarked Gurney Ivory Laid. He concluded after microscopic examination that two Ripper letters and three pieces of Sickert's correspondence came from the same batch of 24 sheets of paper.

Perhaps her strongest piece of forensic evidence came from DNA examination of both Ripper and Sickert correspondence. Her forensic team found similar sequences of mitochondrial DNA in Sickert's correspondence and a stamp used on an envelope to mail what came to be known as the 'Openshaw' letter. Detractors point out a couple of important issues: Firstly, conditions for DNA examination were not ideal as there were plenty of opportunities for the exhibits to have been contaminated over the years by anyone and everyone who handled them. Secondly, Ms. Cornwell concludes that the results of their mitochondrial DNA analysis show that only 1 per cent of the population of the UK share the DNA found on the Ripper letter, which includes the person who left the DNA on Sickert's correspondence. Although 1 per cent of the population seems small, it would have represented approximately 65,000 people in Greater London in 1901.

Although there is convincing evidence that Sickert was the author of one or more of the Ripper letters, it does not necessarily make him Jack the Ripper. There have been hundreds of letters written from persons reporting to be Jack the Ripper. None have ever been proven to have been authentic and nearly all of them have been generally considered hoaxes, except for one which is often referred to as the 'From Hell' letter. Ironically, that letter was not signed Jack the Ripper.

Dr. Roslyn D'Onston Stephenson (Dr. Robert Donston Stephenson)

Dr. Roslyn D'Onston Stephenson, born April 20, 1841, whose real name was Robert Donston Stephenson, was a patient of the London Hospital in Whitechapel during the murders. He had apparently checked himself in on July 26, 1888, suffering from neurasthenia (chronic fatigue) and left the hospital on Friday December 7, 1888. The body of Jack the Ripper's first victim, Mary Ann Nichols, was discovered approximately 150 yards from that hospital. According to *The Complete Jack the Ripper A to Z* (p. 489) Stephenson was in the Currie Ward until at least October 16, 1888, and in 2007 the curator of the London Hospital Museum told researchers that Currie Ward patients were prevented from leaving the ward at night.

Stephenson injected himself into the investigation on October 16, 1888, by writing a letter to the city police responding to Chief Commissioner Sir Charles Warren's claim that 'no language or dialogue is known in which the word Jews is spelled JUWES'. This was in reference to the sentence 'The Juwes are the men that Will not be Blamed for nothing' which was written in chalk above the entrance of a building where a piece of the bloody apron belonging to victim Catherine Eddowes was located. It was his belief the author actually wrote Juives instead of the word Juwes and that it was incorrectly recorded due to the poor lighting conditions at the time. He indicated that Juives is the French word for Jews and that the murderer unconsciously reverted for a moment to his native language. This caused Stephenson to deduce that the murderer was a Frenchman.

Stephenson's interest in the cases intensified from there, and he even managed to profit from them by writing a few articles for the *Pall Mall Gazette*. He was paid a few pounds for each article, one of which related to the writing on the wall. He is reported to have offered his services to the editor to track the murderer, but the editor declined the offer.

On December 26, 1888, Stephenson wrote another letter to the police. This letter was to draw their attention to Dr. Morgan Davies, who made numerous visits to the London hospital to visit another patient and while there often discussed the murderers. These discussions included his own theories on the murderer, and on one occasion Dr. Davies actually took a knife and acted out how the murderer killed and slashed up the victim's body. Stephenson felt that Dr. Davies knew more about the murders than he should have and that there were other things connecting him to the cases.

This included his opinion that Davies was a woman-hater, with a powerful frame and of strong sexual passions. The letter included a P.S. which stated that he had mentioned this matter to George Marsh with whom he had a written agreement to share any reward which he may derive from his information. The agreement, dated '24. Dec. 88', was included with the letter.

George Marsh was an unemployed salesman and self-professed amateur detective. After speaking to Stephenson about the case and seeing him act out how the murderer would have committed the crimes according to Dr. Davies, he concluded, 'From his manner I am of the opinion he is the murderer in the first six cases, if not the last one'. Marsh was so concerned that on December 24, 1888, he went to the police station and provided a statement to Inspector Thomas Roots of Scotland Yard.

Marsh described Stephenson as

Age 48, height 5 ft 10 in, full face, sallow complexion, moustache heavy—mouse coloured—waxed and turned up, hair brown turning grey, eyes sunken. When looking at a stranger generally has an eyeglass. Dress, grey suit and light brown felt hat all well worn; military appearance: says he has been in 42 battles: well educated.

He also said Stephenson was not a drunkard:

He is what I call a regular soaker—can drink from 8 o'clock in the morning until closing time but keep a clear head.

On December 26, 1888, Inspector Roots filed a report indicating that Stephenson came there that evening regarding his suspicions of Dr. Davies. He left Inspector Roots with a statement detailing his suspicions along with his agreement with Marsh relating to the collection of the reward. This statement may have been the letter discussed earlier.

Inspector Roots noted in the file that he had known Stephenson for 20 years and described him in the following manner:

He is a travelled man of education and ability, a doctor of medicine upon diplomas of Paris & New York; a major from the Italian Army—he fought under Garibalidi: and a newspaper writer.

Roots also said,

He has led a Bohemian life, drinks very heavily, and always carries drugs to sober him and stave off delirium tremens.

Further research of Stephenson indicates that he had an interest in the occult. In his younger life he ran up gambling debts and had regular contact with a prostitute. On February 14, 1876, he married Anne Deary. It is unclear how long this marriage lasted or what became of her, but he appeared to be separated from her around the time of the murders. Some speculate that he may have been responsible for her death, but there is no solid evidence to support that hypothesis.

Francis Tumblety

Francis Tumblety is believed to have been born in Ireland in 1833 and immigrated to Rochester, New York, with his family at a young age. He was not well known as a Jack the Ripper suspect until a letter, which came to be known as 'The Littlechild Letter', was discovered among some correspondence of journalist George Sims which had been purchased by crime historian Stewart Evans in 1993.

The letter was written on September 23, 1913, by Chief Inspector Littlechild to George Sims in apparent reply to a letter he had received from him inquiring about a 'Dr. D.' who Sims may have believed had a connection to the Whitechapel murders. The following paragraph from that letter addresses his inquiry of 'Dr. D' and introduces Tumblety as a very likely suspect:

> I never heard of a Dr. D. in connection with the Whitechapel murders but amongst the suspects, and to my mind a very likely one, was a Dr. T. (which sounds much like D). He was an American quack named Tumblety and was at one time a frequent visitor to London and on these occasions constantly brought under the notice of police, there being a large dossier concerning him at Scotland Yard. Although a 'Sycopathia Sexualis' subject he was not known as a 'Sadist' (which the murderer unquestionably was) but his feelings toward women were remarkable and bitter in the extreme, a fact on record. Tumblety was arrested at the time of the murders in connection with unnatural offences and charged at Marlborough Street, remanded on bail, jumped his bail, and got away to Boulogne. He shortly left Boulogne and was never heard of afterwards. It was believed he committed suicide but certain it is that from this time the 'Ripper' murders came to an end.

The paragraph undoubtedly refers to Francis Tumblety, who was known as Dr. Tumblety, a doctor of herbal medicine although there is some question as to whether he ever had any formal training as a medical doctor. Chief Inspector Littlechild was correct that at the time of the murders Tumblety did jump bail for France, but rather than never being heard of afterwards, the police were in fact able to track him from France to the United States where he became well known as a suspect in the Whitechapel murders.

Prior to being in London around the time of the Whitechapel murders, Tumblety had a very colourful past, moving from various cities in the United States, Canada and the United Kingdom. He is believed to have begun his interest in medicine with the aid of a Dr. Lispenard, who was of somewhat questionable character himself. One newspaper reported that Lispenard had pleaded guilty to sending obscene material through the mail.

After having worked with an Indian herb doctor in Rochester, he opened his own practice. He turned up in Canada around 1857 operating as an herbalist in Toronto. He was arrested in Montreal on September 23, 1857, for attempting to induce a miscarriage. He was supposed to have sold some pills and a bottle of liquid to a young prostitute for that purpose. The charges were later dismissed. He moved back and forth between the United States and Canada between 1857 and 1860. In 1860, he was fined in Saint John, New Brunswick, for assuming the title of MD which was against the Medical Act. His conviction was overturned.

He was then charged for causing the death of a James Portmore, a patient of his who apparently died after taking medicine prescribed by him. He was subsequently convicted of manslaughter and quickly fled across the US border into the state of Maine. In 1861 he set up shop in New York and eventually moved to Washington, DC, where he became quite well known. He then moved to a number of other cities including St. Louis where he was arrested in 1865 for wearing military clothing that he was not qualified to wear.

Tumblety was again arrested in St. Louis because he had apparently used an alias of J. H. Blackburn which caused authorities to confuse him with L. P. Blackburn who was believed to have plotted to import clothing infected with yellow fever into the Northern states during the Civil War. He was released from custody once the confusion was cleared up.

In 1873 Tumblety travelled to England where he met a young man in London who he hired as his secretary and convinced to move to Liverpool with him. The youth returned to London a short time later where he attempted to pawn a watch Tumblety had given him. He was arrested but charges were dismissed. The boy, however, told police a story which caused them to issue a warrant for Tumblety.

Tumblety set up shop in Liverpool as a 'Great American Doctor'. During his time there he got in trouble when Edward Hanratty died after taking medicines prescribed to him by Tumblety. At the inquest, his widow said 'the American Doctor' whose name she didn't know sold her husband a bottle of medicine, a box of pills and some herbs. He died a few hours after taking some of the medicine. The January 28, 1875, issue of the *Liverpool Mercury* reported that the inquest jury delivered a verdict to the following effect:

Death was the result of natural causes, but whether it was accelerated by unskilful treatment or not was left an open question. 'The jury strongly censured the conduct of Mr. Tumilty [sic] in administering medicine, he being in total ignorance of the condition of his patient'.

Tumblety returned once again to the United States where he unsuccessfully sued a number of individuals relating to financial matters. According to the April 4, 1881, edition of the *Rochester Daily Union and Advertiser*:

> He was arrested while 'practising his profession' in Toronto, Ont., for a serious offense which, however, was reduced to a common assault.

In 1881 in New Orleans, he was arrested and charged for pickpocketing but charges were later dismissed in court because they could not be substantiated.

Tumblety returned to England where he again ran afoul of the law which included being arrested in London in November 1888 for suspicion of the Whitechapel murders. Although no charges were laid against him in the Whitechapel murders, he was charged with eight counts of 'gross indecency, and indecent assault with force and arms' against four men which allegedly occurred between July 27 and November 2, 1888.

He was released on bail which he skipped out on by travelling to France and then the United States using the alias Frank Townsend. Police were quickly able to trace him to New York where he gained notoriety as being suspected of being Jack the Ripper. Police were unable to return him to London because, as Chief Inspector Byrnes of the New York Police Department said,

> There is no proof of his complicity in the Whitechapel Murders and the crime for which he was under bond in London is not extraditable.

Tumblety actually placed himself in Whitechapel during the crimes in an interview with a reporter for the *New York World* in January 1891. Explaining why he was arrested as a suspect, he was quoted in the article as saying:

> 'My arrest came about this way', said he. 'I had been going over to England for a long time-ever since 1869, indeed-and I used to go about the city a great deal until every part of it became familiar to me.
> I happened to be there when these Whitechapel murders attracted the attention of the whole world and, in the company with thousands of other people, I went down to the Whitechapel district. I was not dressed in a way to attract attention, I thought, though it afterwards turned out that I did. I was interested by the excitement and the crowds and the queer scenes and sights, and did not know that all the time I was being followed by English detectives'.

His stature as a suspect in the Whitechapel murders was enhanced by an article printed in the *Williamsport Sunday Grit* on December 9, 1888. The article portrayed him as a woman-hater who kept their internal organs in jars in his office. Much of the information in the article was sourced to Col. C. S. Dunham, who some believe was an alias of Sanford Conover who was reported to have significant issues of credibility himself. In the article Dunham speaks of a party hosted by Tumblety in Washington, DC, many years previous that Dunham and his lieutenant-colonel attended. According to Dunham when Tumblety was asked why he didn't invite women to the dinner, he responded in the following manner:

> His face instantly became as black as a thunder cloud. He had a pack of cards in his hands but he laid them down and said, almost savagely: 'No, Colonel, I don't know any such cattle, and if I did I would, as your friend, sooner give you a dose of quick poison then to take you into such danger'. He then broke into a homily on the sin and folly of dissipation, fiercely denounced all women and especially fallen women.

Dunham said he then invited them into a library where he showed them a piece of furniture containing tiers of shelves with many glass jars each containing an assortment of anatomical specimens. He said,

> The 'doctor' placed on a table a dozen or more jars containing, he said, the matrices[1] of every class of woman.

Dunham also claimed in the article that when Tumblety was asked why he hated women, he explained the following:

> He said that when quite a young man he fell desperately in love with a pretty girl, rather his senior, who promised to reciprocate his affection. After a brief courtship he married her. The honeymoon was not over when he noticed a disposition on the part of his wife to flirt with other men. He remonstrated, she kissed him, called him a dear, jealous fool—and he believed her. Happening to pass one day in a cab through the worst part of the town he saw his wife and a man enter a gloomy looking house. Then he learned that before her marriage his wife had been an inmate of that and many similar houses. Then he gave up on all womankind.

Tumblety moved around between different cities and had a few minor issues with the law after his return to the United States. He lived with his sister for a number of years in Rochester and eventually died in a hospital in St. Louis in 1903 under the assumed name of Dr. Townsend.

Endnote

1. Wombs.

Scoring the Jack the Ripper Suspects

13

Introduction

If you read the previous chapter, you likely have formed an opinion as to who you believe from the list of suspects presented there is the most likely to have been the real Jack the Ripper. Your opinion was probably impacted not only by the information provided to you but also by your own life experiences, perceptions, biases, prejudices and even intuition, all of which make your evaluation of the suspects highly subjective.

The Jack the Ripper POIPAT we created in a previous chapter was designed to significantly reduce the subjectivity from the evaluation process. Ideally, even when that POIPAT is utilized by different evaluators, they will score each suspect similarly. One issue that will have an impact on scoring each of the elements on the Jack the Ripper POIPAT is how the information on each suspect is presented.

Unfortunately, the suspect files in this case were lost, so much of the information gathered on these suspects came from secondary sources such as news articles, books, websites and movies. In many cases the evaluator may have to draw some inferences or make conclusions based on his or her interpretation of the information presented in order to address some of the elements on the POIPAT. This would not be so much of an issue in today's investigations as most of the suspect background information would come from law enforcement sources such as police reports, criminal records checks and other databases which tend to be much more black and white.

In order to get the most out of this chapter, it is recommended that you start by rank ordering the suspects strictly based on your own opinion as to who is most likely the killer. Then utilize the Jack the Ripper POIPAT available in Appendix E or on the companion CD in the Jack the Ripper sub-directory to score each of the suspects. You should take the time to review the Jack the Ripper POIPAT Instructional Guide which is available in Appendix F and on the companion CD in the Jack the Ripper sub-directory to ensure you understand how each element should be assessed as well as the rationale before you begin scoring the suspects. Once you are finished scoring each of the subjects, rank order them based on their POIPAT score. Then compare that list with the one you created based on your opinion.

Once you have completed those tasks, follow along in this chapter as we score the suspects together using the Jack the Ripper POIPAT. It will explain in detail the rationale for the scoring of each suspect. Then in the next chapter we will provide our list of rank-ordered suspects based on their POIPAT score as well as explain how to use the scores to create a priority range. The actual POIPAT for each suspect will be listed alphabetically in Appendix G.

Thomas Hayne Cutbush

Residence/Comfort Zone

No points were awarded to Cutbush in the Residence section for having lived in either London or Whitechapel. Nor was he given points in the Comfort Zone section for being connected to the Whitechapel area. According to the information provided, he lived with his mother and aunt in Kennington, England, and although there was no account of his whereabouts during the murders, he could not be linked to Whitechapel which was a substantial distance from his home.

		PP	Score
Residence (Aug. 31, 1888–Nov. 9, 1888)			
1	London (includes suburbs)	20	
2	Whitechapel (10 mile radius)	20	
Comfort Zone			
3	Resides in, works in or known to frequent Whitechapel or surrounding area (10 mile radius)	20	

Physical Description

He was awarded 50 points for being a male in the Physical Description section but no points for age or physical abnormality. He was 23 years old at the time of the murders which puts him outside the age parameters of between 25 and 45. Nor is there information about him suffering from any physical abnormality.

Physical Description			
4	Male	50	50
5	Age (25–45)	10	
6	Physical abnormality (i.e. speech impediment, scarred complexion, physical illness or injury)	5	

Lifestyle

He was not awarded any points in the Lifestyle section because there was no information that he used prostitutes or was nocturnal.

Lifestyle			
7	Uses prostitutes	30	
8	Nocturnal due to choice or circumstance (night person)	10	

Marital Status

He was not awarded points in the Marital Status section because his background information indicated that he was living with his mother and aunt at the time of the murders. It would have been possible for Cutbush to have been married and also living with his mother and aunt but there was no information to that effect.

It is also worth noting that this element is used to increase the score of someone who was not accountable to others and would therefore have more freedom to commit these murders. Given that Cutbush was living with his mother and aunt at the time, it is likely he would have been accountable to some degree to them.

Marital Status (Aug. 31, 1888–Nov. 9, 1888) (Select One Only)			
9	Unattached (i.e. single, divorced, separated)	5	
10	Unaccountable (i.e. married but wife is extremely passive)	5	

Employment Status

Cutbush was not assigned any points in the Employment Status section because the information suggests he was not employed *at the time of the offences*. Although it did indicate that at one time he worked as a clerk and traveller in the tea trade and canvassed for a Directory in the East End, he was believed to have contracted syphilis around 1888 which was followed by an idle and useless life.

Employment Status (Aug. 31, 1888–Nov. 9, 1888)			
11	Employed—at time of offences	10	
12	Engaged in an occupation, hobby or other activity where the use of a knife was common	20	

Criminal History

He was given 10 points in the 'history of property crimes, of assault causing bodily harm and of domestic violence' element of the Criminal History section because he stabbed a woman in the buttocks when he was at large from an infirmary in 1891. Other than the stabbing incident, there was no other information supporting a criminal history, sex related offences or throat slashing.

Criminal History (Charges and/or Conviction Not Necessary)			
13	History of property crimes, of assault causing bodily harm and of domestic violence	10	**10**
14	History of sex related offences	20	
15	History of throat slashing (includes attempts)	20	

Linked to Victim

There was no known connection between Cutbush and any of the victims so he received no points in the Linked to Victim section.

Linked to Victim			
16	Mary Ann Nichols	20	
	Annie Chapman	20	
	Elizabeth Stride	20	
	Catherine Eddowes	20	
	Mary Jane Kelly	20	

Availability

There is no information regarding Cutbush's whereabouts during the homicides. The Jack the Ripper POIPAT Instructional Guide says, 'If you do not have any information that clears the POI assume he or she was available and had the opportunity'; therefore he was scored 10 points for being available for each victim.

Availability (Subject Was Available [i.e. Not Incarcerated at the Time of the Offences])			
17	Mary Ann Nichols (Aug. 31, 1888)	10	**10**
	Annie Chapman (Sept. 8, 1888)	10	**10**
	Elizabeth Stride (Sept. 29–30, 1888)	10	**10**
	Catherine Eddowes (Sept. 30, 1888)	10	**10**
	Mary Jane Kelly (Nov. 9, 1888)	10	**10**

Weapon

Cutbush was assigned 20 points in the Weapon section for being known to carry a knife as a result of the incident when he stabbed a woman in the buttocks. Later investigation determined that the knife he used on that occasion was purchased a week before the incident. There was no information that he carried a knife around the time of the Ripper murders, but there are no time limitations on this element and the Jack the Ripper POIPAT Instructional Guide directs: 'If the POI is known to carry a knife no matter how often, score this element 20 points'.

Weapon			
18	Known to carry a knife (does not matter how often)	20	**20**

Other

There was no information that Cutbush had a history of setting fires or torturing small animals or had a history of or documented fantasy of evisceration or mutilation of sexual areas of the body, so he received no points in the Other section.

Other			
19	History of setting fires or torturing small animals	10	
20	History of or documented fantasy of evisceration or mutilation of sexual areas of the body	50	

Total Points

Thomas Cutbush's total POIPAT score was 130 points.

Montague John Druitt

Residence/Comfort Zone

Druitt was an assistant schoolmaster at a boarding school in Blackheath, London, England, where he resided in chambers during the Whitechapel murders. Blackheath is about 7.5 miles from Whitechapel so he received 20 points for living in London and another 20 points for living within 10 miles of Whitechapel between August 31 and November 9, 1888. He was also assigned 20 points in the Comfort Zone section for residing within 10 miles of Whitechapel.

		PP	Score
Residence (Aug. 31, 1888–Nov. 9, 1888)			
1	London (Includes suburbs)	20	20
2	Whitechapel (10 mile radius)	20	20
Comfort Zone			
3	Resides, works or known to frequent Whitechapel or surrounding area (10 mile radius)	20	20

Physical Description

Druitt was 31 years old during the Whitechapel murders so he was scored 50 points for being a male and 10 points for being between the age of 25 and 45. There was no information of him having a physical abnormality.

Physical Description			
4	Male	50	50
5	Age (25–45)	10	10
6	Physical abnormality (i.e. speech impediment, scarred complexion, physical illness or injury)	5	

Lifestyle

There was no information that Druitt used prostitutes or was a night person so he did not receive any points in the Lifestyle section.

Lifestyle			
7	Uses prostitutes	30	
8	Nocturnal due to choice or circumstance (night person)	10	

Marital Status

Although there was no specific information about Druitt's marital status, it is logical to conclude that he was not married during the homicides based on the fact that he lived alone at the boarding school during this time, and there was no mention of a wife in any of his background information. He was therefore scored five points for being single.

He may also have been unaccountable during this time but he was not assigned points for that because the Jack the Ripper POIPAT Instructional Guide directs: 'If you scored item 9, do *not* score this item'.

Marital Status (Aug. 31, 1888–Nov. 9, 1888) (Select One Only)			
9	Unattached (i.e. single, divorced, separated)	5	5
10	Unaccountable (i.e. married but wife is extremely passive)	5	

Employment Status

Druitt was employed at the boarding school during the date range of the murders so he was given 10 points for being employed at the time. He was not given any points for being engaged in an occupation, hobby or other activity where the use of a knife was common as there was no information to support that.

Employment Status (Aug. 31, 1888–Nov. 9, 1888)			
11	Employed—at time of offences	10	10
12	Engaged in an occupation, hobby or other activity where the use of a knife was common	20	

Criminal History

None of the information available indicated that he had any type of criminal history so he was not awarded points in the Criminal History section.

Criminal History (Charges and/or Conviction Not Necessary)			
13	History of property crimes, of assault causing bodily harm and of domestic violence	10	
14	History of sex related offences	20	
15	History of throat slashing (includes attempts)	50	

Linked to Victim

There was no information that linked Druitt to any of the victims so he received no points in this section.

Linked to Victim			
16	Mary Ann Nichols	20	
	Annie Chapman	20	
	Elizabeth Stride	20	
	Catherine Eddowes	20	
	Mary Jane Kelly	20	

Availability

There was no information that indicated Druitt had an alibi during the time of these offences, so in keeping with instructions he was assumed to be available and as such awarded 10 points for each victim. It would likely have been relatively easy for investigators at the time to rule Druitt out if it could have been confirmed by school records or witnesses that he was in Blackheath at the time of the homicides. However, the role of the POIPAT is to prioritize the POIs based on information that is available to the evaluator at the time of scoring, and then it is up to investigators to conduct follow-up to establish, confirm or refute the POI's alibi.

Availability (Subject Was Available [i.e. Not Incarcerated at the Time of the Offences])			
17	Mary Ann Nichols (Aug. 31, 1888)	10	10
	Annie Chapman (Sept. 8, 1888)	10	10
	Elizabeth Stride (Sept. 29–30, 1888)	10	10
	Catherine Eddowes (Sept. 30, 1888)	10	10
	Mary Jane Kelly (Nov. 9, 1888)	10	10

Weapon

There was no information that Druitt ever carried a knife so no points were assigned to him in this section.

Weapon			
18	Known to carry a knife (does not matter how often)	20	

Other

Druitt was not known to have a history of setting fires or torturing small animals or a history or fantasy of evisceration or mutilation of sexual areas of the body so he did not receive any points in this section.

Other			
19	History of setting fires or torturing small animals	10	
20	History of or documented fantasy of evisceration or mutilation of sexual areas of the body	50	

Total Points

Montague Druitt's total POIPAT score was 185 points.

Sir William Withey Gull

Residence/Comfort Zone

Sir William Gull lived in London, England during the Whitechapel murders, but there is no information that he lived in, worked in or ever visited the Whitechapel area. As such, he was only assigned 20 points for living in London at the time but no points for residing or having a connection to the Whitechapel area.

		PP	Score
Residence (Aug. 31, 1888–Nov. 9, 1888)			
1	London (includes suburbs)	20	**20**
2	Whitechapel (10 mile radius)	20	
Comfort Zone			
3	Resides in, works in or known to frequent Whitechapel or surrounding area (10 mile radius)	20	**20**

Physical Description

Gull was nearly 72 years old at the time of the Whitechapel murders so he did not receive points for being between 25 and 45. He did get 50 points for being male and 5 points for having a physical abnormality. He was slightly paralyzed on his right side at the time.

Physical Description			
4	Male	50	**50**
5	Age (25–45)	10	**0**
6	Physical abnormality (i.e. speech impediment, scarred complexion, physical illness or injury)	5	**5**

Lifestyle

He did not receive points in the Lifestyle section because there was no information linking him to prostitutes or indicating that he was a night person.

Lifestyle			
7	Uses prostitutes	30	
8	Nocturnal due to choice or circumstance (night person)	10	

Marital Status

There is information Gull was married in 1848 and none that he was divorced, separated or widowed at the time of the murders so he was not assigned any points for being unattached. There was no information to support that he was unaccountable or that his wife was passive so he was not awarded points for being unaccountable either.

Marital Status (Aug. 31, 1888–Nov. 9, 1888) (Select One Only)			
9	Unattached (i.e. single, divorced, separated)	5	
10	Unaccountable (i.e. married but wife is extremely passive)	5	

Employment Status

Gull had a long and distinguished career as a doctor of medicine and had obtained degrees with honours in surgery, physiology, medicine and comparative anatomy. Although he did suffer a stroke in 1887, there was no information that he retired from his profession or could no longer work at that time. Therefore in the absence of information to the contrary, it can be concluded he was still employed at the time of the murders. Additionally, given that he was a surgeon, it is likely he had unrestricted access to surgical tools which would have included a variety of surgical knives. In view of these details, he was awarded 10 points for being employed at the time and 20 points for being engaged in an occupation where the use of a knife was common.

Employment Status (Aug. 31, 1888–Nov. 9, 1888)			
11	Employed—at time of offences	10	**10**
12	Engaged in an occupation, hobby or other activity where the use of a knife was common	20	**20**

Criminal History

There was no information that Gull had a criminal history; therefore, he was not awarded any points in this section.

Criminal History (Charges and/or Conviction Not Necessary)			
13	History of property crimes, of assault causing bodily harm and of domestic violence	10	
14	History of sex related offences	20	
15	History of throat slashing (includes attempts)	50	

Linked to Victim

Although there has been a significant amount of speculation including the royal conspiracy plot that Gull was responsible for the homicides, there has been no credible independent evidence linking him to any of the victims. Therefore he was not assigned any points for being linked to any of the victims in this section.

Linked to Victim			
16	Mary Ann Nichols	20	
	Annie Chapman	20	
	Elizabeth Stride	20	
	Catherine Eddowes	20	
	Mary Jane Kelly	20	

Availability

It is not likely that a 71 year old man suffering from partial paralysis would be capable of committing these violent murders; however, this question deals with his availability and not his capacity. This is a reverse onus question wherein if there is no information available to provide an alibi for the POI, he is to be awarded points for being available. This is the case for Gull so he was given 10 points for each victim in this section.

Availability (Subject Was Available [i.e. Not Incarcerated at the Time of the Offences])			
17	Mary Ann Nichols (Aug. 31, 1888)	10	**10**
	Annie Chapman (Sept. 8, 1888)	10	**10**
	Elizabeth Stride (Sept. 29–30, 1888)	10	**10**
	Catherine Eddowes (Sept. 30, 1888)	10	**10**
	Mary Jane Kelly (Nov. 9, 1888)	10	**10**

Weapon

Even though Gull was a qualified surgeon and likely had access to surgical knives, there is no information that he carried them around with him. It may very well have been the practice for doctors to carry such instruments back in 1888, but there was no specific information that this was the case for Dr. Gull so he was not awarded points for being known to carry a knife.

Weapon		
18	Known to carry a knife (does not matter how often)	20	

Other

There was no information Gull had a history of setting fires or torturing animals or a history or fantasy of evisceration or mutilation of sexual areas of the body so he was not assigned any points in this section.

Other			
19	History of setting fires or torturing small animals	10	
20	History of or documented fantasy of evisceration or mutilation of sexual areas of the body	50	

Total Points

Sir William Gull's total POIPAT score was 155 points.

Severin Antoinovich Klosowski, aka George Chapman

Residence/Comfort Zone

Klosowski is believed to have lived at 126 Cable Street, St. George's-in-the-East, which was situated next to Whitechapel during the time of the murders, so he was assigned 20 points for residing in London and 20 points for living within 10 miles of Whitechapel. He was also assigned 20 points in the Comfort Zone section for living near Whitechapel.

		PP	Score
Residence (Aug. 31, 1888–Nov. 9, 1888)			
1	London (includes suburbs)	20	20
2	Whitechapel (10 mile radius)	20	20
Comfort Zone			
3	Resides, works or known to frequent Whitechapel or surrounding area (10 mile radius)	20	20

Physical Description

Klosowski was assigned 50 points for being male in this section, but he was born December 14, 1865, which would have made him 22 at the time of the homicides so he was not awarded any points for being between 25 and 45 years old. There was no information that he suffered from any type of physical abnormality so he was not awarded any points for that element either.

Physical Description			
4	Male	50	50
5	Age (25–45) *22 age time of offences*	10	
6	Physical abnormality (i.e. speech impediment, scarred complexion, physical illness or injury)	5	

Lifestyle

There was no information indicating that Klosowski used prostitutes or was a night person so he was not given any points in the Lifestyle section.

Lifestyle			
7	Uses prostitutes	30	
8	Nocturnal due to choice or circumstance (night person)	10	

Marital Status

There is information that Klosowski was married when he moved to London sometime between 1887 and 1888, but he left his wife behind in Poland. There is also information that he married Lucy Baderski in 1889 even though he was still married to his Polish wife. This would have meant that he was legally married but separated from his wife at the time of the murders. Given that he was still legally married, this separation was a physical separation but not a legal separation.

This may seem to complicate the scoring of the 'unattached' element; however, the Jack the Ripper POIPAT Instructional Guide explains that the rationale for this element is to identify situations where the POI 'does not have to account for his whereabouts for extended periods of time particularly during the late night or early morning hours'. As such, this is not a legal issue so in Klosowski's case he was awarded five points for the 'unattached' element for being separated from his wife because she was living in another country at the time.

Marital Status (Aug. 31, 1888–Nov. 9, 1888) (Select One Only)			
9	Unattached (i.e. single, divorced, separated)	5	5
10	Unaccountable (i.e. married but wife is extremely passive)	5	

Employment Status

Klosowski is believed to have been running his own barber shop near Whitechapel at the time of the murders; so he was assigned five points for being employed. However, deciding if working in a barber shop qualified him to receive points for the next element of 'engaged in an occupation, hobby or other activity where the use of a knife was common' was more difficult.

On one hand most barber shops, particular in the 1800s, would have been equipped with shaving razors and sharpening straps. As an experienced barber Klosowski would have been quite comfortable using one. Additionally, most of these razors folded in two and would have been easy to carry around discreetly in a pocket without anyone taking notice.

On the other hand, the rationale for this element comes from SSA John Douglas' profile report which says the following about the offender:

> He would seek a position where he could work alone and vicariously experience his destructive fantasies. Such employment would include work as a butcher, mortician's helper, medical examiner's assistant, or hospital attendant.

These are all occupations where the employee would have an opportunity to have some interaction with the anatomies of either human beings or animals. He was likely not thinking of a barber when he wrote that.

However, when there are situations like this where there are conflicting feelings on whether or not points should be scored for any given element, one should err on the side of caution and award the points. The worst that can happen in that situation is that the POI's priority level will increase, and there is no significant harm if that occurs. That is why Klosowski was awarded the 20 points for this element.

Employment Status (Aug. 31, 1888–Nov. 9, 1888)			
11	Employed—at time of offences	10	5
12	Engaged in an occupation, hobby or other activity where the use of a knife was common.	20	20

Criminal History

There is ample information regarding a history of domestic violence by Klosowski. He is known to have physically and mentally abused his wives and eventually was convicted of slowly poisoning three of them to death. This justified assigning him 10 points for the 'history of property crimes, of assault causing bodily harm and of domestic violence' element.

He did not have a history of sex crimes so he was not awarded points for that. Although there was one incident in his past in America where if he had not been interrupted by a customer coming into his barber shop he may have killed his wife with a knife he had tucked under a pillow, there is no known history of him slashing or attempting to slash anyone's throat.

Criminal History (Charges and/or Conviction Not Necessary)			
13	History of property crimes, of assault causing bodily harm and of domestic violence	10	10
14	History of sex related offences	20	
15	History of throat slashing (includes attempts)	50	

Linked to Victim

In a strange coincidence Klosowski met a lady named Annie Chapman in 1893 when he went to work at a barber shop in South Tottenham. They lived together for about a year. This obviously was not the same Annie Chapman who had been murdered by Jack the Ripper five years previous. There was no known connection between Klosowski and any of the victims so he did not receive any points in this section.

Linked to Victim			
16	Mary Ann Nichols	20	
	Annie Chapman	20	
	Elizabeth Stride	20	
	Catherine Eddowes	20	
	Mary Jane Kelly	20	

Availability

There is no information that would indicate that Klosowski was not available during the crucial times of these homicides so he was assigned 10 points for being available for each victim.

Availability (Subject Was Available [i.e. Not Incarcerated at the Time of the Offences])			
17	Mary Ann Nichols (Aug. 31, 1888)	10	**10**
	Annie Chapman (Sept. 8, 1888)	10	**10**
	Elizabeth Stride (Sept. 29–30, 1888)	10	**10**
	Catherine Eddowes (Sept. 30, 1888)	10	**10**
	Mary Jane Kelly (Nov. 9, 1888)	10	**10**

Weapon

Klosowski was a barber, so as indicated previously he would have had access to a barber's shaving razor which could be considered a knife but there is no information that he carried one around. There was information, however, as mentioned previously about an incident where if Klosowski had not been interrupted by a customer coming into the barber shop, he may have killed his wife with a knife he had hidden under his pillow. She discovered the knife and hid it while he was tending to the customer. Klosowski later admitted to her that he had planned on killing her and even showed her where he planned on burying her body.

Some may view this incident as not actually carrying a knife because it was discovered by his wife under their pillow. Whereas this may be technically true, the idea of this question is to identify and elevate those subjects who have been known to carry a knife as a weapon. Although his wife did not see him put the knife under the pillow, it was obvious from his actions and admitted intentions that it was he who placed the knife there to use as a weapon against his wife. Therefore he was assigned 20 points for being known to carry a knife.

Weapon			
18	Known to carry a knife (does not matter how often)	20	**20**

Other

There was no information that Klosowski had a history of setting fires or torturing small animals. Nor did he have a history of or a documented fantasy of evisceration or mutilation of sexual areas of the body so he was not awarded points in this section.

Other			
19	History of setting fires or torturing small animals	10	
20	History of or documented fantasy of evisceration or mutilation of sexual areas of the body	50	

Total Points

Severn Klosowski's total POIPAT score was 220 points.

Aaron Kosminski

Residences/Comfort Zone

Kosminski is believed to have moved from Poland to Whitechapel with his sisters and their husbands in 1880 or 1881. There is no information that he resided anywhere other than Whitechapel after this until 1890 when he began his residency in a number of asylums until his death in 1919. Therefore he was award 20 points in all three elements associated with the Residence and Comfort Zone sections.

		PP	Score
Residence (Aug. 31, 1888–Nov. 9, 1888)			
1	London (includes suburbs)	20	20
2	Whitechapel (10 mile radius)	20	20
Comfort Zone			
3	Resides in, works in or known to frequent Whitechapel or surrounding area (10 mile radius)	20	20

Physical Description

Kosminski was assigned 50 points for being male but received no points for being between 25 and 45 or having a physical abnormality. He was not noted to have any outstanding physical issues, and actually turned 23 years of age on September 11, 1888, which was between the first murder which occurred on August 31, 1888, and the second on September 8, 1888.

Physical Description			
4	Male	50	50
5	Age (25–45)	10	0
6	Physical abnormality (i.e. speech impediment, scarred complexion, physical illness or injury)	5	0

Lifestyle

There was no information that Kosminski regularly used prostitutes. However, it is believed that he was identified by a witness as having been with one of the victims just prior to her murder. This information came from handwritten notes of the lead investigator on the case so it was assumed to be true. That being the case, Kosminski was assigned 30 points for the 'uses prostitutes' element.

Some might argue that being seen with a prostitute doesn't necessarily mean you use them. In theory that may be true; however, anyone talking to a prostitute late at night or in the early morning hours in the dark, isolated back alleys of Whitechapel where they plied their trade could quite appropriately be assumed to be a consumer of their services. This is analogous in today's world to someone pulling over his vehicle late at night to speak to a prostitute in an area known for prostitution. It may be possible that he is not discussing a sex deal, but you can be assured that person would end up on the police 'john' list if the encounter were observed by police.

Considering that all of the victims were murdered either very late at night or early in the morning and that Kosminski was seen with one of them just prior to her murder, it can also be assumed that he was nocturnal. Therefore he was assigned 10 points for the 'nocturnal' element in this section.

Lifestyle			
7	Uses prostitutes	30	30
8	Nocturnal due to choice or circumstance (night person)	10	10

Marital Status

There was no information that Kosminski was ever married so he was assigned five points for being unattached in this section.

Marital Status (Aug. 31, 1888–Nov. 9, 1888) (Select One Only)			
9	Unattached (i.e. single, divorced, separated)	5	5
10	Unaccountable (i.e. married but wife is extremely passive)	5	

Employment Status

There is no indication that Kosminski ever worked after moving to England from Poland so he was not assigned any points in this section.

Employment Status (Aug. 31, 1888–Nov. 9, 1888)			
11	Employed—at time of offences	10	
12	Engaged in an occupation, hobby or other activity where the use of a knife was common	20	

Criminal History

There is no record of Kosminski having any type of criminal history. There was a mention in his asylum records of an incident where he took up a chair and attempted to strike an attendant with it. There was also some mention of an incident from a second-hand source in his admissions record that he took up a knife and threatened his sister's life with it. However, there is no information that he ever actually physically harmed anyone. Therefore he was not awarded points in any of the elements in this section.

Criminal History (Charges and/or Conviction Not Necessary)			
13	History of property crimes, of assault causing bodily harm and of domestic violence	10	
14	History of sex related offences	20	
15	History of throat slashing (includes attempts)	50	

Linked to Victim

As indicated earlier Kosminski was identified by a witness as having been with one of the victims just prior to her murder. It is not certain who the witness was or which victim he or she was speaking about. However, it is believed the witness referred to was either Israel Schwartz, who saw a male with Elizabeth Stride 15 minutes before her murder, or Joseph Lawende, who saw a male with Catherine Eddowes about 10 minutes before her murder.

For the purposes of the POIPAT, it does not really matter which victim he is linked to so long as his POIPAT score reflects that he was linked to one of the victims. Therefore he was awarded 20 points for being linked to Elizabeth Stride.

Linked to Victim			
16	Mary Ann Nichols	20	
	Annie Chapman	20	
	Elizabeth Stride	20	20
	Catherine Eddowes	20	
	Mary Jane Kelly	20	

Availability

There is no information that Kosminski was unavailable or had a solid alibi during the murders so he was assigned 10 points for being linked to each victim.

	Availability (Subject Was Available [i.e. Not Incarcerated at the Time of the Offences])		
17	Mary Ann Nichols (Aug. 31, 1888)	10	**10**
	Annie Chapman (Sept. 8, 1888)	10	**10**
	Elizabeth Stride (Sept. 29–30, 1888)	10	**10**
	Catherine Eddowes (Sept. 30, 1888)	10	**10**
	Mary Jane Kelly (Nov. 9, 1888)	10	**10**

Weapon

There was no information that Kosminski carried a knife except for the incident previously mentioned on his intake record where he was reported by a second-hand source to have threatened his sister with a knife. This may have been an insignificant one-time incident; however, the instructions require that points be awarded no matter how often the POI carried a knife. Therefore to err on the side of caution we award 20 points in this 'known to carry a knife' element.

	Weapon		
18	Known to carry a knife (does not matter how often)	20	**20**

Other

There was no information that Kosminski had a history of any of the elements listed in this section so he was not assigned any points here.

	Other		
19	History of setting fires or torturing small animals	10	
20	History of or documented fantasy of evisceration or mutilation of sexual areas of the body	50	

Total Points

Aaron Kosminski's total POIPAT score was 245 points.

Michael Ostrog

Residence/Comfort Zone

There was no information that Ostrog was a resident of London or Whitechapel during these offences. There was also no information that indicates he ever had any connection to Whitechapel or the surrounding area so he was not assigned any points in these sections.

		PP	Score
Residence (Aug. 31, 1888–Nov. 9, 1888)			
1	London (includes suburbs)	20	
2	Whitechapel (10 mile radius)	20	
Comfort Zone			
3	Resides, works or known to frequent Whitechapel or surrounding area (10 mile radius)	20	

Physical Description

Ostrog was assigned 50 points for being male, but he was in his late 50s at the time of the murders so he was not awarded points for being between 25 and 45 years old. There also no evidence that he had any physical abnormalities so he received no points there either.

	Physical Description		
4	Male	50	**50**
5	Age (25–45)	10	**10**
6	Physical abnormality (i.e. speech impediment, scarred complexion, physical illness or injury)	5	

Lifestyle

He was not assigned any points in this section because there was no information that he used prostitutes or was nocturnal.

	Lifestyle		
7	Uses prostitutes	30	
8	Nocturnal due to choice or circumstance (night person)	10	

Marital Status

There was not a great deal of information available about Ostrog's marital status. On September 30, 1887, he was registered as a 50 year old, married Jewish surgeon suffering mania at the Surrey Pauper Lunatic Asylum in Tooting. Other than that reference, there is no information to indicate if at the time of the homicides he was still married, separated or divorced; therefore, he was not assigned any points for being unattached or unaccountable.

	Marital Status (Aug. 31, 1888–Nov. 9, 1888) (Select One Only)		
9	Unattached (i.e. single, divorced, separated)	5	
10	Unaccountable (i.e. married but wife is extremely passive)	5	

Employment Status

Although there were a number of documents that described him as a surgeon, there is no evidence that he was actually a doctor or had any medical training. If in fact he did have medical training, there was no information that he had a medical practice or was a practising surgeon in England or France. Additionally, there is information that he was in prison in France during the time period of Whitechapel murders so it would not have been possible for him to be employed during that time. Therefore he was not awarded any points in this section.

Employment Status (Aug. 31, 1888–Nov. 9, 1888)			
11	Employed—at time of offences	10	
12	Engaged in an occupation, hobby or other activity where the use of a knife was common	20	

Criminal History

Ostrog had an extensive criminal history of petty theft so he was assigned 10 points in the 'history of property crimes, of assault causing bodily harm and of domestic violence' element. However, there was no information that he had a history of sex related offences or throat slashing so he received no points for those elements.

Criminal History (Charges and/or Conviction Not Necessary)			
13	History of property crimes, of assault causing bodily harm and of domestic violence	10	**10**
14	History of sex related offences	20	
15	History of throat slashing (includes attempts)	50	

Linked to Victim

There is no information that links Ostrog to any of the victims so he was not awarded any points in this section.

Linked to Victim			
16	Mary Ann Nichols	20	
	Annie Chapman	20	
	Elizabeth Stride	20	
	Catherine Eddowes	20	
	Mary Jane Kelly	20	

Availability

There was information Ostrog was in custody in France during the Whitechapel murders so he was not assigned any points for being available.

Availability (Subject Was Available [i.e. Not Incarcerated at the Time of the Offences])			
17	Mary Ann Nichols (Aug. 31, 1888)	10	
	Annie Chapman (Sept. 8, 1888)	10	
	Elizabeth Stride (Sept. 29–30, 1888)	10	
	Catherine Eddowes (Sept. 30, 1888)	10	
	Mary Jane Kelly (Nov. 9, 1888)	10	

Weapon

Although there was one incident where he was found in possession of a gun, there was no evidence to support that Ostrog carried a knife. Therefore he was not assigned any points for this element.

Weapon			
18	Known to carry a knife (does not matter how often)	20	

Other

Ostrog did not have a history of setting fires or torturing small animals. He also did not have a history or documented fantasy of evisceration or mutilation of sexual areas of the body. As such, he was not assigned any points in this section.

Other			
19	History of setting fires or torturing small animals	10	
20	History of or documented fantasy of evisceration or mutilation of sexual areas of the body	50	

Total Points

Michael Ostrog's total POIPAT score was 60 points.

John Pizer, aka Leather Apron

Residence/Comfort Zone

According to an alibi witness, Pizer was staying at a common lodging house on Holloway Road on the night of the Nichols murder. Holloway Road is about five miles from Whitechapel. He was staying with relatives at 22 Mulberry Street in Whitechapel on the night of Annie Chapman's homicide which had been his home for a number of years. Based on this information he was assigned 20 points in all of the elements in both the Residence and Comfort Zone sections.

		PP	Score
Residence (Aug. 31, 1888–Nov. 9, 1888)			
1	London (includes suburbs)	20	**20**
2	Whitechapel (10 mile radius)	20	**20**
Comfort Zone			
3	Resides in, works in or known to frequent Whitechapel or surrounding area (10 mile radius)	20	**20**

Physical Description

Pizer was believed to have been born in 1850 which would have made him 38 at the time of the homicides. As a result, he was assigned 10 points for being between 25 and 45 and 50 points for being male. There is no information that he suffered from any physical abnormalities; so he was not assigned points for that element.

Physical Description			
4	Male	50	**50**
5	Age (25–45)	10	**10**
6	Physical abnormality (i.e. speech impediment, scarred complexion, physical illness or injury)	5	

Lifestyle

Pizer came to the attention of the police from a number of prostitutes who accused him of violence and blackmail against them. Although there is no information that he actually had sex with them, the Jack the Ripper POIPAT Instructional Guide specifically says,

> 'Uses' does not necessarily mean having sex with them. It could also mean he interacts with them in other ways such as buying drugs from or for them, living off them or drinking with them.

As such, he was assigned 30 points for the 'uses prostitutes' element.

If he was interacting with prostitutes, it is likely he was also nocturnal. However, there was no specific information to that effect, and given that prostitution is not restricted to night hours, he was not assigned points for the 'nocturnal' element.

Lifestyle			
7	Uses prostitutes	30	**30**
8	Nocturnal due to choice or circumstance (night person)	10	

Marital Status

Pizer was not married at the time of the homicides so he was assigned five points for being unattached.

Marital Status (Aug. 31, 1888–Nov. 9, 1888) (Select One Only)			
9	Unattached (i.e. single, divorced, separated)	5	5
10	Unaccountable (i.e. married but wife is extremely passive)	5	

Employment Status

Although there was information that Pizer was a boot finisher by trade, there was no information that he actually had full-time employment at the time of the homicides. Boot finishing was a profession where the use of knifes was common, and it was reported in one of the local papers that Detective-Sergeant Thicke seized five long-bladed knifes when he apprehended Pizer. As a result he was not assigned any points for being employed at the time of the offences but was assigned 20 points for being engaged in an occupation where the use of a knife was common.

Employment Status (Aug. 31, 1888–Nov. 9, 1888)			
11	Employed—at time of offences	10	
12	Engaged in an occupation, hobby or other activity where the use of a knife was common.	20	20

Criminal History

There was no information that Pizer had a criminal history; consequently, he was not assigned any points in this section.

Criminal History (Charges and/or Conviction Not Necessary)			
13	History of property crimes, of assault causing bodily harm and of domestic violence	10	
14	History of sex related offences	20	
15	History of throat slashing (includes attempts)	50	

Linked to Victim

There was no information that Pizer had a connection to any of the victims; therefore, he was not assigned any points in this section.

Linked to Victim			
16	Mary Ann Nichols	20	
	Annie Chapman	20	
	Elizabeth Stride	20	
	Catherine Eddowes	20	
	Mary Jane Kelly	20	

Availability

Police investigation was able to confirm alibis for Pizer for both the Nichols and Chapman homicides, thus he was not assigned points for those. There is no information that precludes him from having been available for the subsequent homicides; so he was awarded points for being available for the Stride, Eddowes and Kelly homicides.

Availability (Subject Was Available [i.e. Not Incarcerated at the Time of the Offences])		
17	Mary Ann Nichols (Aug. 31, 1888)	10	0
	Annie Chapman (Sept. 8, 1888)	10	0
	Elizabeth Stride (Sept. 29–30, 1888)	10	10
	Catherine Eddowes (Sept. 30, 1888)	10	10
	Mary Jane Kelly (Nov. 9, 1888)	10	10

Some might argue that if these cases were believed to have been committed by the same offender, then if he had an alibi for one, he had an alibi for them all and therefore there is no point in doing a POIPAT. There may be some merit in that view; however, there are two important points to consider. Firstly, even though there is good reason to believe that all these offences were committed by the same offender, that conclusion is based on professional opinion but not proven fact supported by scientific forensic evidence. Secondly, the alibis were based on the word of witnesses. It has been well established that alibi witnesses can and often do change their stories after the fact. In this case, Pizer's alibi for the Chapman homicide came from family members, who may not have been the most unbiased witnesses.

Weapon

The *Star* newspaper made a couple of references to a knife in a story they had written about 'Leather Apron' prior to his identity being established as follows:

> He carries a razor-like knife, and two weeks ago drew it on a woman called 'Widow Annie' as she was crossing near London Hospital, threatening at the same time, with his ugly grin and his malignant eyes, to 'rip her up'.

and

> He has never cut anybody so far as known, but always carries a leather knife, presumably as sharp as leather knives are wont to be.

Except for that article there was no other information that Pizer carried a knife.

Even though there was this newspaper story that claimed that 'Leather Apron', who was later confirmed to be Pizer, carried a knife, we did not assign points for being 'known to carry a knife'. The reason for this comes from the Jack the Ripper POIPAT Instructional Guide which says:

> The source of the information to support a true or false response does not have to be an official document such as a criminal record but *it must be believed to be accurate, credible and reliable*. This could include but would not be restricted to police reports, records management systems, intelligence reports, court records, municipal records, government databases and medical records.

Although the story may have been true, newspapers have been known to be wrong. In this case, the source(s) for their description of 'Leather Apron' reportedly came from '50 of the unfortunates'. It is not possible to determine the accuracy of these sources. What we do not know is whether all 50 claimed he carried a knife, just a few or only 1. We also do not know the credibility or reliability of these source(s). Were they always truthful, deceptive or prone to exaggeration? Additionally, although it is not quite clear why, Pizer is believed to have received compensation from the media for their portrayal of him.

Weapon			
18	Known to carry a knife (does not matter how often)	20	

Other

Pizer was not known to set fires or torture small animals. Nor did he have a history of or documented fantasy of evisceration or mutilation of sexual areas of the body. Therefore he was not assigned any points in this section.

Other			
19	History of setting fires or torturing small animals	10	
20	History of or documented fantasy of evisceration or mutilation of sexual areas of the body	50	

Although there were no points assigned to him for this element, there was a note made in the Comments section at the end of the POIPAT to make investigators aware of the newspaper report.

Comments
According to a newspaper article, he was known to carry a razor-like knife. No points were awarded for 'known to carry a knife' because it was not possible to conclude that the source was accurate, credible or reliable.

Total Points

John Pizer's total POIPAT score was 205 points.

Walter Richard Sickert

Residence/Comfort Zone

Walter Sickert was married to Ellen Cobden 1885 and lived at 54 Broadhurst Gardens, South Hampstead, London, until their divorce in 1899. South Hampstead is about nine miles from Whitechapel, so Sickert was assigned 20 points each for living in London and within 10 miles of Whitechapel respectively. This would have also qualified him to receive 20 points in the Comfort Zone section for having a connection to an area within 10 miles of Whitechapel.

		PP	Score
Residence (Aug. 31, 1888–Nov. 9, 1888)			
1	London (includes suburbs)	20	20
2	Whitechapel (10 mile radius)	20	20
Comfort Zone			
3	Resides in, works in or known to frequent Whitechapel or surrounding area (10 mile radius)	20	20

Physical Description

Sickert was a 28 year old male at the time of the murders, but there was no information that he suffered from any physical abnormalities. Therefore he was assigned 50 points for being male and 10 points for being between 25 and 45.

Physical Description			
4	Male	50	50
5	Age (25–45)	10	10
6	Physical abnormality (i.e. speech impediment, scarred complexion, physical illness or injury)	5	

Lifestyle

Although there is no information that Sickert used the sexual services of prostitutes, there is information he used them as models in many of his paintings. According to the Jack the Ripper POIPAT Instructional Guide, it is not necessary for the POI to have had sex with prostitutes in order to receive points here. The important issue is that he felt comfortable around them and they likely felt comfortable and perhaps safe around him. As a result he was awarded 30 points for the 'uses prostitutes' element.

There was no information that he was nocturnal; so he was not awarded points for that element.

Lifestyle			
7	Uses prostitutes	30	30
8	Nocturnal due to choice or circumstance (night person)	10	

Marital Status

Sickert was married to Ellen Cobden from 1885 to 1899 which would have been during the crucial time period. Additionally, although there was speculation that he may have had a number of romantic affairs, there was no specific information that he was not accountable to his wife during this time. Therefore he received no points in this section.

Marital Status (Aug. 31, 1888–Nov. 9, 1888) (Select One Only)			
9	Unattached (i.e. single, divorced, separated)	5	
10	Unaccountable (i.e. married but wife is extremely passive)	5	

Employment Status

Sickert was a self-employed painter at the time of the murders so he was assigned 10 points for being employed at the time of the offences. He was not assigned points for being engaged in an occupation, hobby or other activity where the use of a knife was common as there was no information to support it.

Employment Status (Aug. 31, 1888–Nov. 9, 1888)			
11	Employed—at time of offences	10	**10**
12	Engaged in an occupation, hobby or other activity where the use of a knife was common	20	

Criminal History

There was no information that Sickert had a criminal history of any type so he was not awarded points in any of the elements in this section.

Criminal History (Charges and/or Conviction Not Necessary)			
13	History of property crimes, of assault causing bodily harm and of domestic violence	10	
14	History of sex related offences	20	
15	History of throat slashing (includes attempts)	50	

Linked to Victim

There was no information that Sickert had a connection to any of the victims with the exception of Mary Jane Kelly. According to the royal conspiracy theory (see Sir William Gull above), Sickert raised a child who was at the center of the theory with the help of Mary Jane Kelly, who was purportedly one of his models. This link to Mary Kelly was also alluded to in Jean Fuller's book which suggested that Mary Kelly was employed by Sickert as a nanny who left him and later began to blackmail him.

There are a number of problems with relying on this information. Firstly, much of the information in Ms. Fuller's book comes to her third-hand from a person who originally provided the information to her mother. Secondly, Joseph Sickert, who claimed to be Walter Sickert's illegitimate son, suggested the royal conspiracy theory for a 1973 docudrama titled 'Jack the Ripper'. However, several years later he admitted that it was a hoax he had made up.

Therefore no points were assigned in this section for having links to any of the victims.

Linked to Victim		
16	Mary Ann Nichols	20
	Annie Chapman	20
	Elizabeth Stride	20
	Catherine Eddowes	20
	Mary Jane Kelly	20

Availability

There was no information that provided Sickert with a solid alibi during any of the homicides so he was assumed available for them all and awarded 10 points for each victim.

Availability (Subject Was Available [i.e. Not Incarcerated at the Time of the Offences])			
17	Mary Ann Nichols (Aug. 31, 1888)	10	**10**
	Annie Chapman (Sept. 8, 1888)	10	**10**
	Elizabeth Stride (Sept. 29–30, 1888)	10	**10**
	Catherine Eddowes (Sept. 30, 1888)	10	**10**
	Mary Jane Kelly (Nov. 9, 1888)	10	**10**

Weapon

Sickert was not assigned any points for this element as there was no information that he was known to carry a knife.

Weapon		
18	Known to carry a knife (does not matter how often)	20

Other

There was no information that Sickert had a history of setting fires or torturing small animals so he was not assigned points for that element. However, the next element in this section, 'History of or documented fantasy of evisceration or mutilation of sexual areas of the body' is a bit more complex.

There was no information that he had a history of evisceration or mutilation of sexual areas of the body, but part of the element allows for a 'documented fantasy' of those interests. Determining if Sickert had such morbid fantasies may seem impossible because people don't often share these types of thoughts with others. However, Sickert was an artist and if he had those specific interests, it is likely that his fantasies were manifested through his artwork (see Chapter 2 for more information on fantasy driven behaviour and collateral material).

It would be quite an onerous task and not very practical to collect and review all of Sickert's many works of art for this purpose. However, there is information from other sources which may provide some insight. Both Jean Overton Fuller and Patricia Cornwell commented in their respective books about the violent and graphic nature of many of his paintings. They both mentioned the 'Camden Town Murder' series which were apparently inspired by the brutal death of a prostitute in 1907 who had her throat cut. Patricia Cornwell goes further and points out some similarities between some of his other paintings and some of the Whitechapel victims.

Ms. Fuller says in her book that artist Florence Pash suggested that Sickert painted a series of paintings that could never be exhibited because they were too horrible. They were apparently paintings of bleeding and mutilated corpses which he could have painted only from memory. These paintings have never surfaced.

Regardless of the existence of the paintings that were too horrible to exhibit, many of his works that have surfaced and survived may reflect a fascination with prostitutes and violence against women. However, there is no indication that they specifically depicted 'evisceration or mutilation of sexual areas of the body' which was clearly Jack the Ripper's focus. Therefore he was not assigned points for that element.

Other			
19	History of setting fires or torturing small animals	10	
20	History of or documented fantasy of evisceration or mutilation of sexual areas of the body	50	

Comments

Although there were no points assigned, it was worth noting in this section that there is some forensic evidence that suggests Sickert may be linked to some of the letters written claiming to be Jack the Ripper. It is likely that this piece of information would be significant enough to investigators that Sickert would have been identified as a high investigative priority regardless of his total POIPAT score.

Comments
There is some forensic evidence that suggests he may be linked to some of the letters written claiming to be Jack the Ripper.

Total Points

Walter Sickert's total POIPAT score was 210 points.

Dr. Roslyn D'Onston Stephenson (Dr. Robert Donston Stephenson)

Residence/Comfort Zone

Dr. Stephenson was reported to have checked himself into the London Hospital in Whitechapel on July 26, 1888, and left on December 7, 1888. This would have made him a resident of Whitechapel during the murders so he was assigned full points for all of the elements of the Residence and Comfort Zone sections.

		PP	Score
Residence (Aug. 31, 1888–Nov. 9, 1888)			
1	London (includes suburbs)	20	20
2	Whitechapel (10 mile radius)	20	20
Comfort Zone			
3	Resides in, works in or known to frequent Whitechapel or surrounding area (10 mile radius)	20	20

Physical Description

Stephenson was 47 years old at the time of the homicides so he was outside the 25 to 45 age range, and he was not known to suffer from any physical abnormalities. Therefore he was not assigned any points for either of those elements but did receive 50 points for being male.

Physical Description			
4	Male	50	50
5	Age (25–45) *47 at time of offences*	10	
6	Physical abnormality (i.e. speech impediment, scarred complexion, physical illness or injury)	5	

Lifestyle

There was information that in his younger days Stephenson did have regular contact with a prostitute. He was awarded 30 points for that element, but there was no information he was nocturnal so he was not assigned points for that.

Lifestyle			
7	Uses prostitutes	30	30
8	Nocturnal due to choice or circumstance (night person)	10	

Marital Status

Stephenson married in 1876 but was believed to have been separated from her around the time of the murders. It was speculated that he may have murdered her, but there is no substantial evidence to support that. Therefore he was assigned five points in this section for being separated.

Marital Status (Aug. 31st, 1888 - Nov. 9th, 1888) (Select One Only)			
9	Unattached (i.e. single, divorced, separated)	5	5
10	Unaccountable (i.e. married but wife is extremely passive)	5	

Employment Status

Stephenson was a full-time patient at the London Hospital during the murders so he was not assigned any points in this section which addresses his employment only during this crucial time.

Employment Status (Aug. 31, 1888–Nov. 9, 1888)			
11	Employed—at time of offences	10	
12	Engaged in an occupation, hobby or other activity where the use of a knife was common	20	

Criminal History

Although there was unsupported speculation that he may have been involved in his wife's apparent disappearance, there is no evidence that he had any form of criminal history. As such, he was not assigned any points in this section.

Criminal History (Charges and/or Conviction Not Necessary)			
13	History of property crimes, of assault causing bodily harm and of domestic violence	10	
14	History of sex related offences	20	
15	History of throat slashing (includes attempts)	50	

Linked to Victim

There was no information that Stephenson was linked to any of the victims; so he was not assigned any points in this section.

Linked to Victim			
16	Mary Ann Nichols	20	
	Annie Chapman	20	
	Elizabeth Stride	20	
	Catherine Eddowes	20	
	Mary Jane Kelly	20	

Availability

There is information that Stephenson was staying in the Currie Ward of the London Hospital until at least October 16, 1888, and that residents were prevented from leaving that wing of the hospital at night. However, we do not know how patients were 'prevented' from leaving. It could have ranged from verbal direction not to leave to being locked up during that time. Given that there is no information on the type of controls, if any, that prevented patients from leaving the hospital at night, we erred on the side of caution and assigned 10 points for being available for each of the victims.

Availability (Subject Was Available [i.e. Not Incarcerated at the Time of the Offences])			
17	Mary Ann Nichols (Aug. 31, 1888)	10	10
	Annie Chapman (Sept. 8, 1888)	10	10
	Elizabeth Stride (Sept. 29–30, 1888)	10	10
	Catherine Eddowes (Sept. 30, 1888)	10	10
	Mary Jane Kelly (Nov. 9, 1888)	10	10

Weapon

Stephenson was not assigned points for this element as there was no information he was known to carry a knife.

Weapon			
18	Known to carry a knife (does not matter how often)	20	

Other

Stephenson did not have a history of any of the elements listed in this section; so he was not assigned any points.

Other			
19	History of setting fires or torturing small animals	10	
20	History of or documented fantasy of evisceration or mutilation of sexual areas of the body	50	

Total Points

Roslyn Stephenson's total POIPAT score was 195 points.

Francis Tumblety

Residence/Comfort Zone

There is information that Tumblety was in London, but there is no information he had a residence there. Therefore he was not assigned any points in the Residence section. However, he did admit in an interview with a reporter to having been in Whitechapel during the murders so he was given 20 points in the Comfort Zone section for being known to frequent Whitechapel.

		PP	Score
Residence (Aug. 31, 1888–Nov. 9, 1888)			
1	London (includes suburbs)	20	
2	Whitechapel (10 mile radius)	20	
Comfort Zone			
3	Resides in, works in or known to frequent Whitechapel or surrounding area (10 mile radius)	20	**20**

Physical Description

Tumblety was assigned 50 points in this section for being male but did not receive any points for the other elements. He was 55 years old at the time of the murders, and there is no information that he had any physical abnormalities.

Physical Description			
4	Male	50	50
5	Age (25–45) *55 at time of offences*	10	
6	Physical abnormality (i.e. speech impediment, scarred complexion, physical illness or injury)	5	

Lifestyle

Other than information that he was supposed to have been arrested in Montreal in 1857 for attempting to induce a miscarriage in a young prostitute, there is no other information that links him to prostitutes. Additionally, there was no information that he was nocturnal either. Consequently, he was not assigned any points for either element in this section.

Lifestyle			
7	Uses prostitutes	30	
8	Nocturnal due to choice or circumstance (night person)	10	

Marital Status

There was no information that Tumblety was married so he was assigned five points for being single during the homicides.

Marital Status (Aug. 31, 1888–Nov. 9, 1888) (Select One Only)			
9	Unattached (i.e. single, divorced, separated)	5	5
10	Unaccountable (i.e. married but wife is extremely passive)	5	

Employment Status

Tumblety was awarded 10 points for being employed at the time of the offences because he was a self-professed and self-employed doctor of herbal medicine. There is nothing to support that the use of a knife was common in that particular field of employment.

Employment Status (Aug. 31, 1888–Nov. 9, 1888)			
11	Employed—at time of offences	10	10
12	Engaged in an occupation, hobby or other activity where the use of a knife was common	20	

Criminal History

Tumblety had an extensive criminal history having been arrested for a variety of offences from pickpocketing to gross indecency and indecent assault. As such, he was assigned 10 points for having a history of property crimes and 20 points for having a history of sex related offences. There is no information that he had a history of throat slashing; so he was not awarded any points for that element.

Criminal History (Charges and/or Conviction Not Necessary)			
13	History of property crimes, of assault causing bodily harm and of domestic violence	10	10
14	History of sex related offences	20	20
15	History of throat slashing (includes attempts)	50	

Linked to Victim

Tumblety was a suspect in the Whitechapel murders, but there was no evidence to connect him to any of the victims. Therefore, he was not awarded any points in this section.

Linked to Victim			
16	Mary Ann Nichols	20	
	Annie Chapman	20	
	Elizabeth Stride	20	
	Catherine Eddowes	20	
	Mary Jane Kelly	20	

Availability

There is no information that provides Tumblety an alibi for any of the Whitechapel cases; so he was assigned 10 points for being available for each case.

Availability (Subject Was Available [i.e. Not Incarcerated at the Time of the Offences])			
17	Mary Ann Nichols (Aug. 31, 1888)	10	10
	Annie Chapman (Sept. 8, 1888)	10	10
	Elizabeth Stride (Sept. 29–30, 1888)	10	10
	Catherine Eddowes (Sept. 30, 1888)	10	10
	Mary Jane Kelly (Nov. 9, 1888)	10	10

Weapon

There was no information that Tumblety was known to carry a knife so he was not assigned points for this element.

Weapon			
18	Known to carry a knife (does not matter how often)	20	

Other

Tumblety was not known to have a history of setting fires or torturing small animals so no points were assigned to him for that element. There was information, however, that Tumblety kept a collection of women's wombs in jars in his library. If this were true, it may have been possible to interpret that as a 'fantasy of evisceration or mutilation of sexual areas of the body'. However, that would have been a bit of a stretch; but more importantly the source and reliability of the information was questionable and therefore no points were awarded for that element either.

Other			
19	History of setting fires or torturing small animals	10	
20	History of or documented fantasy of evisceration or mutilation of sexual areas of the body	50	

Comments

Although the information that Tumblety had a collection of wombs in his library came from a questionable source of unknown reliability, it was included in the Comments section so investigators would be aware of it and make their own assessment of its importance.

Comments
Reported by subject of questionable credibility that he hated women and had a collection women's wombs in jars in his library.

Total Points

Francis Tumblety's total POIPAT score was 165 points.

Conclusion

If you took the time to score these POIs on your own using the Jack the Ripper POIPAT created in a previous chapter prior to following along in this chapter, there were likely some scoring differences between how you scored them and how we scored them. This is probably because the source of the information used to score each of the elements required some interpretation and judgement calls. If this was a current case, the background information would have been much more definitive and require much less interpretation.

There may also be those who take issue with some of the scoring because they disagree with some of the background information provided in the previous chapter or they have information that was not provided there. It is, however, important to note that POIPATs are scored based on the information that is available to the assessor about the POI at the time he or she scores the POIPAT. That is why each POIPAT contains a date at the bottom to indicate that it was based on the information available at that time.

Even if your scoring was a bit off, it is likely that it did not drastically affect the order in which the POIs were rank ordered based on their scores. It is important to keep in mind that the POIPAT is not meant to be an investigative tool that solves the case by identifying who scored highest on the POIPAT. It is an administrative case management tool that prioritizes POIs based on how likely they are to have committed the offence(s) compared to all of the other POIs. Therefore placing them at the correct priority level of high, medium or low is more important than their individual POIPAT score. If for example a POI's score places them in the high priority range, they should be treated the same as any other POI in that category regardless of individual score.

We will use the POIPAT scores for the suspects identified in this chapter in the next chapter to demonstrate how our Jack the Ripper suspects ranked against each other and to identify a priority scoring range.

Jack the Ripper— Establishing a Priority Range

14

Introduction

In the previous chapter we scored our entire list of Jack the Ripper suspects using the POIPAT we created specifically for that purpose. In this chapter we will use those scores not only to rank order the suspects but also to create a priority range. The priority range will determine if their scores place them in the high, medium or low priority range. If this was a current investigation where POIs were still being identified on an ongoing basis, this priority range would be used to determine where those new POIs fit on the priority scale.

We will identify our priority range for this Jack the Ripper investigation by following the instructions from Chapter 5, 'Establishing Priority Levels Points Ranges'.

Identity POIs to Be Scored

The instructions in Chapter 5 tell you to start this exercise by selecting a certain number of POIs at random. They suggest that 20 is a reasonable number but mention that the more cases used, the better. Although there were many Jack the Ripper suspects we could have chosen from, we selected only 10 of the better known subjects for our case study so we will use them all for this exercise. Luckily, they provided us with a wide range of scores from 60 to 245.

The following is our list of subjects in alphabetical order by surname:

- Thomas Hayne Cutbush
- Montague John Druitt
- Sir William Withey Gull
- Severin Antoniovich Klosowski, aka George Chapman
- Aaron Kosminski
- Michael Ostrog
- John Pizer, aka Leather Apron
- Walter Richard Sickert
- Roslyn D'Onston Stephenson, aka Dr. Robert Donston Stephenson
- Francis Tumblety

Doing the Calculations

Chapter 5 suggests that 25 per cent of the POIs should be high priority, 50 per cent should be medium priority and 25 per cent should be low priority. In our case we had 10 POIs, and we know that 25 per cent of 10 is 2.5. However, you can't have 2.5 POIs, so we rounded 2.5 up to 3. Now we know the top three scores will represent the high priority range, the bottom three will represent the low priority range and the scores between the high and low range will be the medium range, as the following chart illustrates:

#	Priority Level	POIPAT Score	Name of POI
1	High		
2	High		
3	High		
4	Medium		
5	Medium		
6	Medium		
7	Medium		
8	Low		
9	Low		
10	Low		

Plugging in the Names with POIPAT Scores

Now that we have created a chart, the next step is to add the names of the suspects starting with the one who scored highest and listing them in descending order of their POIPAT score as the following chart demonstrates:

#	Priority Level	POIPAT Score	Name of POI
1	High	245	Aaron Kosminski
2	High	220	Severin Antoniovich Klosowski (George Chapman)
3	High	210	Walter Richard Sickert
4	Medium	205	John Pizer (Leather Apron)
5	Medium	195	Roslyn D'Onston Stephenson (Dr. Robert Donston Stephenson
6	Medium	185	Montague John Druitt
7	Medium	165	Francis Tumblety
8	Low	150	Sir William Withey Gull
9	Low	130	Thomas Hayne Cutbush
10	Low	60	Michael Ostrog

Identifying Priority Ranges

Now that we plugged in the names and corresponding POIPAT scores, we can determine what the priority ranges should be for this case. We can start with the high priority range first. Note that the top three scores ranged from a low of 210 to a high of 245, so you might conclude that 210 to 245 should be the high priority range. However, what we have not considered is that the maximum possible score for the Jack the Ripper POIPAT is 510, so it would be possible for future POIs to score higher than 245 up to a maximum of 510. In order to address this, the high priority range should be set at from a low of 210 to a high of 510.

Next we will look at the low priority because once we have determined the low priority, everything between the high and low range will automatically be medium priority. The bottom three scores in the chart were between a low of 60 to a high of 150 points. However, in this case we must consider that it is possible although unlikely for future POIs to score less than 60 down to a possible 0. In order to adjust for this possibility, the low range should be set at from 0 to 150.

By default, if the highest score in the low priority range is 150, then the lowest possible score in the medium range would be 151. However, all of the scores on the Jack the Ripper POIPAT were divisible by 5 so in fact the lowest possible score would be 155. Conversely, the lowest possible score in the high priority range is 210, so the highest possible score in the medium priority range would be 205 when the requirement of being divisible by 5 is factored in.

Therefore the following are the priority ranges for the Jack the Ripper investigation:

Low Priority = 0–150
Medium Priority = 155–205
High Priority = 210–510

Now that the priority range has been established for this investigation, those scores should be reflected at the bottom of the Jack the Ripper POIPAT as follows:

Other			
19	History of setting fires or torturing small animals	10	
20	History of or documented fantasy of evisceration or mutilation of sexual areas of the body	50	
		Total Points	

Comments
Priority Point Range: Low = 0–150; Medium = 155–205; High = 210–510
Completed by: _____Date: ____/____/____
Reviewed by: _____Date: ____/____/____
Note: This assessment was completed with the information available to the assessor at the time of the file review. Additional information could change this assessment.

Conclusion

Establishing the priority level ranges is the last significant process in implementing a POIPAT system in any investigation. These ranges would determine where new POIs introduced to the investigation would fit once they were assessed with the POIPAT. Although the Jack the Ripper case is over 100 years old, new suspects are constantly being introduced. As such, this POIPAT could be used as a subjective method of determining how those new suspects compared to those already scored using this POIPAT and also what investigative priority they would have been given if it were a current investigation.

Now that we have rank ordered our Jack the Ripper POIs in order of who was the most likely to have committed the offences based on how they scored on our POIPAT, should we conclude that Aaron Kosminski, who had the highest score, was the real Jack the Ripper? We will address that very question in the next chapter.

Jack the Ripper Case Study—Epilogue 15

Who Was the Real Jack the Ripper?

There are many individuals who are convinced they know who Jack the Ripper was and can provide some very convincing arguments to support their views. However, the reality is that there is no forensic evidence that conclusively proves any one individual is responsible for any of the cases generally believed to be the work of a person who came to be known as Jack the Ripper. In fact, there is no absolute proof that any or all of the cases being attributed to him were committed by the same person.

Unfortunately, there is little, if any, trace evidence left from any of the crime scenes that could be subjected to current advancements in forensic science such as fingerprint examination or DNA. Therefore it is unlikely that investigators, researchers and Ripperologists will ever be able to conclusively prove that their favorite suspect was the real Jack the Ripper. The best they can ever hope to do is make a strong circumstantial case.

The POIPAT is not intended to be a replacement for forensic evidence nor a means of providing proof that any individual was responsible for any given offence or offences. It was designed as an administrative case management tool that allows managers to assign POIs to investigators in priority of those who are most likely to have committed the offence(s) based on the information that was available to the assessor at the time the POIPAT was scored.

This is true of the Jack the Ripper POIPAT. Although it may be tempting to conclude that Aaron Kosminski was Jack the Ripper because he scored highest and as a result finished at the top of the priority list, caution should be exercised. The Jack the Ripper POIPAT was not created to identify who Jack the Ripper was. If this POIPAT had been created back in 1888, it would have been used to identify which of the many suspects identified at that time should be assigned to investigators first.

Kosminski's specific score or overall ranking in the list of suspects was not as important as what priority level he was determined to be at. His score placed him in the high priority range, but Severin Klosowski and Walter Sickert were also assessed at that level. As such, they should all be regarded as high priorities and treated no differently regardless of their individual score.

#	Priority Level	POIPAT Score	Name of POI
1	High	245	Aaron Kosminski
2	High	220	Severin Antoniovich Klosowski (George Chapman)
3	High	210	Walter Richard Sickert
4	Medium	205	John Pizer (Leather Apron)
5	Medium	195	Roslyn D'Onston Stephenson (Dr. Robert Donston Stephenson
6	Medium	185	Montague John Druitt
7	Medium	165	Francis Tumblety
8	Low	150	Sir William Withey Gull
9	Low	130	Thomas Hayne Cutbush
10	Low	60	Michael Ostrog

It may seem obvious that POIs should be assigned in order of their POIPAT score; however, it is not always as simple as that. In cases where there are several investigators, in order to be the most efficient and effective investigators may be assigned to investigate POIs based on specific geographic zones. In this case, if Kosminski, Klosowski and Sickert lived in different zones, they could have been assigned to three different investigators. Those investigators could be assigned POIs from all three priority ranges. It would then be up to the investigators to prioritize them based on their rankings. For example, if an investigator was assigned Sickert (high), Druitt (medium) and Ostrog (low), it would be up to that investigator to give investigative priority to Sickert.

It is also important to understand that a person could receive a low score on the POIPAT and still be the person responsible for the offence(s). There could be a number of reasons for this, but the most likely cause would have to do with the information that is available about the POI at the time he or she is assessed. The less information that is known about a POI, the less likely they are to receive a high score on the POIPAT.

The POIPAT scores for the Jack the Ripper suspects in our case study were based solely on the information available in Chapter 12 of this book. That chapter provided only a brief summary of the vast volumes of information available on these individuals. It is possible that if the assessor had all the information written about each suspect and the time to read it all, their POIPAT scores would have been higher.

Another important factor to consider is that the POIPAT system cannot place the actual offender in the high priority category if that offender was not subjected to a POIPAT. For example, our case study looked at only 10 of the better known Jack the Ripper suspects. However, there were likely hundreds of other POIs identified during that investigation. In fact, the actual suspect file from the investigation has been missing for some time. It is possible that Jack the Ripper was one of the individuals listed in the missing file.

It is interesting, however, that the author based many of the elements in this Jack the Ripper POIPAT on SSA Douglas' profile report, and that when it was utilized to assess the better known POIs, Kosminski bubbled up as the number one suspect. This is interesting because the profile Mr. Douglas wrote was in preparation for a two hour television documentary on Jack the Ripper in which he was challenged to solve the mystery. Douglas asked another very well known FBI profiler, SSA Robert Hazelwood, to assist him. Although they were very well prepared to defend the profile, they were surprised their first day on the set when the production company asked them to consider five suspects that their investigative research department had identified. The suspects included Roslyn D'Onston Stephenson, Montague Druitt, Sir William Gull, Prince Albert Victor and Aaron Kosminski. These were very well known suspects, two of whom, Stephenson and Druitt, surfaced in the famous Macnaghten report.

The television program was hosted by Peter Ustinov, and in addition to Douglas and Hazelwood, the panel guests included the late William Eckerd, a forensic pathologist; Queens Counsel Anne Mallalieu; and William Waddell, who was a British criminologist and the curator of Scotland Yard's Black Museum. They were all given access to research material on the five suspects.

When Peter Ustinov asked the panel to select their favourite suspect, all of the panel members selected Kosminski for a variety of reasons. The fact that several renowned experts unanimously selected Kosminski as their favourite suspect provides support that the POIPAT works and can be even more effective when used with a criminal investigative analysis unknown offender profile.

So the answer to the question 'Who was the real Jack the Ripper?' is that we still do not know. The best we can say is that based on the information we had about the investigations and what we knew about each of the suspects from Chapter 12, Aaron Kosminski scored the highest of the 10 suspects who were assessed on the Jack the Ripper POIPAT we created for this case and as a result should have been a high investigative priority.

Unfortunately, we were unable to conclusively solve the Jack the Ripper mystery, but the good news is, if you read the first part of this book and followed along with the Jack the Ripper case study, you should now be able to create a POIPAT for any investigation no matter how unique or complex it may be. Your newly acquired skill could save your agency a significant amount of time and resources and more importantly may even save lives. Also, remember that if you are having difficulty getting started, you can use the Standard POIPAT Elements Library in Chapter 6 along with the General POIPAT Template available in the POIPAT Utilities sub-directory on the companion CD.

Appendix A: Sample POIPAT

Persons of Interest Priority Assessment Tool						
Name of POI	**Surname**			**First Given**		**Second Given**
	Linderman			Mathew		Nelson
DOB	**YYYY**	**MM**	**DD**	**Fingerprint Number**		**Task/Tip #**
▮▮▮	1963	07	25	A374658C		1456
					PP	**Score**
Residence						
1	Alberta (June 1, 2009–Dec. 31, 2009)				20	**20**
2	Calgary (June 01, 2009–Dec. 31, 2009)				20	**20**
Comfort Zone						
3	Resides in, works in or known to frequent Calgary or surrounding area (25 km radius)				20	**20**
4	Resides in, works in or known to frequent Okotoks or surrounding area (25 km radius)				20	
Physical Description						
5	Tattoo of lion on right arm				30	
6	Very tall (over 6' 2")				20	**20**
7	Age (between 20 and 45)				10	
8	Age (between 46 and 60)				5	
Gender						
9	Male				50	**50**
Speech Characteristic						
10	Speech impediment				15	
Lifestyle						
11	Uses sex trade workers				50	
12	Nocturnal due to choice or circumstance (night person)				5	
13	Engages in activities of an outdoor nature such as hunting or fishing				5	**5**
Marital Status (June 1, 2009–Dec. 31, 2009) (Select One Only)						
14	Unattached (i.e. single, divorced, separated)				5	**5**
15	Unaccountable (i.e. married but wife is extremely passive or compliant)				5	
Employment Status (June 1, 2009–Dec. 31, 2009)						
16	Employed—at time of offences				5	**5**
17	Employed professional—at the time of the incident(s)				5	
18	Linked to medical industry				20	

Education			
19	Post-secondary education or higher	10	
Criminal History (Score All That Are Applicable)			
20	Has criminal history	5	5
21	Has history of violence	20	
22	Has history of sex related offences	20	
23	Has history of sex offences against children	50	
Linked to Victim			
24	Jane Smith	20	
	Sally Jones	20	
	Bobbi Olson	20	
	Jackie Simpson	20	
Availability (Subject Was Available [i.e. Not Incarcerated at the Time of the Offences])			
25	Jane Smith (2009/06/01–2009/07/30)	10	10
	Sally Jones (2009/08/27–2009/09/14)	10	10
	Bobbi Olson (2009/10/22–2009/10/29)	10	10
	Jackie Simpson (2009/12/14–2009/12/31)	10	10
Vehicle			
26	Owns or has access to a vehicle	5	
27	Owns or has access to truck, SUV or van	15	
Other			
28	Has access to rifle	20	
29	Has access to a Ruger 10-22 CRR rifle	50	
		Total Points	190

Comments

An intelligence report revealed that he has a large collection of Soldier of Fortune, Gun and True Crime magazines. It also advises that he has been downloading graphic images from the Internet of homicide victims who have been killed by gunshot.

Priority Point Range: Low = 0–175; Medium = 176–225; High = 226–595

Completed by: _____ **Cpl. P. Jones** _____ **Date: 2011/10/31**

Reviewed by: _____ **Date:** ___ / ___ / ___

Note: This assessment was completed with the information available to the assessor at the time of the file review. Additional information could change this assessment.

Appendix B: POIPAT Process Map

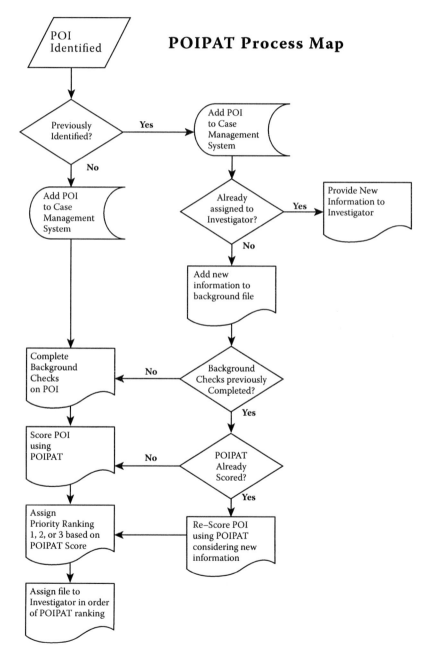

POIPAT Process Map

- POI Identified
- Previously Identified? — **Yes** → Add POI to Case Management System
  - **No** → Add POI to Case Management System
- Add POI to Case Management System → Already assigned to Investigator? — **Yes** → Provide New Information to Investigator
  - **No** → Add new information to background file
- Add new information to background file → Background Checks previously Completed?
  - **No** → Complete Background Checks on POI
  - **Yes** → POIPAT Already Scored?
- POIPAT Already Scored?
  - **No** → Score POI using POIPAT
  - **Yes** → Re-Score POI using POIPAT considering new information
- Complete Background Checks on POI → Score POI using POIPAT
- Score POI using POIPAT → Assign Priority Ranking 1, 2, or 3 based on POIPAT Score
- Re-Score POI using POIPAT considering new information → Assign Priority Ranking 1, 2, or 3 based on POIPAT Score
- Assign Priority Ranking 1, 2, or 3 based on POIPAT Score → Assign file to Investigator in order of POIPAT ranking

Appendix C: SSA John Douglas Profile Report

July 6, 1988
UNSUB: AKA JACK THE RIPPER;
SERIES OF HOMICIDES
LONDON, ENGLAND
1888
NCAVC- HOMICIDE (CRIMINAL INVESTIGATIVE ANALYSIS)

The following criminal investigative analysis was prepared by Supervisory Special Agent (SSA) John E. Douglas, FBI National Center for the Analysis of Violent Crime (NCAVC), Program Manager of Criminal Investigative Analysis. At the request of Cosgrove-Meurer Productions, SSA Douglas was requested to prepare an analysis of a 100-year-old, unsolved serial murder case that occurred in England. This historical case was known as "Jack the Ripper."

SSA Douglas was provided basic background information relative to each case; however, it is noted that forensic technology and other investigative techniques, as we know of today, were nonexistent a century ago. Medical examiners' reports were incomplete, crime scene photography was used sparingly and police investigative reports do not reflect the type of thoroughness evidenced today.

When a case is submitted for investigative analysis, the reliability and validity of the overall analysis is hinged on the thoroughness displayed by the medical examiners, technicians, investigators, etc. Although materials provided were not as complete as cases submitted today by much more sophisticated law enforcement agencies, SSA Douglas filled in the missing pieces of information by making certain probable assumptions.

This analysis will address the following areas: Victimology or profile of victims; medical examiner's findings; crime and crime scene analysis; offender traits and characteristics; pre- and post-offense behavioral patterns; investigative and/or proactive techniques; and interview/interrogation suggestions.

Rather than address each homicide separately, SSA Douglas' comments will relate to the entire series of homicides as a whole.

Victimology

In each homicide, the victim was a prostitute with a reputation of drinking quite heavily. These two ingredients place the victim in a "high risk" category. By "high risk," we define this as someone who is very likely to be the victim of violent crime. From an investigative perspective, this makes it extremely difficult in reference to developing logical suspects. From a forensic viewpoint, if any evidence is obtained such as hairs and fibers, semen, etc., law enforcement would not know for certain if this evidence did in fact come from the subject.

One hundred years ago, prostitution was not as organized as it is today, where we have pimps controlling, monitoring and protecting their stables. During the "Jack the Ripper" era, women worked independently. A female prostitute who drank heavily was looking for trouble. We would suspect that there were numerous instances of these women being physically assaulted, raped and ripped off.

Prostitutes 100 years ago did not dress differently than other women at that time. In most cases, they performed their "services" in dark alleys or in "flop" houses. The prostitutes targeted by Jack the Ripper were nearly twice the age of prostitutes soliciting today. They were not particularly attractive and other than their age, there were no striking similarities between them. (It is noted that the last victim was 25.)

The Jack the Ripper victims were targeted because they were readily accessible. Jack the Ripper did not have to initiate the contact. This was done for him by the prostitute. This is an important feature in a case such as this and will be addressed later on this analysis "Offender Traits and Characteristics."

Medical Examination

As stated earlier, the medical examinations conducted at that time were not very thorough when compared to autopsy examinations conducted today by experienced forensic pathologists. However, even in some parts of the United States today, autopsy examinations are something less than desired.

The primary areas noted in this analysis were as follows:

1. No evidence of sexual assault.
2. Subject killed victims swiftly.
3. Subject was able to maintain control of victims during the initial "blitz style" of attack.
4. Subject removed body organs (i.e. kidney, vagina, nose) on some of the victims, indicating some anatomical knowledge.
5. No evidence of physical torture prior to death.
6. Postmortem mutilation.
7. Possible manual strangulation.
8. Blood from victims was concentrated in small areas.
9. Rings were taken from one of the victims.
10. The last victim was killed indoors and was the most mutilated. Subject spent a considerable amount of time at the scene.
11. Time of death was in the early morning hours.

The above-listed autopsy findings will contribute to the overall offender analysis that will be addressed later on in this report.

Crime and Crime Scene Analysis

With the exception of the last case, all victims were killed outdoors. All victims were killed swiftly, with the victims consequently receiving postmortem mutilation. All homicides occurred within one-fourth of a mile from each other and occurred either on Friday, Saturday, or Sunday during early morning hours. After the first homicide at Whitechapel Station, the subject moved slightly across town (one-fourth of a mile). If a line is drawn from crime scenes 2, 3, 4, and 5, a triangular configuration is formed. This is observed in other types of serial crimes. This triangular configuration is viewed as a secondary comfort zone for the Ripper. This movement is caused when a subject believes that the investigation is heating up in his primary comfort zone. The primary comfort zone would be the location of the first homicide in the vicinity of Whitechapel Station. It is the opinion of this crime analyst that there were other attacks in the Whitechapel area that either went unreported or for some reason were not considered by authorities to be crimes of Jack the Ripper.

Some criminologist and behavioral scientists have written in the past that subjects will maintain their modus operandi and that is what links so-called "signature crimes." This conclusion is incorrect. A subject will change his *modus operandi* as he gains additional experience. This is learned behavior. However, the personal desires and needs of the subject are expressed in the *ritual* aspect of a crime. The ritual is something that he must always do because it is the acting out of the fantasy. With Jack the Ripper, the target selection, the approach, the method of his initial attack, are his modus operandi. What takes place after this is the ritual. The ritual may become more elaborate as was in the last homicide case. Here, the Ripper had time to act out his fantasies. As investigators, we should not necessarily expect the same type of homicides in the future, particularly if subsequent victims are killed outdoors. Once again, he would not have the time to carry out all of his fantasies and consequently mutilation will not be as advanced.

Communiques Allegedly Received from the Ripper

Another aspect of this case worth mentioning was the communiques allegedly received from Jack the Ripper. It is quite rare when a serial murderer of this type communicates with police, media, family, etc. When they do communicate, they generally provide specifics relative to the crime that only are known by the subject. In addition, they generally provide information relative to their motivation for committing such a heinous crime. It is my opinion that this series of homicides was not perpetrated by someone who set up a challenge against law enforcement. While the killer knew he would be receiving national as well as international publicity, this was not his primary motivation.

In summary, I would not put emphasis on the communiques during this investigation. However, I would develop an investigative technique with the goal in mind to identify the author of the communiques.

Offender Traits and Characteristics

These homicides are referred to as Lust Murders. Roy Hazelwood and I wrote an article several years ago which appeared in the FBI's *Law Enforcement Bulletin*. The word "lust" does not mean love or have any sexual meaning, other than the fact that the subject attacks the genital areas of his victims. The vaginal area and breast are the focal point of attack in a woman and the penis and scrotum are the attack area of the male offender. Generally, males who are attacked in this fashion are victims that were involved in a homosexual relationship.

I have never experienced a female serial lust murder either in research or in cases received at the NCAVC. It is for this reason that Jack the Ripper was a male. He was of white race in view of the fact that white was the predominant race at the scene locations, and generally crimes such as these are intraracial.

The age of onset for these types of homicides is generally between the mid to late 20's. Based upon the high degree of psychopathology exhibited at the scene, the ability of the subject to converse with the victim until a suitable location is found, and the ability to avoid detection, places him between the age bracket of 28 to 36 years of age. However, it should be noted that age is a difficult characteristic to categorize and consequently we would not eliminate a viable suspect exclusively because of age.

This offender does not look out of the ordinary. However, the clothing he wears at the time of the assaults is not his everyday dress. He wants to project to unsuspecting females (prostitutes) that he has money; consequently this relieves him from initiating contact.

He comes from a family where he was raised by a domineering mother and weak, passive and/or absent father. In all likelihood, his mother drank heavily and enjoyed the company of many men. As a result, he failed to receive consistent care and contact with stable adult role models. Consequently, he became detached socially and developed a diminished emotional response towards his fellow man. He became asocial, preferring to be alone. His anger became internalized and in his younger years, he expressed his pent-up destructive emotions by setting fires and torturing small animals. By perpetrating these acts, he discovered increased areas of dominance, power and control, and learned how to continue violent destructive acts without detection or punishment.

As he grew older, his *fantasy* developed a strong component that included domination, cruelty and mutilation of women. We would expect to find evidence of this violent destructive fantasy life through personal writings of his as well as drawings of women being mutilated.

For employment, he would seek a position where he could work alone and vicariously experience his destructive fantasies. Such employment would include work as a butcher, mortician's helper, medical examiner's assistant, or hospital attendant. He is employed Monday through Friday and on Friday night, Saturday and Sunday is off from work. He has carried a knife for defense purposes—just in case he was ever attacked, he would be ready.

This paranoid-type of thinking is in part justified because of the poor self-image he has of himself. He would be expected to have some type of physical abnormality. However, although not severe, he perceives this as being psychologically crippling. We would look for someone below or above average in height and/or weight. May have problems with speech, scarred complexion, physical illness, or injury.

We would not expect this type of offender to be married. If he was married in the past, it would have been to someone older than himself and the marriage would have been for a short duration.

He is not adept in meeting people socially and the major extent of his heterosexual relationships would be with prostitutes. Due to lack of hygiene practices by prostitutes at that time and the absence of treatment for venereal disease, he may have been infected. If infected, this would further fuel his hatred and disgust for women.

He would be perceived as being quiet, a loner, shy, slightly withdrawn, obedient, and neat and orderly in appearance and when working. He drinks in the local pubs and after a few spirits, he becomes more relaxed and finds it easier to engage in conversation. He lives or works in the Whitechapel area. The first homicide should be in closed proximity to either his home or workplace. It is noted that London Hospital is only one block from the first homicide and as stated earlier in this analysis, we would expect other violent crimes in this vicinity.

Investigators would have interviewed him during the course of the investigation, and he was probably talked to by police on several occasions. Unfortunately at this time, there was no way to correlate this type of information; therefore, he was overlooked. Investigators and citizens in the community had a preconceived idea or picture of what Jack the Ripper would look like. Because of the belief that he would appear odd or ghoulish in appearance, he was overlooked and/or eliminated as a potential suspect.

Pre- and Post-Offense Behavior

Prior to each homicide, the subject was in a local pub drinking spirits, while at the same time lowering his inhibitions. He would be observed walking all over the Whitechapel area during the early evening hours. He did not specifically seek a certain look in a women; however, it was by no accident that he killed prostitutes. He had the sense to know when and where to attack his victims. There would have been many other women who confronted Jack the Ripper and were not assaulted because the location was not secure enough.

Post-offense behavior would include returning to an area where he could wash his hands of blood and remove his clothing. We would not expect him to inject himself into the police investigation or provide bogus information.

Jack the Ripper hunted nightly for his victims. When he could not find another, he returned to the locations where he killed his previous victims. If the victims were buried locally, he would visit the gravesites of his victims during the early morning hours for the purpose of reliving his lust murders.

Jack the Ripper would not have committed suicide after the last homicide. Generally, when crimes such as these cease, it is because he came close to being identified, was interviewed by police, or was arrested for some other type of offense. As stated previously in this report, we would be surprised if

Jack the Ripper would suddenly stop. However, we've seen this happen before and generally it has been because of the above-stated reasons.

Investigative and/or Prosecutive Techniques

Jack the Ripper would be best suited to be interviewed during the early morning hours. He would feel more relaxed and secure to confess to homicides. He would feel more relaxed to express himself by writing about his motivation for killing the women. He would not be visibly shaken or upset if directly accused of the homicides. However, he would be psychologically and physiologically stressed if confronted with the fact that he became personally soiled by the victim's blood. Jack the Ripper believed the homicides were justified, and he was only removing perishable items—who were like garbage.

This analysis was prepared for the exclusive use of Cosgrove-Meurer Productions, Inc. Any reproduction or use of this analysis for publication must have the written consent of SSA John E. Douglas.*

---

* This report was completed by SSA John E. Douglas while he worked for the FBI, and the report is now in the Public Domain.

Appendix D: Dr. Thomas Bond Profile Report

The following is extracted from a letter written to Assistant Commissioner Robert Anderson of the Home Officer from Dr. Thomas Bond. Although he did not refer to it as a 'Profile Report', it is believed by some to be the first criminal profile:

Dear Sir,
I beg to report that I have read the notes of the 4 Whitechapel Murders viz:

1. Buck's Row.
2. Hanbury Street.
3. Berner's Street.
4. Mitre Square.

I have also made a Post Mortem Examination of the mutilated remains of a woman found yesterday in a small room in Dorset Street —

1. All five murders were no doubt committed by the same hand. In the first four the throats appear to have been cut from left to right. In the last case owing to the extensive mutilation it is impossible to say in what direction the fatal cut was made, but arterial blood was found on the wall in splashes close to where the woman's head must have been lying.
2. All the circumstances surrounding the murders lead me to form the opinion that the women must have been lying down when murdered and in every case the throat was first cut.
3. In the four murders of which I have seen the notes only, I cannot form a very definite opinion as to the time that had elapsed between the murder and the discovering of the body.
In one case, that of Berner's Street, the discovery appears to have been made immediately after the deed — In Buck's Row, Hanbury Street, and Mitre Square three or four hours only could have elapsed. In the Dorset Street case the body was lying on the bed at the time of my visit, 2 o'clock, quite naked and mutilated as in the annexed report —
Rigor Mortis had set in, but increased during the progress of the examination. From this it is difficult to say with any degree of certainty the exact time that had elapsed since death as the period varies from 6 to 12 hours before rigidity sets in. The body was comparatively cold at 2 o'clock and the remains of a recently taken meal were found in

the stomach and scattered about over the intestines. It is, therefore, pretty certain that the woman must have been dead about 12 hours and the partly digested food would indicate: that death took place about 3 or 4 hours after the food was taken, so one or two o'clock in the morning would be the probable time of the murder.

4. In all the cases there appears to be no evidence of struggling and the attacks were probably so sudden and made in such a position that the women could neither resist nor cry out. In the Dorset Street case the corner of the sheet to the right of the woman's head was much cut and saturated with blood, indicating that the face may have been covered with the sheet at the time of the attack.

5. In the four first cases the murderer must have attacked from the right side of the victim. In the Dorset Street case, he must have attacked from in front or from the left, as there would be no room for him between the wall and the part of the bed on which the woman was lying. Again, the blood had flowed down on the right side of the woman and spurted on to the wall.

6. The murderer would not necessarily be splashed or deluged with blood, but his hands and arms must have been covered and parts of his clothing must certainly have been smeared with blood.

7. The mutilations in each case excepting the Berner's Street one were all of the same character and showed clearly that in all the murders, the object was mutilation.

8. In each case the mutilation was inflicted by a person who had no scientific nor anatomical knowledge. In my opinion he does not even possess the technical knowledge of a butcher or horse slaughterer or any person accustomed to cut up dead animals.

9. The instrument must have been a strong knife at least six inches long, very sharp, pointed at the top and about an inch in width. It may have been a clasp knife, a butcher's knife or a surgeon's knife. I think it was no doubt a straight knife.

10. The murderer must have been a man of physical strength and of great coolness and daring. There is no evidence that he had an accomplice. He must in my opinion be a man subject to periodical attacks of Homicidal and erotic mania. The character of the mutilations indicate that the man may be in a condition sexually, that may be called satyriasis. It is of course possible that the Homicidal impulse may have developed from a revengeful or brooding condition of the mind, or that Religious Mania may have been the original disease, but I do not think either hypothesis is likely. The murderer in external appearance is quite likely to be a quiet inoffensive looking man probably middle aged and neatly and respectably dressed. I think he must be in the habit of wearing a cloak or overcoat or he could hardly have escaped notice in the streets if the blood on his hands or clothes were visible.

11. Assuming the murderer to be such a person as I have just described he would probably be solitary and eccentric in his habits, also he is most likely to be a man without regular occupation, but with some small income or pension. He is possibly living among respectable persons who have some knowledge of his character and habits and who may have grounds for suspicion that he is not quite right in his mind at times. Such persons would probably be unwilling to communicate suspicions to the Police for fear of trouble or notoriety, whereas if there were a prospect of reward it might overcome their scruples.

I am, Dear Sir,
Yours faithfully,
Thos. Bond.

Appendix E: Jack the Ripper POIPAT

Persons of Interest Priority Assessment Tool—Jack the Ripper Investigation							
Name of POI	**Surname**		**First Given**		**Second Given**		
DOB	**YYYY**	**MM**	**DD**	**Fingerprint Number**		**Task/Tip #**	
						PP	**Score**
Residence (Aug. 31, 1888–Nov. 9, 1888)							
1	London (includes suburbs)					20	
2	Whitechapel (10 mile radius)					20	
Comfort Zone							
3	Resides in, works in or known to frequent Whitechapel or surrounding area (10 mile radius)					20	
Physical Description							
4	Male					50	
5	Age (25–45)					10	
6	Physical abnormality (i.e. speech impediment, scarred complexion, physical illness or injury)					5	
Lifestyle							
7	Uses prostitutes					30	
8	Nocturnal due to choice or circumstance (night person)					10	
Marital Status (Aug. 31, 1888–Nov. 9, 1888) (Select One Only)							
9	Unattached (i.e. single, divorced, separated)					5	
10	Unaccountable (i.e. married but wife is extremely passive)					5	
Employment Status (Aug. 31, 1888–Nov. 9, 1888)							
11	Employed—at time of offences					10	
12	Engaged in an occupation, hobby or other activity where the use of a knife is common					20	
Criminal History (Charges and/or Conviction Not Necessary)							
13	History of property crimes, of assault causing bodily harm and of domestic violence					10	
14	History of sex related offences					20	
15	History of throat slashing (includes attempts)					50	

Linked to Victim			
16	Mary Ann Nichols	20	
	Annie Chapman	20	
	Elizabeth Stride	20	
	Catherine Eddowes	20	
	Mary Jane Kelly	20	
Availability (Subject Was Available [i.e. Not Incarcerated at the Time of the Offences])			
17	Mary Ann Nichols (Aug. 31, 1888)	10	
	Annie Chapman (Sept. 8, 1888)	10	
	Elizabeth Stride (Sept. 29–30, 1888)	10	
	Catherine Eddowes (Sept. 30, 1888)	10	
	Mary Jane Kelly (Nov. 9, 1888)	10	
Weapon			
18	Known to carry a knife (does not matter how often)	20	
Other			
19	History of setting fires or torturing small animals	10	
20	History of or documented fantasy of evisceration or mutilation of sexual areas of the body	50	
		Total Point	
Comments			

Priority Point Range: Low = 0–150; Medium = 155–205; High = 210–510

Completed by: _____Date: ____/_____/____

Reviewed by: _____Date: ____/_____/____

Note: This assessment was completed with the information available to the assessor at the time of the file review. Additional information could change this assessment.

Appendix F: Jack the Ripper—POIPAT Instructional Guide

Introduction

Numerous persons of interest (POIs) have been identified in the Jack the Ripper investigation for consideration and follow-up. There are a number of factors that determine the likelihood of being the person responsible for one or more of these offences. Establishing the priority that should be placed on subjects who have been identified as POIs is a very subjective process but extremely important to ensure the most effective and efficient use of resources.

The purpose of this POIPAT is to provide the Jack the Ripper investigative team an objective means of assessing the priority level for each subject. It is important to note that this POIPAT is not absolute or all encompassing. There may be factors not included in the POIPAT that make an individual more or less likely to be a suspect. In these cases the POIPAT is designed to take these additional factors into consideration.

Important Note: The POIPAT is designed as an administrative tool to establish a priority level for each of the POIs. It should *not* be used as justification to eliminate a POI as a potential suspect. All available investigative steps should be taken to eliminate POIs regardless of their POIPAT score.

Methodology

This POIPAT has been created specifically for the Jack the Ripper investigation. It is premised on the belief the same offender is responsible for the homicides of Mary Ann Nichols, Annie Chapman, Elizabeth Stride, Catherine Eddowes and Mary Jane Kelly.

It includes a series of traits and characteristics believed to be true of the offender. It considers where the offender resided at the time of the offences; his comfort zone, lifestyle, marital status, physical characteristics, employment and criminal history; any known association to any or all of the victims; and his availability to commit the offence. This composite of the offender was developed after a thorough review of the material available at the time and in consideration of retired SSA John Douglas' profile.

Each of the elements on the POIPAT has been assigned a score. The base score for each element was 20 points. Then each item was weighted based on a number of factors including how important it is compared to the other elements; availability and accessibility of the information; frequency or uniqueness of the element; subjectivity of information; and the reliability of the source. Once this weighting process is completed, it could increase, decease or have no effect on the initial base score of 20 points.

Once the POIPAT is completed, all the items are added up. The higher the total score, the higher the priority rating that will be assigned to the POI being assessed. The priority ratings are 'low', 'medium' and 'high'. See the 'Priority Point Range' at the end of the POIPAT for the specific point range for each priority level.

General Rules

When scoring each of these elements give them either full points or no points. No element should receive partial points. Each item is to be considered either true or false. If the element is true, full points are awarded. If the element is false, no points are awarded.

The source of the information to support a true or false response does not have to be an official document such as a criminal record, but it must be believed to be accurate, credible and reliable. This could include but would not be restricted to police reports, records management systems, intelligence reports, court records, municipal records, government databases and medical records. It is always a good practice to identify the source of the information that supported the responses to each of the items on POIPAT.

POIPAT Element Assessment

The following sections explain the rationale for each element as well as instruction on how each of the items should be assessed. The number preceding each item is the same as the number of its matching element on the POIPAT.

Residence

1. **Rationale:** All of these incidents occurred in London, England; therefore, it is likely the offender resided in London during the time of the offences.

   Instruction: If the POI resided in London, England, between August 31, 1888 and November 9, 1888, score this element 20. This item is independent of element 2. You score this regardless of whether or not the POI was a resident of Whitechapel at the time.

2. **Rationale:** All of the victims in these cases were believed to have been murdered in or near Whitechapel. It is likely the offender lived in or near Whitechapel.

Instruction: If the POI resided within 10 miles of Whitechapel, England, between August 31, 1888 and November 9, 1888, score this element 20. This item is independent of item 1. You score this 20 even if you gave the POI points in item 1 for being a resident of London, England.

Comfort Zone

3. **Rationale:** All of the victims in these cases were believed to have been murdered in or near Whitechapel. It likely that even if the offender did not live there, he was familiar with and comfortable in that area. That comfort may have been a result of living in, working in or visiting the area. For scoring purposes it does not matter how strong the POI's familiarity is with the area. Full points should be scored regardless of the length or extent of the POI's connection to the area.

Instruction: If the POI resided in, worked in or was known to frequent within 10 miles of the Whitechapel area, score this item 20 points. It does not matter when.

Physical Description

4. **Rationale:** It is virtually unheard of for a female to be responsible for these types of crimes; so it is not very likely Jack the Ripper was a female. However, under POIPAT scoring rules it is not possible to give negative points, so we added 'male' as an element and weighted it very high. This ensures that males receive significantly more points than females.

Instruction: If the POI is male, score this element 50 points.

5. **Rationale:** Retired SSA John Douglas' profile report estimated the offender to be between 28 and 36 years old. This age range seems to fit with the age one might expect of someone who would be comfortable engaging prostitutes in the early morning hours in the back alleys of Whitechapel. In the interests of caution, we expanded the age range to between 25 and 45 years old.

Instruction: If the POI was between 25 and 45 years at the time of *any* of these incidents, score this item 10 points.

6. **Rationale:** Retired SSA John Douglas indicated in his profile report that he felt that among other physical characteristics, the offender would have problems with speech, a scarred complexion, physical illness or injury.

Instruction: If the POI has any known physical abnormality such as a speech impediment, scarred complexion or injury, score this item 5.

Lifestyle

7. **Rationale:** All of the victims in this investigation were prostitutes, and it is likely that the offender did not kill the first one he met. Furthermore, it is likely that he knew from experience how to interact with them so they would feel comfortable and not in danger around him.

Instruction: If the POI is known to use prostitutes, score this element 30 points. 'Uses' does not necessarily mean having sex with them. It could also mean that he interacts with them in other ways such as buying drugs from or for them, living off them or drinking with them. He does not have to have a criminal record to receive points for this item.

8. **Rationale:** All of the offences occurred after dark between midnight and 6:00 a.m. This would tend to support the belief Jack the Ripper was comfortable being out at this time of the night. This may have been a lifestyle choice or a result of his employment.

Instruction: If the POI is known to be nocturnal (i.e. works shift work or is known to be out all hours of the night partying or picking up prostitutes), score this element 10 points.

Marital Status

9. **Rationale:** The nature of these crimes is such that the offender likely does not have to account for his whereabouts for extended periods of time, particularly during the late night or early morning hours. This is consistent with someone who is single, divorced or separated or has a passive partner. Retired FBI profiler John Douglas' profile report agreed that he would likely not be married: 'We would not expect this type of offender to be married'.

Instruction: If the POI was single, divorced or separated (includes common-law relationships), score this item 5.

10. **Rationale:** See item 9.

Instruction: If the POI was married (includes common-law relationship) but had a very passive wife during the time of the incidents, score this item 5. If you awarded points in item 9, do *not* score this item.

Employment Status

11. **Rationale:** All of these offences happened during the early morning hours of Friday, Saturday or Sunday. This was likely because the offender had a conventional Monday to Friday day job which precluded him from being able to stay out late during the regular week days. Mr. Douglas said the following in his profile report: 'He would seek a position where he could work alone and vicariously experience his destructive fantasies. Such employment would include work as a butcher, mortician's helper, medical examiner's assistant, or hospital attendant. He is employed Monday through Friday and on Friday night, Saturday, and Sunday is off from work'.

Instruction: If the POI was employed at the time of the offences, score this item 10 points. Item 12 is related to this element but each is to be scored separately.

12. **Rationale:** See item 11.

Instruction: If the POI was employed in an occupation, hobby or other activity where the use of a knife was common, score this item 20 points.

Criminal History

13. **Rationale:** It is common for sex offenders to have a history of property offences such as break and enter, possession of stolen property and/or theft. It is also likely that the offender had a history of violent crimes such as assault causing bodily harm and domestic violence.

Instruction: If the POI has a criminal history involving theft, break and enter, minor frauds, domestic violence, assault causing bodily harm and other such similar crimes, this item should be scored 10 points.

14. **Rationale:** Chances are, given the number of cases the offender is believed to be responsible for and the fact that criminals don't usually start committing offences at the most extreme end of their crime category, it is likely that Jack the Ripper was involved in other sex crimes. It is also known that it is common for sex offenders to have a number of psychosexual disorders such as exhibitionism and voyeurism.

Instruction: If the POI has been known to be involved in any sex related criminal offences of any type, this item is to be scored 20 points.

15. **Rationale:** All of the victims had their throats slashed. In most, if not all of the cases, this led to the incapacitation and death of the victims. This was a consistent behaviour for Jack the Ripper and is very likely to be present in any other offences he committed or attempted. It does not necessarily have to have led to the victim's death.

Instruction: If the POI has been known to have slashed or attempted to slash a victim's throat whether or not it led to his or her death, score this item 50 points.

Linked to Victims

16. **Rationale:** The purpose of this item is to acknowledge any linkages that can be identified between the POI and any or all of the victims. The more victims the POI can be linked to, the higher the probability this POI is the offender. The linkage may be a result of but not restricted to the following examples: the POI is a relative, a customer or client, an employer/employee or an acquaintance of the victim(s), or briefly met the offender on some occasion.

The victim(s) may not even be aware of the linkage. For example, the POI was an attendant at the hospital where the victims were patients. The POI may know the victim(s) from seeing them there often but the victim never took notice of the attendant.

Instruction: Score 20 points for each of the cases where there is a linkage between the POI and the victim.

Availability

17. **Rationale:** The purpose of this element is to assess the POI's opportunity and availability to commit any or all of the offences. If for example it can be proven he was in prison at the time of Mary Ann Nichols' murder, then he would not be available or have the opportunity to commit that particular murder.

Instruction: Score 10 points for each case where the POI would have been available and had the opportunity at the time of the offence. In this case, *if you do not have any information that clears the POI, assume that he or she was available and had the opportunity.*

Weapon

18. **Rationale:** Given that all the victims had their throats slashed and most were cut open and had parts of their bodies removed, there is no doubt that Jack the Ripper used a knife as a weapon. Dr. Bond,

who conducted one of the autopsies, said he thought the knife was 'a strong knife at least six inches long, very sharp, pointed at the top and about an inch in width. It may have been a clasp knife, a butcher's knife or a surgeon's knife. I think it was no doubt a straight knife'.

It is also likely Jack the Ripper brought the knife to each of the crime scenes, so we can be quite confident he carried a knife even if it was only on those occasions he planned to murder.

Instruction: If the POI is known to carry a knife no matter how often, score this element 20 points.

Other

19. **Rationale:** This element comes from retired SSA John Douglas' profile report: 'His anger became internalized and in his younger years, he expressed his pent-up destructive emotions by setting fires and torturing small animals'.

Instruction: If the POI has a history of setting fires or torturing animals, score this item 10 points.

20. **Rationale:** Almost all of the victims were eviscerated and had parts of their body removed post-mortem. It is highly likely Jack the Ripper derived psychosexual gratification from this activity which would likely be present in other similar cases he was involved in.

Instruction: Score 50 points if the POI has a history of or documented fantasy of evisceration, mutilation and/or removal of body parts. This information can come from any believed reliable source such as police information systems or sources close to the offender such as a girlfriend or ex-wife.

Comments

Rationale: The 'Comments' box was designed for important information that may not have been addressed in other areas of the POIPAT. Although this item is not scored, it may be very important to the investigation and regardless of the total POIPAT score may cause this POI's priority level to be elevated.

Instruction: If during the course of the review of this POI's background material you discover information that you believe has not been covered in other areas of the POIPAT but may be of interest to investigators or management, record the information here.

The End Section

Once all of the elements have been considered and scored, they should be added and the total score placed in the 'Total Points' box. This score will determine the priority ranking for the POI. These priority rankings are located under the 'Comments' box. If the total points are between 0 and 149, the priority ranking will be 'low'. If they are between 150 and 199, the priority ranking will be 'medium'. If the total score is higher than 199, it will be a 'high' priority. You can circle the applicable priority level that matches the total score.

There is a location for two signature blocks including a place for a date. The person conducting the POI assessment should sign the 'Completed by' signature block. It is very important that it be dated when the assessment was completed, because the score is based on the information that was available to the assessor on that date. New information could be received later that could change the score.

The second signature block is there for the person who reviews the POIPAT once it has been completed. This could be a supervisor, file manager, lead investigator or whoever's job it is to oversee the POIPAT system for this case.

Appendix G: Jack the Ripper Suspect POIPATs

Persons of Interest Priority Assessment Tool—Jack the Ripper Investigation			
Name of POI	**Surname**	**First Given**	**Second Given**
	Cutbush	Thomas	Hayne

DOB	**YYYY**	**MM**	**DD**	**Fingerprint Number**	**Task/Tip #**	
	1866					
					PP	**Score**
Residence (Aug. 31, 1888–Nov. 9, 1888)						
1	London (includes suburbs)				20	
2	Whitechapel (10 mile radius)				20	
Comfort Zone						
3	Resides in, works in or known to frequent Whitechapel or surrounding area (10 mile radius)				20	
Physical Description						
4	Male				50	50
5	Age (25–45)				10	0
6	Physical abnormality (i.e. speech impediment, scarred complexion, physical illness or injury)				5	
Lifestyle						
7	Uses prostitutes				30	
8	Nocturnal due to choice or circumstance (night person)				10	
Marital Status (Aug. 31, 1888–Nov. 9, 1888) (Select One Only)						
9	Unattached (i.e. single, divorced, separated)				5	
10	Unaccountable (i.e. married but wife is extremely passive)				5	
Employment Status (Aug. 31, 1888–Nov. 9, 1888)						
11	Employed—at time of offences				10	
12	Engaged in an occupation, hobby or other activity where the use of a knife is common				20	
Criminal History (Charges and/or Conviction Not Necessary)						
13	History of property crimes, of assault causing bodily harm and of domestic violence				10	10
14	History of sex related offences				20	
15	History of throat slashing (includes attempts)				20	

Linked to Victim			
16	Mary Ann Nichols	20	
	Annie Chapman	20	
	Elizabeth Stride	20	
	Catherine Eddowes	20	
	Mary Jane Kelly	20	
Availability (Subject Was Available [i.e. Not Incarcerated at the Time of the Offences])			
17	Mary Ann Nichols (Aug. 31, 1888)	10	10
	Annie Chapman (Sept. 8, 1888)	10	10
	Elizabeth Stride (Sept. 29–30, 1888)	10	10
	Catherine Eddowes (Sept. 30, 1888)	10	10
	Mary Jane Kelly (Nov. 9, 1888)	10	10
Weapon			
18	Known to carry a knife (does not matter how often)	20	20
Other			
19	History of setting fires or torturing small animals	10	
20	History of or documented fantasy of evisceration or mutilation of sexual areas of the body	50	
	Total Points		130
Comments			

Priority Point Range: Low = 0–150; Medium = 155–205; High = 210–510

Completed by: _____Date: ____/_____/_____

Reviewed by: _____Date: ____/_____/_____

Note: This assessment was completed with the information available to the assessor at the time of the file review. Additional information could change this assessment.

Persons of Interest Priority Assessment Tool—Jack the Ripper Investigation							
Name of POI	Surname		First Given		Second Given		
	Druitt		Montague		John		
DOB	YYYY	MM	DD	Fingerprint Number		Task/Tip #	
	1857	08	15				
						PP	Score
Residence (Aug. 31, 1888–Nov. 9, 1888)							
1	London (Includes suburbs)					20	20
2	Whitechapel (10 mile radius)					20	20
Comfort Zone							
3	Resides, works or known to frequent Whitechapel or surrounding area (10 mile radius)					20	20
Physical Description							
4	Male					50	50
5	Age (25–45)					10	10
6	Physical abnormality (i.e. speech impediment, scarred complexion, physical illness or injury)					5	
Lifestyle							
7	Uses prostitutes					30	
8	Nocturnal due to choice or circumstance (night person)					10	
Marital Status (Aug. 31, 1888–Nov. 9, 1888) (Select One Only)							
9	Unattached (i.e. single, divorced, separated)					5	5
10	Unaccountable (i.e. married but wife is extremely passive)					5	
Employment Status (Aug. 31, 1888–Nov. 9, 1888)							
11	Employed—at time of offences					10	10
12	Engaged in an occupation, hobby or other activity where the use of a knife was common					20	
Criminal History (Charges and/or Conviction Not Necessary)							
13	History of property crimes, of assault causing bodily harm and of domestic violence					10	
14	History of sex related offences					20	
15	History of throat slashing (includes attempts)					50	
Linked to Victim							
16	Mary Ann Nichols					20	
	Annie Chapman					20	
	Elizabeth Stride					20	
	Catherine Eddowes					20	
	Mary Jane Kelly					20	

Availability (Subject Was Available [i.e. Not Incarcerated at the Time of the Offences])			
17	Mary Ann Nichols (Aug. 31, 1888)	10	**10**
	Annie Chapman (Sept. 8, 1888)	10	**10**
	Elizabeth Stride (Sept. 29–30, 1888)	10	**10**
	Catherine Eddowes (Sept. 30, 1888)	10	**10**
	Mary Jane Kelly (Nov. 9, 1888)	10	**10**
Weapon			
18	Known to carry a knife (does not matter how often)	20	
Other			
19	History of setting fires or torturing small animals	10	
20	History of or documented fantasy of evisceration or mutilation of sexual areas of the body	50	
		Total Points	185
Comments			

Priority Point Range: Low = 0–150; Medium = 155–205; High = 210–510

Completed by: _____Date: ____ /_____ /____

Reviewed by: _____Date: ____ /_____ /____

Note: This assessment was completed with the information available to the assessor at the time of the file review. Additional information could change this assessment.

Persons of Interest Priority Assessment Tool—Jack the Ripper Investigation				
Name of POI	**Surname**	**First Given**		**Second Given**
	Gull	William		Withey

DOB	**YYYY**	**MM**	**DD**	**Fingerprint Number**		**Task/Tip #**	
■	1816	12	31				
						PP	**Score**
Residence (Aug. 31, 1888–Nov. 9, 1888)							
1	London (includes suburbs)					20	20
2	Whitechapel (10 mile radius)					20	
Comfort Zone							
3	Resides in, works in or known to frequent Whitechapel or surrounding area (10 mile radius)					20	
Physical Description							
4	Male					50	50
5	Age (25–45)					10	0
6	Physical abnormality (i.e. speech impediment, scarred complexion, physical illness or injury)					5	5
Lifestyle							
7	Uses prostitutes					30	
8	Nocturnal due to choice or circumstance (night person)					10	
Marital Status (Aug. 31, 1888–Nov. 9, 1888) (Select One Only)							
9	Unattached (i.e. single, divorced, separated)					5	
10	Unaccountable (i.e. married but wife is extremely passive)					5	
Employment Status (Aug. 31, 1888–Nov. 9, 1888)							
11	Employed—at time of offences					10	10
12	Engaged in an occupation, hobby or other activity where the use of a knife was common					20	20
Criminal History (Charges and/or Conviction Not Necessary)							
13	History of property crimes, of assault causing bodily harm and of domestic violence					10	
14	History of sex related offences					20	
15	History of throat slashing (includes attempts)					50	
Linked to Victim							
16	Mary Ann Nichols					20	
	Annie Chapman					20	
	Elizabeth Stride					20	
	Catherine Eddowes					20	
	Mary Jane Kelly					20	

	Availability (Subject Was Available [i.e. Not Incarcerated at the Time of the Offences])		
17	Mary Ann Nichols (Aug. 31, 1888)	10	**10**
	Annie Chapman (Sept. 8, 1888)	10	**10**
	Elizabeth Stride (Sept. 29–30, 1888)	10	**10**
	Catherine Eddowes (Sept. 30, 1888)	10	**10**
	Mary Jane Kelly (Nov. 9, 1888)	10	**10**
Weapon			
18	Known to carry a knife (does not matter how often)	20	
Other			
19	History of setting fires or torturing small animals	10	
20	History of or documented fantasy of evisceration or mutilation of sexual areas of the body	50	
	Total Points		155

Comments

Priority Point Range: Low = 0–150; Medium = 155–205; High = 210–510

Completed by: _____ Date: ____/_____/_____

Reviewed by: _____ Date: ____/_____/_____

Note: This assessment was completed with the information available to the assessor at the time of the file review. Additional information could change this assessment.

Persons of Interest Priority Assessment Tool–Jack the Ripper Investigation			
Name of POI	**Surname**	**First Given**	**Second Given**
	Klosowski	Severin	Antoinovich

DOB	**YYYY**	**MM**	**DD**	**Fingerprint Number**		**Task/Tip #**	
	1865	12	14				
						PP	**Score**
Residence (Aug. 31, 1888–Nov. 9, 1888)							
1	London (includes suburbs)					20	20
2	Whitechapel (10 mile radius)					20	20
Comfort Zone							
3	Resides, works or known to frequent Whitechapel or surrounding area (10 mile radius)					20	20
Physical Description							
4	Male					50	50
5	Age (25–45) *22 age time of offences*					10	
6	Physical abnormality (i.e. speech impediment, scarred complexion, physical illness or injury)					5	
Lifestyle							
7	Uses prostitutes					30	
8	Nocturnal due to choice or circumstance (night person)					10	
Marital Status (Aug. 31, 1888–Nov. 9, 1888) (Select One Only)							
9	Unattached (i.e. single, divorced, separated)					5	5
10	Unaccountable (i.e. married but wife is extremely passive)					5	
Employment Status (Aug. 31, 1888–Nov. 9, 1888)							
11	Employed—at time of offences					10	5
12	Engaged in an occupation, hobby or other activity where the use of a knife was common.					20	20
Criminal History (Charges and/or Conviction Not Necessary)							
13	History of property crimes, of assault causing bodily harm and of domestic violence					10	10
14	History of sex related offences					20	
15	History of throat slashing (includes attempts)					50	
Linked to Victim							
16	Mary Ann Nichols					20	
	Annie Chapman					20	
	Elizabeth Stride					20	
	Catherine Eddowes					20	
	Mary Jane Kelly					20	

Availability (Subject Was Available [i.e. Not Incarcerated at the Time of the Offences])			
17	Mary Ann Nichols (Aug. 31, 1888)	10	**10**
	Annie Chapman (Sept. 8, 1888)	10	**10**
	Elizabeth Stride (Sept. 29–30, 1888)	10	**10**
	Catherine Eddowes (Sept. 30, 1888)	10	**10**
	Mary Jane Kelly (Nov. 9, 1888)	10	**10**
Weapon			
18	Known to carry a knife (does not matter how often)	20	**20**
Other			
19	History of setting fires or torturing small animals	10	
20	History of or documented fantasy of evisceration or mutilation of sexual areas of the body	50	
	Total Points		**220**
Comments			

Priority Point Range: Low = 0–150; Medium = 155–205; High = 210–510

Completed by: _____Date: ____ / ____ / ____

Reviewed by: _____Date: ____ / ____ / ____

Note: This assessment was completed with the information available to the assessor at the time of the file review. Additional information could change this assessment.

Persons of Interest Priority Assessment Tool—Jack the Ripper Investigation						
Name of POI	**Surname**			**First Given**	**Second Given**	
	Kosminski			Aaron		
DOB	**YYYY**	**MM**	**DD**	**Fingerprint Number**	**Task/Tip #**	
	1864/65	09	11			
					PP	**Score**
Residence (Aug. 31, 1888–Nov. 9, 1888)						
1	London (includes suburbs)				20	20
2	Whitechapel (10 mile radius)				20	20
Comfort Zone						
3	Resides in, works in or known to frequent Whitechapel or surrounding area (10 mile radius)				20	20
Physical Description						
4	Male				50	50
5	Age (25–45)				10	0
6	Physical abnormality (i.e. speech impediment, scarred complexion, physical illness or injury)				5	0
Lifestyle						
7	Uses prostitutes				30	30
8	Nocturnal due to choice or circumstance (night person)				10	10
Marital Status (Aug. 31, 1888–Nov. 9, 1888) (Select One Only)						
9	Unattached (i.e. single, divorced, separated)				5	5
10	Unaccountable (i.e. married but wife is extremely passive)				5	
Employment Status (Aug. 31, 1888–Nov. 9, 1888)						
11	Employed—at time of offences				10	
12	Engaged in an occupation, hobby or other activity where the use of a knife was common				20	
Criminal History (Charges and/or Conviction Not Necessary)						
13	History of property crimes, of assault causing bodily harm and of domestic violence				10	
14	History of sex related offences				20	
15	History of throat slashing (includes attempts)				50	
Linked to Victim						
16	Mary Ann Nichols				20	
	Annie Chapman				20	
	Elizabeth Stride				20	20
	Catherine Eddowes				20	
	Mary Jane Kelly				20	

Availability (Subject Was Available [i.e. Not Incarcerated at the Time of the Offences])			
17	Mary Ann Nichols (Aug. 31, 1888)	10	10
	Annie Chapman (Sept. 8, 1888)	10	10
	Elizabeth Stride (Sept. 29–30, 1888)	10	10
	Catherine Eddowes (Sept. 30, 1888)	10	10
	Mary Jane Kelly (Nov. 9, 1888)	10	10
Weapon			
18	Known to carry a knife (does not matter how often)	20	20
Other			
19	History of setting fires or torturing small animals	10	
20	History of or documented fantasy of evisceration or mutilation of sexual areas of the body	50	
	Total Points		245
Comments			

Priority Point Range: Low = 0–150; Medium = 155–205; High = 210–510

Completed by: _____Date: ____ / ____ / ____

Reviewed by: _____Date: ____ / ____ / ____

Note: This assessment was completed with the information available to the assessor at the time of the file review. Additional information could change this assessment.

Persons of Interest Priority Assessment Tool—Jack the Ripper Investigation							
Name of POI	**Surname**		**First Given**			**Second Given**	
	Ostrog		Michael				
DOB	**YYYY**	**MM**	**DD**	**Fingerprint Number**			**Task/Tip #**
	1830						
						PP	**Score**
Residence (Aug. 31, 1888–Nov. 9, 1888)							
1	London (includes suburbs)					20	
2	Whitechapel (10 mile radius)					20	
Comfort Zone							
3	Resides, works or known to frequent Whitechapel or surrounding area (10 mile radius)					20	
Physical Description							
4	Male					50	50
5	Age (25–45)					10	
6	Physical abnormality (i.e. speech impediment, scarred complexion, physical illness or injury)					5	
Lifestyle							
7	Uses prostitutes					30	
8	Nocturnal due to choice or circumstance (night person)					10	
Marital Status (Aug. 31, 1888–Nov. 9, 1888) (Select One Only)							
9	Unattached (i.e. single, divorced, separated)					5	
10	Unaccountable (i.e. married but wife is extremely passive)					5	
Employment Status (Aug. 31, 1888–Nov. 9, 1888)							
11	Employed—at time of offences					10	
12	Engaged in an occupation, hobby or other activity where the use of a knife was common					20	
Criminal History (Charges and/or Conviction Not Necessary)							
13	History of property crimes, of assault causing bodily harm and of domestic violence					10	10
14	History of sex related offences					20	
15	History of throat slashing (includes attempts)					50	
Linked to Victim							
16	Mary Ann Nichols					20	
	Annie Chapman					20	
	Elizabeth Stride					20	
	Catherine Eddowes					20	
	Mary Jane Kelly					20	

Availability (Subject Was Available [i.e. Not Incarcerated at the Time of the Offences])			
17	Mary Ann Nichols (Aug. 31, 1888)	10	
	Annie Chapman (Sept. 8, 1888)	10	
	Elizabeth Stride (Sept. 29–30, 1888)	10	
	Catherine Eddowes (Sept. 30, 1888)	10	
	Mary Jane Kelly (Nov. 9, 1888)	10	
Weapon			
18	Known to carry a knife (does not matter how often)	20	
Other			
19	History of setting fires or torturing small animals	10	
20	History of or documented fantasy of evisceration or mutilation of sexual areas of the body	50	
	Total Points		60
Comments			

Priority Point Range: Low = 0–150; Medium = 155–205; High = 210–510

Completed by: _____Date: ____ / ____ / ____

Reviewed by: _____Date: ____ / ____ / ____

Note: This assessment was completed with the information available to the assessor at the time of the file review. Additional information could change this assessment.

Persons of Interest Priority Assessment Tool—Jack the Ripper Investigation							
Name of POI	Surname			First Given		Second Given	
	Pizer			John			
DOB	YYYY	MM	DD	Fingerprint Number		Task/Tip #	
	1850						
						PP	Score
Residence (Aug. 31, 1888–Nov. 9, 1888)							
1	London (includes suburbs)					20	20
2	Whitechapel (10 mile radius)					20	20
Comfort Zone							
3	Resides in, works in or known to frequent Whitechapel or surrounding area (10 mile radius)					20	20
Physical Description							
4	Male					50	50
5	Age (25–45)					10	10
6	Physical abnormality (i.e. speech impediment, scarred complexion, physical illness or injury)					5	
Lifestyle							
7	Uses prostitutes					30	30
8	Nocturnal due to choice or circumstance (night person)					10	
Marital Status (Aug. 31, 1888–Nov. 9, 1888) (Select One Only)							
9	Unattached (i.e. single, divorced, separated)					5	5
10	Unaccountable (i.e. married but wife is extremely passive)					5	
Employment Status (Aug. 31, 1888–Nov. 9, 1888)							
11	Employed—at time of offences					10	
12	Engaged in an occupation, hobby or other activity where the use of a knife was common.					20	20
Criminal History (Charges and/or Conviction Not Necessary)							
13	History of property crimes, of assault causing bodily harm and of domestic violence					10	
14	History of sex related offences					20	
15	History of throat slashing (includes attempts)					50	
Linked to Victim							
16	Mary Ann Nichols					20	
	Annie Chapman					20	
	Elizabeth Stride					20	
	Catherine Eddowes					20	
	Mary Jane Kelly					20	

	Availability (Subject Was Available [i.e. Not Incarcerated at the Time of the Offences])		
17	Mary Ann Nichols (Aug. 31, 1888)	10	0
	Annie Chapman (Sept. 8, 1888)	10	0
	Elizabeth Stride (Sept. 29–30, 1888)	10	10
	Catherine Eddowes (Sept. 30, 1888)	10	10
	Mary Jane Kelly (Nov. 9, 1888)	10	10
Weapon			
18	Known to carry a knife (does not matter how often)	20	
Other			
19	History of setting fires or torturing small animals	10	
20	History of or documented fantasy of evisceration or mutilation of sexual areas of the body	50	
	Total Points		205
Comments			
According to a newspaper article he was known to carry a razor-like knife. No points were awarded for 'known to carry a knife' because it was not possible to conclude the source was accurate, credible or reliable.			

Priority Point Range: Low = 0–150; Medium = 155–205; High = 210–510

Completed by: _____Date: _____/_____/_____

Reviewed by: _____Date: _____/_____/_____

Note: This assessment was completed with the information available to the assessor at the time of the file review. Additional information could change this assessment.

Persons of Interest Priority Assessment Tool—Jack the Ripper Investigation						
Name of POI	**Surname**		**First Given**		**Second Given**	
Sickert			Walter		Richard	
DOB	**YYYY**	**MM**	**DD**	**Fingerprint Number**		**Task/Tip #**
	1860	05	31			
					PP	**Score**
Residence (Aug. 31, 1888–Nov. 9, 1888)						
1	London (includes suburbs)				20	20
2	Whitechapel (10 mile radius)				20	20
Comfort Zone						
3	Resides in, works in or known to frequent Whitechapel or surrounding area (10 mile radius)				20	20
Physical Description						
4	Male				50	50
5	Age (25–45)				10	10
6	Physical abnormality (i.e. speech impediment, scarred complexion, physical illness or injury)				5	
Lifestyle						
7	Uses prostitutes				30	30
8	Nocturnal due to choice or circumstance (night person)				10	
Marital Status (Aug. 31, 1888–Nov. 9, 1888) (Select One Only)						
9	Unattached (i.e. single, divorced, separated)				5	
10	Unaccountable (i.e. married but wife is extremely passive)				5	
Employment Status (Aug. 31, 1888–Nov. 9, 1888)						
11	Employed—at time of offences				10	10
12	Engaged in an occupation, hobby or other activity where the use of a knife was common				20	
Criminal History (Charges and/or Conviction Not Necessary)						
13	History of property crimes, of assault causing bodily harm and of domestic violence				10	
14	History of sex related offences				20	
15	History of throat slashing (includes attempts)				50	
Linked to Victim						
16	Mary Ann Nichols				20	
	Annie Chapman				20	
	Elizabeth Stride				20	
	Catherine Eddowes				20	
	Mary Jane Kelly				20	

Availability (Subject Was Available [i.e. Not Incarcerated at the Time of the Offences])			
17	Mary Ann Nichols (Aug. 31, 1888)	10	**10**
	Annie Chapman (Sept. 8, 1888)	10	**10**
	Elizabeth Stride (Sept. 29–30, 1888)	10	**10**
	Catherine Eddowes (Sept. 30, 1888)	10	**10**
	Mary Jane Kelly (Nov. 9, 1888)	10	**10**
Weapon			
18	Known to carry a knife (does not matter how often)	20	
Other			
19	History of setting fires or torturing small animals	10	
20	History of or documented fantasy of evisceration or mutilation of sexual areas of the body	50	
		Total Points	**210**
Comments			

There is some forensic evidence that suggests he may be linked to some of the letters written claiming to be Jack the Ripper.

Priority Point Range: Low = 0–150; Medium = 155–205; High = 210–510

Completed by: _____ Date: ____ / ____ / ____

Reviewed by: _____ Date: ____ / ____ / ____

Note: This assessment was completed with the information available to the assessor at the time of the file review. Additional information could change this assessment.

Persons of Interest Priority Assessment Tool—Jack the Ripper Investigation			

Name of POI	Surname	First Given	Second Given
Stephenson		Roslyn	D'Onston

DOB	YYYY	MM	DD	Fingerprint Number	Task/Tip #	
	1841	04	20			

			PP	Score
Residence (Aug. 31, 1888–Nov. 9, 1888)				
1	London (includes suburbs)		20	20
2	Whitechapel (10 mile radius)		20	20
Comfort Zone				
3	Resides in, works in or known to frequent Whitechapel or surrounding area (10 mile radius)		20	20
Physical Description				
4	Male		50	50
5	Age (25–45) *47 at time of offences*		10	
6	Physical abnormality (i.e. speech impediment, scarred complexion, physical illness or injury)		5	
Lifestyle				
7	Uses prostitutes		30	30
8	Nocturnal due to choice or circumstance (night person)		10	
Marital Status (Aug. 31st, 1888 - Nov. 9th, 1888) (Select One Only)				
9	Unattached (i.e. single, divorced, separated)		5	5
10	Unaccountable (i.e. married but wife is extremely passive)		5	
Employment Status (Aug. 31, 1888–Nov. 9, 1888)				
11	Employed—at time of offences		10	
12	Engaged in an occupation, hobby or other activity where the use of a knife was common		20	
Criminal History (Charges and/or Conviction Not Necessary)				
13	History of property crimes, of assault causing bodily harm and of domestic violence		10	
14	History of sex related offences		20	
15	History of throat slashing (includes attempts)		50	
Linked to Victim				
16	Mary Ann Nichols		20	
	Annie Chapman		20	
	Elizabeth Stride		20	
	Catherine Eddowes		20	
	Mary Jane Kelly		20	

Availability (Subject Was Available [i.e. Not Incarcerated at the Time of the Offences])			
17	Mary Ann Nichols (Aug. 31, 1888)	10	10
	Annie Chapman (Sept. 8, 1888)	10	10
	Elizabeth Stride (Sept. 29–30, 1888)	10	10
	Catherine Eddowes (Sept. 30, 1888)	10	10
	Mary Jane Kelly (Nov. 9, 1888)	10	10
Weapon			
18	Known to carry a knife (does not matter how often)	20	
Other			
19	History of setting fires or torturing small animals	10	
20	History of or documented fantasy of evisceration or mutilation of sexual areas of the body	50	
	Total Points		**195**
Comments			

Priority Point Range: Low = 0–150; Medium = 155–205; High = 210–510

Completed by: _____ Date: ____/____/____

Reviewed by: _____ Date: ____/____/____

Note: This assessment was completed with the information available to the assessor at the time of the file review. Additional information could change this assessment.

Persons of Interest Priority Assessment Tool—Jack the Ripper Investigation							
Name of POI	**Surname**		**First Given**			**Second Given**	
	Tumblety		Francis				
DOB	**YYYY**	**MM**	**DD**	**Fingerprint Number**		**Task/Tip #**	
	1833						
						PP	**Score**
Residence (Aug. 31, 1888–Nov. 9, 1888)							
1	London (includes suburbs)					20	
2	Whitechapel (10 mile radius)					20	
Comfort Zone							
3	Resides in, works in or known to frequent Whitechapel or surrounding area (10 mile radius)					20	20
Physical Description							
4	Male					50	50
5	Age (25–45) *55 at time of offences*					10	
6	Physical abnormality (i.e. speech impediment, scarred complexion, physical illness or injury)					5	
Lifestyle							
7	Uses prostitutes					30	
8	Nocturnal due to choice or circumstance (night person)					10	
Marital Status (Aug. 31, 1888–Nov. 9, 1888) (Select One Only)							
9	Unattached (i.e. single, divorced, separated)					5	5
10	Unaccountable (i.e. married but wife is extremely passive)					5	
Employment Status (Aug. 31, 1888–Nov. 9, 1888)							
11	Employed—at time of offences					10	10
12	Engaged in an occupation, hobby or other activity where the use of a knife was common					20	
Criminal History (Charges and/or Conviction Not Necessary)							
13	History of property crimes, of assault causing bodily harm and of domestic violence					10	10
14	History of sex related offences					20	20
15	History of throat slashing (includes attempts)					50	
Linked to Victim							
16	Mary Ann Nichols					20	
	Annie Chapman					20	
	Elizabeth Stride					20	
	Catherine Eddowes					20	
	Mary Jane Kelly					20	

Availability (Subject Was Available [i.e. Not Incarcerated at the Time of the Offences])			
17	Mary Ann Nichols (Aug. 31, 1888)	10	**10**
	Annie Chapman (Sept. 8, 1888)	10	**10**
	Elizabeth Stride (Sept. 29–30, 1888)	10	**10**
	Catherine Eddowes (Sept. 30, 1888)	10	**10**
	Mary Jane Kelly (Nov. 9, 1888)	10	**10**
Weapon			
18	Known to carry a knife (does not matter how often)	20	
Other			
19	History of setting fires or torturing small animals	10	
20	History of or documented fantasy of evisceration or mutilation of sexual areas of the body	50	
		Total Points	165
Comments			

Reported by subject of questionable credibility that he hated women and had a collection of women's wombs in jars in his library.

Priority Point Range: Low = 0–150; Medium = 155–205; High = 210–510

Completed by: _____ Date: ____/____/____

Reviewed by: _____ Date: ____/____/____

Note: This assessment was completed with the information available to the assessor at the time of the file review. Additional information could change this assessment.

Bibliography

Much of the information in this book, particularly relating to information on Jack the Ripper victims, suspects and details of the investigations, was sourced from other publications, articles and websites. In many cases there were contradictions or disagreements between sources. We tried to avoid information that was not generally accepted as fact or verifiable through secondary sources. However, when we had to take sides we went with identifiable named sources that had evidence to support their claims.

Publications

Acton, Chiswick & Turnham Green Gazette. January 5, 1889.

Anderson, Robert. 2007. *The Lighter Side of My Official Life*. Seattle, WA: CreateSpace.

Begg, Paul, Fido, Martin, and Keith Skinner. 2010. *The Complete Jack the Ripper A to Z*. London: John Blake Publishing, p. 271.

Begg, Paul. 2005. *Jack the Ripper: The Definitive History*. London: Pearson Education.

Bond, Dr. Thomas. Whitechapel Murders. Letter to Assistant Commissioner Robert Anderson, Home Office, November 10, 1888.

Campbell, Archie. 1996. *Bernardo Investigation Review*. Report of Mr. Justice Archie Campbell, http://www.opconline.ca/depts/omcm/Campbell/Bernardo_Investigation_Review%20PDF.pdf.

Campbell, John H. and Don DeNevi. 2004. *Profilers*. Amherst, NY: Prometheus Books, p. 16.

Collins English Dictionary—Complete and Unabridged. 1991, 1994, 1998, 2000, 2003. London: HarperCollins.

Cornwell, Patricia. 2002. *Portrait of a Killer: Jack the Ripper Case Closed*. New York: G. P. Putnam's Sons.

Douglas, John. 1988. *UNSUB: AKA Jack the Ripper; Series of Homicides, London, England, 1888, NCAVA—Homicide (Criminal Investigative Analysis)*. Washington, DC: Federal Bureau of Investigation.

Evans, Stewart P., and Keith Skinner. 2000. *The Ultimate Jack the Ripper Companion: An Illustrated Encyclopedia*. New York: Carroll & Graf.

Fido, Martin. 1897. *Crimes, Detection and Death of Jack the Ripper*. London: Weidenfeld & Nicolson.

Fuller, Jean Overton. 2003. *Sickert and the Ripper Crimes*. Rev. ed. Oxford: Mandrake of Oxford .

Hazelwood, R. R., and J. E. Douglas. 1980. 'The Lust Murderer'. *FBI Law Enforcement Bulletin* 49: 1–5.

Hazelwood, R. Robert, and Ann W. Burgess. 2001. *Practical Aspects of Rape Investigation*. Boca Raton, FL: CRC Press.

Jones, Richard. 2009. *Jack the Ripper: The Casebook*. London: Andre Deutsch.

Liverpool Mercury, January 28, 1875.

Macnaghten, Melville. *The Macnaghten Memoranda*. February 23, 1894.

Michaud, Stephen G., and Hugh Aynesworth. 1999. *The Only Living Witness: The True Story of Serial Sex Killer Ted Bundy*. Irving, TX: Authorlink Press.

Michaud, Stephen G., with Roy Hazelwood. 2000. *The Evil That Men Do*. New York: St. Martin's Press.

New York World, January 1891.

Pall Mall Gazette, March 24, 1903, and September 11, 1888.

Police Gazette, October 26, 1888.

Ressler, Robert K., Ann W. Burgess and John E. Douglas. 1995. *Sexual Homicide: Patterns and Motives*. New York: The Free Press.

Rochester Daily Union and Advertiser, April 4, 1881.

Sugden, Philip. 2002. *The Complete History of Jack the Ripper*. Rev. ed. New York: Carroll & Graf.

The Star (UK), September 5, 1888.

Twain, Mark. 1962. The Lowest Animal. In Bernard Devoto, ed., *Letters from the Earth*. New York: HarperCollins. Mark Twain Quotations, Newspaper Collections, & Related Resources. 2011. http://www.twainquotes.com/Animals. html. Accessed November 2011.

Williamsport Sunday Grit. December 9, 1888.

Online Sources

Anthropometric Reference Data for Children and Adults: United States, 2003–2006. http://www.cdc.gov/nchs/data/nhsr/nhsr010.pdf.

Merriam-Webster Online Dictionary. 2011. http://www.merriam-webster.com/dictionary.

Environmental Criminology Research Inc. (ECRI). http://www.ecricanada.com/.

Jack the Ripper Tour. 2011. http://www.jack-the-ripper-tour.com/.

Morley, Christopher J. 2005. *Jack the Ripper: A Suspect Guide*. E-book. http://www.casebook.org/ripper_media/book_reviews/non-fiction/cjmorley/index.html.

Marquis de Sade. n.d. Brainy Quote. http://www.brainyquote.com/quotes/authors/m/marquis_de_sade.html (accessed November 2011).

Oxford Dictionaries. 2011. http://oxforddictionaries.com/.

Pegg, Jennifer D. 'Robert D'Onston Stephenson: A Jack the Ripper Suspect'. In *Casebook: Jack the Ripper*. http://www.casebook.org/suspects/donston.html (accessed May 2011).

Royal Canadian Mounted Police. *Geographic Profiling*. http://www.rcmp-grc.gc.ca/tops-opst/geographic-g-profil-eng.htm.

Ryder, Stephen P. (ed.). *Casebook: Jack the Ripper*. http://www.casebook.org/ (accessed 2010–11).

Statistics Canada. 2011. Population Group of Person. http://www.statcan.gc.ca/concepts/definitions/ethnicity-ethnicite-eng.htm (accessed 2010–2011).

View London. 2011. Whitechapel, London—Local Information for Whitechapel, London. http://www.viewlondon.co.uk/whatson/whitechapel-london-feature-1731.html.

Video

Alper, Joshua, John Cosgrove and Mike Mathis. 1988. *The Secret Identity of Jack the Ripper.* TV. Directed by Louis J. Horvitz.

Index